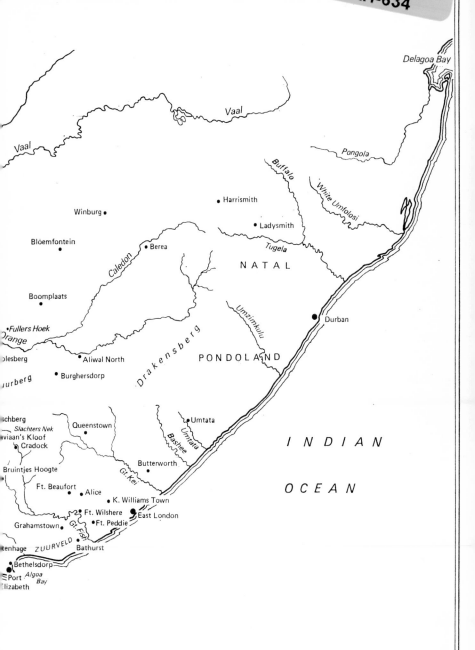

Delagoa Bay

Vaal

Vaal

Pongola

Harrismith

Winburg

Buffalo

White Umfolosi

Blöemfontein

Berea

Ladysmith

Caledon

Tugela

NATAL

Boomplaats

Umzimkulu

Durban

•Fullers Hoek

Orange

PONDOLAND

olesberg

Aliwal North

Drakensberg

uurberg

Burghersdorp

schberg

Queenstown

Umtata

Slachters Nek

Bashee

Umtata

I N D I A N

viaan's Kloof

Cradock

Bruintjes Hoogte

Butterworth

Gt. Kei

O C E A N

Ft. Beaufort

Alice

K. Williams Town

Ft. Wilshere

East London

Grahamstown

Ft. Peddie

Gt. Fish

tenhage

ZUURVELD

Bathurst

Bethelsdorp

Port

Algoa

Bay

lizabeth

0   50   100

miles

The
Kaffir
Wars

19TH CENTURY MILITARY CAMPAIGNS

The Kaffir Wars
1779 - 1877

by
A. J. SMITHERS

LEO COOPER · LONDON

First published in Great Britain 1973
by LEO COOPER LTD
196 Shaftesbury Avenue, London, WC2H 8JL

Copyright © by A. J. Smithers

ISBN 0 85052 107 6

Printed in Great Britain by
Clarke, Doble & Brendon Ltd.
Plymouth

CONTENTS

ILLUSTRATIONS

The author and publishers would like to thank the following for permission to reproduce the above illustrations: The Radio Times Hulton Picture Library, Nos 1 and 2; The Parker Gallery, Nos 3, 4, 5, 6, 13 and 14; The Mansell Collection, Nos 7, 8, 9 and 10; The National Army Museum, Nos 11 and 12.

ACKNOWLEDGEMENTS

I am, as always, greatly indebted to many people and institutions for the help they have given me in the making of this book. His Grace the Duke of Beaufort, the present head of a house which has left such a mark upon South Africa, kindly put me in touch with an essential source of information; Mrs. Honoria Durant, authoress of *The Somerset Sequence*, was kindness itself in bringing to my attention many authorities which I would otherwise have overlooked. The librarians of the Royal United Service Institution, the Royal Commonwealth Society, the South African Embassy and the British Museum, the officials of the Public Records Office, the Ministry of Defence Library, not to mention the owners of various private collections, have given generously of their time and specialized knowledge. Mr. R. G. Hollies-Smith, F.R.G.S., late 4/7th Dragoon Guards, has searched through the apparently inexhaustible archives of the Parker Gallery to produce prints with which to illustrate the text. I owe a particular debt to the Royal Commonwealth Society for kindly permitting one who is not a member to use their library.

There is also an acknowledgement due to a man long dead. George McCall Theal was, in a quiet way, a most distinguished citizen. For decades he was Keeper of the Cape Archives, a member of several learned societies, and probably the greatest authority on the tribes of South Africa. His formidably detailed knowledge of their ethnology, ethnography and every aspect of their life and traditions, together with an encyclopaedic knowledge of the past of the country he loved so well are recorded in some-

A*

thing like 50 books, sadly little read nowadays. His work was not limited to the library, however, for other people write of him about a century ago as personally running a school for young Kaffirs at Lovedale where he taught them to work with their hands as well as their heads. When the last Kaffir war broke out in 1877, Theal went among the tribes and was responsible for the fact that an unhallowed place which had been the worst theatre of the previous war remained untroubled. Only his own very short and reticent account survives but it seems plain that this bookish man placed his life at risk to preserve the lives of others. When accounts of various incidents conflict, as they often do, I have nearly always chosen to rely on George McCall Theal.

Lastly, this book would probably never have been written but for an affection for South Africa and South Africans dating back to a later war. In common with tens of thousands of other people, I passed through both Cape Town and Durban. So many convoys had gone before that one would not have been surprised if the residents had become heartily sick of entertaining troops. I know that I speak for a great many other people in saying that never was there such hospitality as we received. The fact that my own Regiment was composed of black Africans from another part of the continent, whose turn-out, drill and bearing were, apparently, something not seen there before, made no difference. Everything possible was done for all of us and, as annual reunions testify, we have not yet forgotten. Nor has everybody in this country forgotten that the van Rynevelds, Oliviers and de Villiers who fought alongside our own people in the Fish River Bush and who later, for a spell, became our enemies, returned to the ranks at Delville Wood and in the Western Desert. If South Africa today is in a muddle, the British Governments of the nineteenth century are not free from blame for contributing handsomely to it. Perhaps this book will go a little way, by chronicling campaigns now almost forgotten, to reminding us of how it all started.

INTRODUCTION

THE wars against the black races in South Africa lasted for almost a century and were fought within a short, by African standards, distance of Algoa Bay. Before considering them in any detail let us first examine the question 'What is a war?'. When Sir John Fortescue delivered his famous lecture at Trinity College, Cambridge in 1913 even he had to confess that no perfect definition was possible. 'A fight between three drunken men and the police is a scuffle. A fight between three hundred men and the police is a riot. A fight between three hundred thousand and the police is civil war.' His eventual definition was the 'strife of communities expressed through the conflict of organized bands of armed men' and most of the fights which are the subject of this book can just be classified under this heading. There were nine regular wars in all, the first two being exclusively the business of the Dutch East India Company, the third being fought during the first brief British occupation and involving a small British force against its will and rather by accident. The remaining six, which were far more serious affairs and which eventually sucked in substantial numbers of British troops, were wars in any view of the matter.

This is not a history of South Africa, but some exegesis of its early days is unavoidable. The fashionable creed is that the Dutch intruded themselves into a country happily and prosperously occupied by Rousseau's noble savage. That is very far from being the truth. By an accident of history, the Hamitic tribes had been on their southward exodus long before Diaz first set eyes on Table Mountain and the time of their arrival on the Great Fish

River more or less coincided with the appearance in the same place of the first Dutch cattle ranchers. Neither can claim the honourable name of aboriginal. The true aboriginals, the Bushmen, never at any time settled the land. The next arrivals in point of time, the Hottentots, were never strong enough in numbers to become effective settlers and such tribal organization as they had did not survive the smallpox epidemic of 1713. As time went on the great majority of them took service with the Europeans to whom their skill as hunters and cattlemen made them an indispensable complement.

Apart from some early scuffles there were no Hottentot wars and many of them served both as soldiers and auxiliaries to the Europeans later on. The Hottentot, however, was always unpredictable. He easily became bored with anything like routine and his superstition made him vulnerable to outside influences. It will be seen how the Colony suffered its greatest threat to existence as late as the 1850's when the Hottentots turned against their former masters.

The primary characters are, however, Boer and Bantu. Neither word explains much, for Boer, of course, means simply 'farmer' while Bantu is the plural of the Kaffir word for 'man'. The characters of the two underlie everything.

In the beginning the Company did not encourage expansion but bolder spirits were always to be found who were not content to remain in the settled farming and vine-growing districts near Cape Town and struck out for themselves as ranchers. Farms of 6,000 acres were to be had for a single quit-rent of about £5 and once that had been paid the Boer, though technically still subject to the Company, was completely on his own. As generation succeeded generation there grew up a separate race of men and women who owed little to Holland or to any authority. They developed in the Taal a language of their own and evolved a rude society distinguished only by courage, Calvinism and a cantankerous objection to being ruled by any sanctions except family ones. They married young and produced large families; the Boer habit, not obsolete, of addressing elders as 'Oom' or 'Tantie' and contemporaries as 'Nief' or 'Niggie' reflects a time when these were genuine ties of blood.

For their existence they relied on themselves; the farms

produced most essentials of life, save in times of drought or locusts; soap and candles were made from the fats of animals and powder and lead were supplied by the Company. Anything else came from the 'smouse', a travelling pedlar, usually Jewish, or was bought at the 'winkel', or store, at the quarterly gatherings called 'Nagmaal'. This most important feature of frontier life began as a service of Holy Communion but expanded into a great social occasion lasting several days. Brandy, coffee, needles and tobacco were the commodities in which many a smouse made his modest fortune, for the appetite of the frontier people for these things was insatiable. Within their own community they were kindly and hospitable but the life did not lend itself to refinement or squeamishness.

The young Boer, who at an early age was taught to drive his knife into the heart of a zebra and to rip the fat from the warm body in order to soften the leather cut from the hide of a buck shot by his father, could not be expected to grow up like a child of Amsterdam or Norwich. Life has always been cheap in Africa and the regular shooting of marauding Bushmen was not seen as being in the least discreditable. The dour Calvinist faith eschewed the subtleties of educated theologians and was starkly simple; the Old Testament said quite plainly that Ham should serve his brethren and that he was made to do. If Ham misbehaved he was punished, sometimes savagely. To find any other book in a Boer home was almost unknown for they lived in a state of uninterested ignorance of all matters that did not directly affect them. Humourless, unlettered and brave, they formed an essential buffer state between the communities of the Cape and the Rider Haggard world beyond.

If the frontier Boers had had their way the commandos would have been called out in force at the first confrontation with the Bantu and a battle of extermination would have been fought out. The Cape, however, was only a Company out-station under the jurisdiction of Batavia where the Governor, as in India, was in the habit of regulating affairs with native princes who were in control of their subjects and could be expected, within limits, to observe treaties. The object of the Company, to be run at a profit, never left the minds of its rulers and they preferred to manage their affairs in this part of their territories similarly.

They could not or would not understand that the Kaffir tribes did not do business in this way. They had no great rajahs at the head of organized states with settled revenues and standing armies and an arrangement made with one petty chieftain would not of necessity be deemed to bind his neighbour, his successor or indeed himself when it no longer suited him. The consequence of this dependence on the practices of civilization was disastrous, for when the Company consoled itself with the conviction that the Eastern frontier had been settled for all time on the Great Fish River the Xosa, the Tembu and the Pondo with their numerous sub-tribes took an entirely different view. They held, with Lloyd George, that God gave the land to the people. The concept that a man might own a great swathe of Africa in the same way that he owned his horse or his wife had no place in their philosophy. The function of the land was to provide subsistence and grazing which at different seasons demanded different places. If a drought required that the cattle be moved outside their usual pastures then the thing must be done or starvation would follow. Anything that some chieflet might have agreed with a white man about not crossing a certain line became quite irrelevant.

Another factor of great importance in Kaffir thinking was magic. Certainly on two occasions the chiefs were persuaded by their witch-doctors that the time had come to drive the white men back to their ships and that the powers of darkness would make this both easy and certain. As recently as 1857 a shaman (witch-doctor) named Mdhlaka announced that his niece had had a vision. The black men must destroy all their grain and slaughter all their cattle whereupon the sun would move backwards, a hurricane would blow all the white men into the sea and warriors long dead would arise to re-join their people with cattle and grain beyond counting. The Xosa and Tembu did as they were bid and died of starvation in their thousands. The British Colonial Government did its best for them but the generally accepted estimate is that the population of what was then called British Kaffraria fell from about 100,000 to 37,000.

In a pitched battle with European troops the Kaffirs would have been helpless. Their missile weapon, the assegai (a name derived from the tree which provides the shaft) was reasonably effective up to about 50 yards but once the warrior had thrown away the 3 or 4 he carried he had disarmed himself save for shield and club. It was not until the Zulu Chaka took the military affairs of his people in hand that a heavier weapon appeared which would serve as a stabbing spear in the mêlée. The Kaffirs had no battle drills; the mob hurled its assegais and then rushed forward en masse. Once the futility of this practice against firearms had been learnt, they moved over to the traditional tactics of the weaker side, the guerrilla and the ambush.

Sir John Fortescue tells us that Dingiswayo, Chaka's mentor, was present at the first meeting between the Kaffirs and the British infantry in 1799 but he gives no authority for the assertion. I have not been able to find any supporting evidence but it is perfectly feasible. Sir John's standing makes it impossible to dismiss it and it may well be that the sharp lesson given on that occasion had something to do with the rise of the Zulu nation.

The British became embroiled in Kaffir wars with reluctance. During the first brief occupation between the seizure of the Cape in 1796 and its return after the treaty of Amiens there occurred the brush just mentioned, but the red-coats then did no more than shoot off their attackers. After Britain assumed the Government and with it the obligation to defend the frontier farmers, the army found that it was caught up in a kind of warfare unknown since General Wade had pacified the Highlands. The theatre was the coastal strip between the mountains and the Indian Ocean which contains thick bush, steep cliffs and rolling hills with the rivers running to the sea through deep forested valleys. How Wellington's Peninsular army taught itself the arts of bush-warfare against a competent and ferocious enemy this book will try to show. They have left their names behind them for the map shows two Fort Wellingtons and a Waterloo, while Colesberg, Durban, Cradock, Harrismith and many others remember the Duke's old officers. Alice, too, was named by Harry Smith for his sister and the Elizabeth of Port Elizabeth was the recently dead and much-loved wife of Sir Rufane Donkin who had commanded a brigade at Talavera. You will find geographical oddities, for Hamburg is just downstream on the

Keiskamma from Bodiam, Lowestoft is a few miles from Athlone and Shorncliffe marches with Potsdam.

The Transkei Bantu Reserve sprawls over all the old battle-grounds and the Transkei Constitution Act of 1963 conferred a limited self-government on the descendants of the Kaffir warriors who fought there. Grahamstown is the seat of a famous University while Fort Hare has been, since 1915, the home of the African College.

The land is now reserved to the tribes whose old way of life is paternally guarded by the Government. No European may wander from the highway without a pass, which is not given without some good reason for his wanting it. Perhaps the black men were the victors after all.

CHAPTER 1
Setting the Scene

In order to make a coherent story of the wars in Southern Africa in which a considerable part of the British army was engaged during the nineteenth century it is necessary first to reach back in time. The history of what is now the Republic is a strange one, differing considerably from that of the other empty places of the earth which became subject to European settlement, though there are, of course, common features in some respects.

In antiquity the Cape was almost certainly visited by ships from Egypt and Phoenicia and archaeologists have discovered evidence of the existence of some cultures at those times. During the thousand years and more which passed between these first contacts and the end of the fifteenth century these earliest peoples gradually vanished and were replaced by the unique race which we still know as the Bushmen. These seem to have migrated from their original home, somewhere about Uganda and the Sudan, and over a long period of time they drifted south until their hunting grounds met the sea. They have always been a completely unorganized folk to whom the idea of authority of any kind has never been known, their way of life being completely nomadic. A description of the Bushmen contained in a book published in the latter part of the last century, but obviously repeating an earlier source, says of them 'frame dwarfish; colour and general appearance those of the ugliest specimens of Hottentots; weapons bow and poisoned arrow; pursuits those of a hunter; government none but parental; habitations caverns or mats spread over the branches of trees; domestic animal the dog; demeanour that of perfect independence; language abounding in clicks and deep guttural sounds'. The Kaffir name for them was 'San', the name Bushman being given to them by the earliest Dutch settlers. The main characteristic of the Bushman was (and still is, for they are by no means extinct) a cheerful improvidence. They were skilled hunters, experts in the distillation of poisons from centipedes and snake venom but lived in a perpetual Stone Age, seeking no intercourse of any kind with the outside world and totally unimpressed by the wonders of superior civilizations. Though their bodies were small and weak (possessing, incidentally, the unusual quality of being able to store food in their capacious rumps) they had a remarkable turn of speed. On broken ground, they could outpace a galloping horse. Their greatest joy was to sing and to dance by the light of the moon until they collapsed exhausted. However, their inability or unwillingness to draw any distinction between the wild beasts with which Africa abounded and the domesticated cattle of later arrivals was to bring them into collision with the farmers in the course of time.

The first permanent dwellers in the country and the first to be seen by European eyes were the Hottentots. From the same authority comes their picture; 'frame slight but sometimes tall; back hollow, head scantily covered with little tufts of short or crisped hair; cheeks hollow, nose always flat; hands and feet small; colour yellow to olive; weapons assegai, knobkerrie, bow and poisoned arrow, shield; pursuits pastoral, to a very small extent metallurgical; habitation slender wickerwork covered with skin or reed mats; domestic animals ox, sheep and dog; demeanour inconsistent, marked by levity; language abounding in clicks.' The Hottentots are believed to descend from Bushmen women taken long ago by the Hamitic races somewhere in the region of the Great Lakes of Central Africa and they too slowly wended their way southward towards the ocean. They were divided into many tribes, possessing some sort of loose organization but were frequently at war with each other. From their mothers they learned how to train oxen to obey certain calls and to act as beasts of burden as well as the skills of hunting and the knowledge required for the compounding of poisons.

They never engaged in agriculture. Even before the Europeans arrived with their gin and rum the Hottentots were given to drunkenness, employing for this purpose a brew made from honey and dacha (wild hemp) which they smoked in pipes of antelope horn. Their food was mainly milk, game, locusts, fruit, and roots and their clothing, such as it was, of dressed leather. They were an intelligent people, the men being trained from early youth to bring down animals as large as goats with thrown knobkerries at ranges of twenty and even thirty yards. The assegai was effective up to about the same distance but the bow relied entirely for its lethal quality on the poison with which the arrows were invariably tipped. The Hottentots were also lazy and superstitious. They had ready to hand an abundance of solid copper but could not be bothered to smelt it for any purpose more useful than to make ornaments for their bodies. Though they were familiar with the use of iron and supplies of ore were available they used it little, being content to tip their weapons with horn because it was so much less trouble to work. 'A more improvident, unstable, thoughtless people never existed. So long as they had food they were without care or grief. They delighted in dancing and many early travellers speak of the music which they were able to produce from reeds. Active in amusement and in hunting, in all other respects they were extremely indolent. Their filthiness was disgusting to Europeans. This last condition was to a large extent the result of the habit, common both to Hottentot and Bantu, of smearing their bodies with grease and clay. This was not intended as an aid to beauty but was for the entirely practical purpose of giving protection from the sun, the rain and insects. Its justification is the fact that they usually enjoyed excellent health; when they did fall sick or become infirm they did not last long, for it was held to be a kindness then to be left to end a miserable existence as swiftly as possible by starvation or exposure. They called themselves 'Khoikhoi' (roughly translatable as Master Race), Hottentot being again a name of Dutch invention probably derived from some unintelligible word light-heartedly twisted by an early arrival.

These characteristics of intelligence, superstition and un-reliability are of great importance for, as will be seen, the Hottentots figure considerably in the events which are to follow and many people, to their undoing, either misunderstood or forgot them. Their lack of tribal discipline made them grow up without any understanding of right or wrong in many respects and their religion, if such it can be called, did nothing to redress this. It was a vague, dimly understood collection of folk-lore but it contained not a single Commandment.

These were the peoples whom the first Europeans encountered, the very different black races being still in the process of migration from the same heart-lands to the north-east when the first Portuguese sailors sighted Table Mountain. It is, neverthe-less, convenient to introduce them at this stage. First the problem of naming them should be faced. They are variously called Kaffirs or Bantu, the former word being, of course, an Arabic one in common use throughout Africa and meaning no more than 'unbeliever'. Of recent years it has acquired a derogatory meaning and its use is regarded as insulting. The fact remains that Kaffir (or Kafir) is the word used consistently in all the records relating to the subject matter of this book and the wars it chronicles are officially described as the Kaffir Wars. To avoid its use would be an affectation and it is hard to believe that anyone can take offence at its retention. Far more pejorative words have been used about the ancestors of the English.

The Kaffirs, while retaining many common characteristics, differed far more amongst themselves than did either the Bush-men or the Hottentots. Their migration was caused in very large part by the slave trading of Arab peoples who had been in the habit of taking and selling them in the markets of Arabia, India and even China since pre-Christian times. The Central High-lands and the eastern coastal belt were their hunting grounds until quite recently and in two thousand years millions more of these unfortunates must have passed through Arab hands than were ever taken by Europeans from the West Coast. The word Kaffir was first used by the Arabs in the early days of Islam and it was they who introduced into Eastern and Central Africa the art of smelting iron ore. From the same source as before comes the picture of the Kaffir. 'Frame of those on the coast generally robust and as well-formed as Europeans; head covered closely with crispy hair; cheeks full, nose usually flat but occasionally prominent; hands and feet large; colour brown to deep black; weapons, assegai, knobkerrie, shield; pursuits agricultural, pastoral and metallurgic; government firmly constituted with perfect system of laws; habitations, strong framework of wood covered with thatch; domestic animals dog, goat, ox, barnyard poultry; demeanour ceremonious, grave, respectful to superiors in rank; language musical, words abounding in vowels and inflected to produce harmony in sound'.

They were no more addicted to war than were their contemporaries in Europe, for the days of the black military empires for whom life held no vocation other than organized butchery and plunder were far off. Quarrels of a violent kind certainly took place over such issues as grazing, water rights and women but fighting was not for them an end in itself. A man might, with luck, live out his time without having to take up arms except against marauding beasts and was not under the necessity of proving his manhood in battle before he could marry and raise a family. Tradition tells of a war of extermination having taken place at the end of the sixteenth century when a great horde appeared from somewhere north of the Zambesi and surged into Natal destroying everything in its path. The old tribes were broken and from their disparate fragments, amongst whom these nameless invaders eventually settled down, the later ones which we know by name gradually evolved. To their ancestors were certainly added immigrants from India (a number of Indian plants still grow wild in parts of East Africa) and an appreciable number of intruders from the Persian Gulf. Even a solitary Englishman who gave his name as Vaughan Goodwin was found living a Moon and Sixpence life in unexplored Natal in 1699. War was never studied by the early Kaffirs. Their weapons were those designed for the chase, assegai and thrown kerrie being adequate for that purpose but poor things in a man to man fight. They made neither pike nor spear to be used in the phalanx nor sword for the close combat. The best they could contrive, with the skills and materials at their disposal capable of producing armies as well found as those of Hector or Alexander, was to break short the shaft of the last assegai and to prod away with

21

a feeble spike. Until the arrival of Dingiswayo the battles of the Kaffirs, bloody though they could be, were no more than the collisions of ill-armed mobs. Smiths plied their trade as at the start of the Iron Age. A mixture of charcoal and haematite was lumped together in a scooped-out rock and brought to intense heat with bellows made from skins. The molten metal ran down into clay moulds where it cooled in the rough shape of mattock or assegai-head. The crude article was then painstakingly hammered with stones into its final shape and then honed to a sharp edge. Much magic and many incantations went into this.

The magic colour of the Kaffirs was red; it symbolized the strength and power which came from the sun and, in a country as red as Devonshire, there are still to be found many clay-pits whence they extracted the ochre with which to smear their bodies. The skin kaross, which was the original single garment, gave way in time to the woollen blanket but no colour but red was acceptable. The red blanket of the Xosa is still a form of national dress. They knew of gold and obtained it by the classical method familiar to the Argonauts; fleeces were hung at selected places in the sluits of the mountains which retained the alluvium as it washed down. The amount acquired in this way cannot, however, have been very great.

Wealth was represented only by cattle whose tending was strictly man's work. No woman was allowed so much as to milk a cow. The system worked in practice for the beasts were trained to such perfection that they would answer to their owner's whistles and clicks with the discipline of sheep-dogs. Amongst the grandees, ox-racing was the sport of kings; the animals were steered by a bridle through the cartilage of the nose and proved surprisingly tractable. In the great kraals form was studied with as much care as on Newmarket Heath. Oddly enough, the stealing of cattle was not treated as a particularly heinous offence; the detected rustler was obliged to make restitution but suffered only in the estimation of his friends for his want of skill. The ox served as the universal carrier, for the wheel was unknown until the wagons of the Europeans first rolled into sight. When these fell into Kaffir hands the only use made of them was to melt down the iron tyres to make better assegai-heads.

The women ran their homes with economy and skill. It was

for the man to make the house, erecting the strong frame and thatching the whole in the familiar bee-hive shape and building the hard floor of beaten mud and cow-dung which took a high polish.* In the middle would be a circular raised hearth and this was the wife's territory. It answered its purpose of cooking and providing warmth on cold nights well enough; as the hut contained no smoke-hole (the only aperture was a low doorway passable by crawling) it is easy to understand why the huts were not much used by day. One of the more remarkable arts of the Kaffir women was the creation of large and sometimes beautiful pots without the benefit of a wheel; fine symmetrical vessels capable of resisting great heat during cooking were turned out in large numbers. The experts were said to be able to make them of capacities up to 50 gallons and still less than $\frac{1}{4}$ inch in thickness. Such a woman would command a very high bride-price. They were also great weavers of grass, making not only the sleeping-mats which were individually marked and hung, neatly rolled, against the wall when not in use, but also of baskets. It was commonplace for these to be so tightly meshed that water could be carried in them. From millet, pounded in the pots with heavy sticks, they brewed beer in great quantities and many Kaffirs, men and women alike, were heavy smokers. Their pipes were made of horn or stone and for tobacco they, like the Hottentots, inhaled dacha. There is no record of when the Dutch first introduced tobacco into South Africa but when it became known it was a prize much sought after. From wood and horn they made their simple artifacts, bowls and spoons and the garden tools needed by the women for work on the crops, for horticulture was part of their business.

The basic foodstuff was milk, carried when away from home in a skin bag in which it soon reached the desirable degree of acidity, but butter and cheese were not known. Meat was a

* Cattle-dung has always been one of the most important basic commodities of Africa and deserves a word to itself. The excrement of beasts feeding only on grass has little resemblance to our cow-pat. It is a pulp, almost odourless, which soon dries out and, under the Afrikaans name of 'mis' it is the staple fuel where wood is scarce. It burns exactly like peat and, before drying, mixes well with mud for making hard floors. It was at least as important as leather, fat, horn, sinews, bladders and other less earthy animal products and, without it, life would sometimes have been almost impossible.

23

popular article of diet but only grave necessity would make a Kaffir slaughter one of his precious cattle to get it. Only when an animal had succumbed to old age, disease or attack by a predator was beef on the menu. Fish, again, was something easily to be had but quite unused; the boatbuilders and fishermen of Accra show conclusively that the black African can be as competent a seaman as any other man but, centuries after they had seen the sea, no boat had been built nor fishing tackle considered.

The Kaffir men were anything but stupid. More than one European writer has left the comment that in debate, especially when defending themselves, they showed powers of reasoned argument and skill in the examination of witnesses at least equal to that of most white men. Their class-consciousness was equally on a par; amongst the Xosa all descendants of the earliest chiefs ranked as noblemen according to their degrees and they exercised much the same privileges as those which were to provoke revolution in France. The offer of insult, let alone violence, to the least of them brought exemplary punishment. The authority to which the common folk submitted was mostly local, for the government of the kraal was almost exactly that of the Norman-French manor brought to England by Duke William. The chief was Lord of the Manor, dwelling in his demesne and virtually owning his villeins. He would parcel out the available land in a form of customary tenure under which each family had enough on which to grow millet and pumpkins for its own consumption, the grazing land being held and enjoyed by all in common. The right to use and occupy was a personal one which could not be alienated and if the tenant failed to cultivate it properly or went away the grant would be revoked. If the villein should decide to leave his lord he would encounter none of the obstacles that would be put in his way in Europe for Bantu tribal law insisted that a refugee be given asylum and hospitality with no questions asked. As a result it often happened that an unpopular or unjust chief would find a large body of ill-wishers growing up on his border so that he must either reform or fight.

The central authority of the paramount chief was seldom invoked in time of peace except as a final court of appeal. The Bantu councillors who advised him on these solemn occasions

had all the devotion to hair-splitting legalistic pedantry inseparable from a Chancery judge. State trials were conducted with the
utmost decorum though any man might attend if he had a mind
to do so. Bantu common law, like the English variety, dwelt in
the bosoms of the chiefs from which mysterious recesses it was
summoned when needed. Precedents existed for almost every
situation imaginable and the man with the longest memory
was reckoned the greatest jurist. The councillors loved to make
their speeches with a richness of allegory and parables drawn
from the mythical sayings and doings of the animals; their
aphorisms have been passed down by succeeding generations.
Onomatopoeia played a large part in language; the present
capital, Lukisikiki, is named from the noise the wind makes as
it blows gently through the rushes. In criminal cases there were
two punishments only: death or fine, though an exception was
made in the case of witchcraft. Here a defendant was frequently
unaware even that a charge had been levelled at him until the
executioners arrived in the night. An ecclesiastical court, part
Star Chamber part Doctor's Commons, had smelt him out
privily and there was no appeal. Sometimes, of course, the priests
claimed to detect offences from spite or greed but more often
than not their actions were dictated by their monomaniac
consciences. It was all the same to the victim; all his goods were
forfeit and he died under whatever form of torture the chief
fancied; in the vernacular, he was 'eaten up'. The concept of
locking men up in dark prisons never entered the Bantu head;
when they first learnt of it they were genuinely shocked that
white men could be such barbarians.

Thus in their smoky and verminous huts they lived, minimally
dressed in garments of breyed leather, troubled mostly by rain,
drought, leopards, baboons and other incidents of Africa, thought-
lessly exhausting the soil so that their villages could have no
hope of permanency. Their spiritual life was eclectic. Common
men after death were thrown to the aasvogels and hyaenas who
maintained an efficient disposal service but great chiefs must be
reverently interred with their grave-goods. Their spirits demanded
animal sacrifices on occasions of disaster, rejoicing or perplexity,
and the knowledge that the manes of kings long dead could still
influence events tended to prevent clans from fragmenting. There

was a strong bond of fraternity between men who had been circumcised at one of the group ceremonies of this kind which were held from time to time; those who had participated at the same time as the son of a chief were bound to him for the rest of their lives in the same relationship as the Myrmidons had with Achilles. It is stoutly asserted, very probably with truth, that this trust has never been betrayed.

These men were the first settlers in recorded times. The Bushmen came and went like butterflies, leaving little more trace of occupation behind them. The Hottentots set up no permanent buildings, dismantling their rude shelters, loading them on to their pack animals and moving on as their fancy took them. However, when the Kaffirs came they came to stay though they took over many of the Hottentot place names particularly to the West of the river Kei. The two biggest tribes were the Tembu (who do not figure in the wars until 1827) and the Xosa; the name is sometimes spelt Kosa but it is not possible to say with certainty which more accurately represents the initial 'click'. Each of them was divided into a number of clans but all acknowledged a single chieftain. By about 1770 they, with their neighbours the Pondo and the Kesibe, were in occupation of the lower plateaux of the belt of land between the Drakensbergs and the sea although they were thinly spread over this large area.

Before leaving them it would be well to examine their law of succession for it sometimes becomes of importance. The first wives of a chief were usually the daughters of some of his father's retainers; as he grew older and more powerful he would be sought in marriage by other chiefly families and so, perhaps quite late in life, the chief would take from one of these his Great Wife. By tribal law, her eldest son would be the heir. However, the chief was permitted at any time before marriage to his Great Wife to designate one of her predecessors as Wife of the Right Hand, her children thus having the next degree of precedence. Her eldest son, as a consolation prize, was given on reaching manhood a proportion of his father's advisers and was permitted to found a new sub-tribe. He might be considerably older than the official heir and if events showed him to be the abler ruler war between the two became inevitable; if peace reigned, however, the son of the Right Hand would acknowledge the sovereignty of his half-brother but would neither pay him tribute nor be obliged to brook any interference from him in his internal government.

This, then, was the situation in the 1490's; the Bushmen flitted over the land, the Hottentots moved around it in larger companies and at less frequent intervals. The heads of the Kaffir columns, though still hundreds of miles from Table Bay, were moving slowly but inexorably south and west. In the space of a dozen years, thanks to the improvements in hull design and sail-plans but above all to the great strides in the art of navigation brought about by the men of Prince Henry of Portugal at his school in Sagres, the caravels of Europe began to move towards the same terminus.

Of all their great discoveries the Cape of Good Hope was the least valued for by an evil chance it had competitors which proved far more attractive to the rulers of Spain and Portugal, then the only real maritime powers. Standing as it did between the markets of India and the rich islands of the East Indies on the one hand and the precious metals of the Americas on the other the attractions of the Cape seemed scanty enough and for the next hundred years they were largely ignored. The coast was probably the most dangerous in the world and returned ship-wrecked mariners had little good to say of what they had found ashore. Its only use was as a staging post on the way to more rewarding places from which such essentials as water and firewood could be got, for it offered neither trade nor commodities.

In 1620, the year of the *Mayflower*, two English sea-captains named Shilling and Fitzherbert made a landfall at Saldanha Bay and had the distinction, so far as is known, of being the first of their countrymen to set foot there. They found no sign of occupation save for the Post Office stones under which seamen were accustomed to leave their mail in the hope that some passing ship would find it and take it on. The two captains therefore went through the formalities of annexing the bay and its mysterious hinterland to the Crown of England. On their return home they presented to King James a reasoned memorial as to why it would be expedient for him to accept this new dominion but the monarch flatly refused to take it. He had quite enough to occupy him with the new American colonies and the fate of his daughter and her husband in the early stages of the Thirty Years War. If Queen Elizabeth had been born twenty years later than she was, the history of South Africa would have been very different.

The vacuum, however, could not remain indefinitely unfilled and new claimants were appearing. Portugal had been ruined by Philip II and mighty Spain herself was in decay; it had begun, imperceptibly almost, in 1588 and the pace had greatly quickened after her defeat at the hands of Condé at Rocroi in 1643. Now her old captive, Holland, was first amongst the sea-going nations and as long ago as 1602 a charter had been granted to her East India Company; Amsterdam was beginning to see the first of its merchant princes growing rich from trade with the gilded East. Their trading stations at Bantam, Amboyna and Batavia with others as far afield as Ceylon and Macassar came into existence within a few years. In 1648 one of the Company's ships stranded in Table Bay; her crew passed a year there existing in part on the produce which the soil so readily yielded. When he eventually trod the cobble-stones of Amsterdam again, Captain Janssens respectfully urged upon the Council that it would be well worth the Company's while to establish a refreshment station at a place where water, fresh vegetables and, most important, wood for galley fires were to be had for the taking. The English and what was left of the Portuguese ships hardly ever went there as they preferred to use the islands of St Helena and Mozambique. The only apparent inhabitants were a handful of Hottentot 'strandloopers'.

The Council ponderously persuaded itself that the proposition was a sound commercial one and set to work to plan the operation. They took two years over it and eventually decided that, on the strength of what Janssens had told them, Saldanha Bay itself was unsafe but that the peninsula to the south, where stood this mountain of which he spoke, could be defended against attack from either direction. Their biggest doubt was whether there could be sufficient supplies of wood at hand; a ship could carry great quantities of water but for food the passengers and crew relied upon cattle and poultry which were taken aboard alive. If the fuel for cooking them was not to be had they were not merely useless but became themselves large consumers of food and water. Janssens was certain that it was to be had at no great distance.

One rule was inflexible; this was to be a company trading and refreshment station, a purely commercial venture which had nothing whatever in common with a colony as the Romans had understood the word. The Governor would be the servant of the Council and every man and woman whom the Governor might permit to enter its station would be the servants of the Governor. There would be a rigid discipline and any who were foolish enough to misbehave themselves in any way would suffer, in addition to any other punishment which might be inflicted, instant repatriation.

In December, 1651, three tiny ships, the flagship *Drommedaris* being no more than 200 tons burden, cleared the Texel. On board were about 200 men of whom only 80 were to remain at the Cape and only a few of these had been permitted to bring their families. It had been made quite clear to them that this was in no sense emigration but merely a posting abroad for a few years. Their commander and first Governor was the surgeon Jan van Riebeeck. After a passage which was, by the standards of the day, tolerable, the ships arrived in Table Bay on 6 April, 1652. Van Riebeeck disembarked his men and at once put them to work to build a fort. Like the Kaffirs, still far away to the north-east, Europe had come to stay.

Life for the Company's men was desperately hard in the first days. Not only was the work itself tiring to bodies softened by months at sea but every kind of frustration set about them. Storms like nothing the Dutchmen had ever seen before swept away the gardens they had planted with such sweat; baboons ravaged the little crops upon which they were going to depend for survival and the Hottentots expertly stole every portable thing that was not under armed guard or nailed down. Grumbling was rife, a few men deserted into the interior in the belief that nothing they might find there could be worse than the life they knew, and one attempt was made on the life of the Governor. Only the steadfastness of van Riebeeck and the severity of the punishments he meted out to offenders kept the little company in existence. However, by degrees affairs improved and the station began to take shape and made ready to carry out its duties.

The Hottentots, greatly intrigued by some of the toys offered to them, were induced to give cattle in exchange; they grudged doing it, but stealing was becoming more difficult. The Company's men, having finished with the 'all hands to the pumps' stage, began to sort themselves out in accordance with their rigid table of precedence. Though they enjoyed ranks with titles like 'Junior Merchant', trading of a private kind was absolutely forbidden and the permission of the Governor or Council of Policy was needed before a man could do almost anything. It can hardly be wondered that men whose fathers had fought under William the Silent chafed bitterly. It took five years before nine brave men were allowed to leave the station and to carve themselves farms out of the wilderness. Even then, for all that they were designated 'free burghers', they remained Company's men and must sell whatever they were able to produce only to their master. These nine founders must have been men of considerable hardihood to risk everything in an unknown, savage land with no protection better than a matchlock musket which would only fire when it was not raining.

In the same year as the little trek of the free burghers, the Company took one of its more disastrous decisions. It needed labour, lots of labour, and the Hottentots were not proving the tractable and industrious people they should have been; in consequence of their incurable idleness and unreliability, and because the Company had slaves to spare in its other territories, it was resolved to import them into the Cape. From India and Java, from Ceylon, the Celebes and Madagascar, the Dutch imported their bought peoples. As the ship-loads of slaves arrived, the Company took them over, housed, fed and educated them and put them to work. Inevitably with so heterogeneous a crew some had greater abilities than had the Europeans already there and much of the semi-skilled work as well as the hewing of wood and drawing of water was taken out of their hands. The more personable of the female slaves were acquired with or without marriage by lonely Dutchmen and those of the second rank went to the Hottentots when they did not marry amongst themselves. It can hardly be wondered that racial purity was not a feature of South African life. One new hybrid, offspring of Dutchmen and Hottentot women, were officially called Griquas but preferred to be designated by the more lordly name of Bastards. The Company laid down complicated regulations for the manumission of slaves on their fulfilling certain conditions and many in time obtained their freedom in this way.

One cannot be dogmatic about the institution of slavery from the standpoint of the mid-seventeenth century. Without their help the Dutch would never have been able to expand their frontiers as they did nor to run their farms properly. Employers of slave labour varied as widely as they did in, say, Alabama, and the good master received his reward in faithful service. The bad slaves, however, were a menace, for it was they who took refuge with the Kaffirs after they had made the Colony too hot to hold them, who provided them with their first stolen firearms and who guided them during their forays. It is, however, safe to assert that the Company would have done posterity better service if it had let its slaves stay at home and had instead brought in more servants from Europe.

In 1658 came the once and for all show-down with the Hottentots. The novelty of the brass buttons and knives had long worn off and they were beginning to realize that these benefactors were not only never going away but that they were going to take over Hottentot land. This operation can never be painlessly performed and the Hottentots, although many were now hangers-on of the Company, were as resentful and angry as were the miscalled Indians in the Americas or the real Indians of India. They rose up against their supplanters with about the same chances of winning that Briton had had against Roman or Saxon against Norman. The cannon and muskets of Amsterdam shot them down without loss to the Company. The Hottentots, having made their gesture, accepted the inevitable with commendable philosophy. Those to whom a more domesticated life appealed threw in their lot with the Dutch and, on the whole, were faithful to them in spite of much ill-treatment at the hands of some. For the others life was not yet much changed, for the borders had still not moved far from the Cape Peninsula and there was a lot of Africa left.

It is not necessary for the purposes of this book to follow the interesting history of the Cape under Dutch rule except in a general way. Being the meticulous businessmen they have always been, the Dutch clerks kept elaborate records of the most trivial occurrences under their régime. Mr Theal, who was for many years archivist to the government, wrote nearly a hundred years ago that 'the manuscript records are so voluminous that an ordinary lifetime would be too short to read all those relating to the years 1691–1745'. Himself an exact man, he reckoned that in the preparation of his four-volume history of the Cape before 1796 he expended at least two years at a rate of ten hours to each working day. It is possible, should anyone wish to do it, to ascertain with certainty which cleric preached in which church on every Sunday over a century and a half and what was the text he took at both Matins and Evensong. To give an idea of the tightness of the Company's collar around the neck of every burgher, I have taken this extract from the Cape Archives for the year 1757:

6. Butchers; the free; protest before God and man against the charge laid against them that they have been unwilling to slaughter and also careless; and wish the Council to withdraw it otherwise they will have to lay the matter before the Directors. They maintain that they cannot, without ruining themselves, slaughter at the present prices fixed by the Council.

7. Blankenburg, Jacobus Willem, his executors, The Orphan Masters, submit that he desired in his Will the manumission of his slaves Clara of Bengal and Fortuyn of the Cape. Ask permission to give effect to his disposition and offer the required security.

8. Blignaut, Jan; Captain of the first Company of Burgher Dragoons at Stellenbosch. Asks for his discharge in consequence of old age and infirmities.

9. Bergh, Olof Abraham; wishes to open a bakery.

10. Boode, Frederick; Minister of the Divine Word here; wishes to send to Europe for his education his little son Jan Boode, 13 years old.

11. Bernard, Anselmus; late Chief Surgeon on the China Return ship *Hooncop*, asks permission to sell some tea by public auction.

12. Breda, Alexander van; burgher; wishes to erect a small

water mill for grinding corn and barley for his own use in his garden in Table Valley which formerly belonged to the adjutant of the burgher cavalry here, Johannes Jacobus Tesselaar.

13. Grison, Jannetje; widow of the late burgher Jacobus van Os submits that her son Anthony van Os in consequence of his drinking habits which have continued for some time has fallen into very bad habits thus daily causing great sorrow and affliction to his mother and, as to her no less regret, she finds that her continued admonitions have been of no avail to cause him to reform, she is compelled to request you to take her son, Anthony van Os, into the service as a soldier and to send him away.

14. Gruselje, Anna; widow of the late Pieter Nebbens, surgeon on the Middleburg; asks, in consequence of ill-health, to be permitted to remain here for a time with her little son, Johannes.

Governor succeeded Governor, 'good' Governors like Simon van der Stel, Colonel de Chavonnes and Ryk Tulbagh and 'bad' ones such as Van de Graaf. Temptation to belong to the latter category was great, for the Company in its relentless pursuit of dividends had the pernicious habit of deliberately underpaying its servants. By way of compensation they were given perquisites such as the exclusive right to trade in certain commodities and fees of one kind and another which gave the less scrupulous considerable scope for malpractice. It says much for the quality of the men chosen that there were far more good Governors than bad ones. A militia existed in and around the capital but the defence of outlying farms was, from the earliest times, left to the commandos; every able-bodied man between 16 and 60 was liable for service, their obligation being to turn out armed, mounted and with three days' rations of biltong and rusks, at the behest of the landdrost who usually acted as field commander. By them constant petty wars were waged against the ubiquitous little Bushmen which, before their pressure was felt to be too great for endurance, often ended with handshakes and presents.

The first outside district to be settled was Stellenbosch, named for Simon van der Stel, thirty miles from Table Bay and officially called into existence before the end of the seventeenth century. Drakenstein and Paarl soon followed but by 1688 the burgher population had still not reached 600. After the Revocation of the Edict of Nantes there came a welcome infusion of homeless

B   33

Huguenots, about 200 in all, who settled about the area which became known as Frenchman's Hoek. Van der Stel was at pains to see that they were not all congregated too closely together for, wisely, he did not want to see a colony within a colony.

In 1713 there was a near disaster; some passengers calling at the Cape on their way home from India carried with them the first germs of smallpox. Within six months some 200 of the slave population of 570 were dead and before the winter was over nearly a quarter of the European population had been wiped out. Between 1712 and 1716 the burgher roll dropped from 1,939 to 1,697 even after taking into account the births and new arrivals of four years. Far worse hit were the Hottentots whose dirty habits made them particularly vulnerable to an unknown disease. Those who tried to escape from the colony were killed or driven back by others further away and those who avoided the massacre came back to die. The number of deaths was impossible to calculate but visitors in the following year remarked that 'the Hottentot population had almost disappeared'. Further inland whole tribes were blotted out never to appear again and even their names have been lost. It was to be a very long time before the numbers among both races were made up and in the meantime great tracts of land stood empty.

During all these years the Kaffir tribes had been slowly moving down into lands to the east of the Colony. In May, 1736, they came into collision with the vedettes of Europe. Three English sailors, Thomas Willer, Henry Clark and William Bilyert, had survived the wreck of their ship some years before and had made homes for themselves amongst the Kaffirs, marrying their women and earning their keep as elephant hunters. A party of Dutchmen in search of ivory happened across them somewhere on the border of Natal and Pondoland. The Englishmen agreed to sell ten wagon-loads of ivory on credit and to accompany the buyers home to collect the goods which were to be bartered for them. The party trekked through Tembu country and were offered hospitality at the kraal of a chief named Palo. Palo's people found the temptation to possess themselves of their belongings too great to be endured and, when the white men were off their guard, they attacked and killed five of them. The seven survivors escaped and managed to reach the Sunday River where they were lucky enough to find another hunting party which took them back to Cape Town. The Governor, who was on the point of resignation, took no action for there was nothing he could do.

The tribes, with the Xosa in the van, continued to move like a black glacier. In 1752 an expedition was sent out to ascertain how far they had got and what they appeared to be intending. It reported back that already they were to be found as near as the Keiskamma river; four years later the tide had flowed yet nearer and the smoke of their fires was observed on the banks of the Great Fish River. Within a short time the Xosa were in some sort of occupation of all the country between the Winterberg and Amatolas to one side and the sea on the other. Boer and Bantu now confronted each other in the place which was to be their battleground for a long time to come.

CHAPTER 2

Cattle and Commandos

THE First Kaffir War was fought in the year 1779. It was brought about by the misbehaviour of the Xosa, an organized people but adept and conscienceless cattle thieves. There are conflicting accounts as to the proximate cause of it, though by then this was not important for collision was inevitable. One story insists that its author was Willem Prinsloo, a masterful man who had, eight years previously, obtained the consent of Governor Tulbagh to his taking up two farms within the colony near the present village of Somerset West. Prinsloo, in fact, had spread himself well over on to the east side of the Great Fish River which, in 1775, had been pronounced to mark the frontier, and had been deaf to all orders to move back. He had angered Mahuta, the nearest Kaffir chief, by shooting one of his men whom he had caught stealing a sheep and had seized some of the tribe's cattle as what he called compensation. Another account declares that Prinsloo's son Marthinus had, in defiance of the Governor, crossed the Keiskamma with a party in order to buy cattle and had there killed a tribal elder in a fight. The third version is that a petty chief named Koba having accepted the Fish River boundary nevertheless crossed over into the colony and was driven back with what seemed to him needless violence. Whichever may be true, the *casus belli* was a boundary dispute and the Prinsloos were almost certainly the culprits.

The Fish River was as bad a boundary as can be imagined.

Its only merit lay in the fact that it was an identifiable feature representing law on one side and barbarism on the other. It snaked its way to the sea by reaches which seemed to aim at every point of the compass; sometimes it was overhung by trees and, after rain, ran in a mad torrent of foaming, muddy water; in other places its bed was a chain of stagnant, buzzing pools of filthy water from which even the unfastidious baboons refused to drink. The banks were high, sometimes rising a sheer 200 feet, and below them were quicksands that could swallow both man and horse. Even at some of the drifts the water came up to a rider's saddle-flaps. Worst of all was the bush, both banks being clothed with it as thickly as anywhere in Africa and turning it into a secret country. In parts it was so close that a man had to lead his horse through tunnels in the foliage to which the sun never penetrated and the only paths were those made by game. The depths were heavy with the scent of wild jasmine, rank willows trailed their roots down the shallower banks and the universal colour varied from the light green of the spekboom to the dark olive of the naboom.

Everywhere the bush was alive; elephant, hippopotamus, gemsbok, duiker and all the animals of the continent had their places there. Down by the river were sandpipers and heron and away from it partridge and guinea-fowl roosted undisturbed. The occasional traveller would find himself importuned by the honey-guides which would flutter chirruping around his head until he gave in and allowed himself to be led to the nest of wild bees the bird had discovered; once there, he would be allowed to take all the honey (a great Kaffir delicacy), the guide receiving his reward from the grubs and wax in the broken comb. The nights were urgent with animal and bird calls and daylight only brought a change in them. Beyond the bush and in open country once more lay the foot-hills of the mountains, good sheep country of short-cropped grass with kranzes of streaked sandstone rising from them. The cliff faces were beautiful with their clinging aloes but the kloofs, cuttings as exact as if wedges had been driven into the hillsides, were dark and fearsome. In them lay the unseen, savage things: leopards, snakes and wild Kaffirs. An army could hide here and none would know it.

The Kaffirs invaded the colony in some force but they insisted, to begin with, that it was not an act of war against the white men. They claimed to be no more than a punitive expedition sent out to exact retribution from a clan named the Gunukwebe by lifting their cattle and the Gunukwebe, warned in time, were seeking sanctuary in the colony. Though they did assegai a few Hottentots and took their cattle, Mahuta's warriors did not, at first, molest the Boers. The restraint, however, was of short duration for by the end of September they had turned their attention to Prinsloo and those others who had followed his example by taking up land near to the frontier. The farmers of the district then called the Zuurveld (now Albany and Bathurst) were forced to take to their wagons. Rarabe, chief of the Xosa, sent word that the offending raiders were rebels and said that he would be glad of help in dealing with them. Unfortunately for Rarabe, several of his senior councillors had been recognized amongst the marauders. This kind of mendacity was to become a feature common to nearly all the future wars but this was the first occasion on which infiltration under cover of deceit was practised. It might have had serious results for the Boers but for the accident of recognition.

Two commandos were called out and for the first time the famous names of Joubert and Ferreira appear in the records as their leaders. They attacked the Xosa and routed them several times, the biggest engagement being at a place called Naudes Hoek, re-taking many stolen cattle in the process. They failed, however, to get most of them back across the river for the drought had reduced them to skin and bone.

During the winter months the Kaffirs came back in far greater numbers and all pretence about their purpose was dropped. More forces were needed and in October the Council of Policy conferred plenary powers over the whole eastern frontier and its inhabitants on Adriaan van Jaarsveld. He was an experienced fighter against the Bushmen and had a reputation for bravery and determination which were not lessened by a streak of cruelty. On one occasion he was said to have thrown a fistful of tobacco to some Kaffirs and as they scrambled for it he fired his *roer* into the midst of them just for fun. This quality, however, would not have made him less welcome as a leader.

Van Jaarsveld's orders from the council were to reach an

agreement if he could but to expel the intruders by force if they could not be persuaded to go back peaceably. He mustered only about a hundred burghers and forty Hottentots but they were well armed and mounted. Above all, van Jaarsveld knew exactly how his battle was to be fought in order to make the most of those factors in which he was superior—mobility and fire-power.

Rarabe's brother, Langa, with more prudence than his colleagues, agreed to restore his spoils and to retire but all the other chiefs refused to budge or to give up anything. Van Jaarsveld therefore first secured all his non-combatants, the European and Hottentot families, in two wagon-laagers protected mainly by the boys and the old men. The wagons were drawn up in two circles in a fashion not seen since they had been similarly used by the Hussites in fifteenth-century Bohemia; wheels were lashed together and the interstices packed with thorn bush; but as the Kaffirs did not use fire-arrows the later precaution of stretching wetted buffalo hide over the outside was not necessary. With his brave horsemen he then attacked the Kaffir masses, galloping to within gun-shot, firing a volley into them, wheeling round to re-load in the saddle and charging back again and again until the Kaffirs, their knobkerries and assegais useless to them, broke and fled across the river. The most formidable mounted warriors since the Mongols, as Winston Churchill was to call their descendants, had come. No other soldiers in the world at this date could have achieved the same effect. Their marksmanship had not yet reached the perfection of later days for the weapons available were not good enough but the big double-barrelled *roers*, usually 4 or 8 bore, loaded with the large slugs about the size of swan-shot which the Boers called 'lopers', did terrible execution at short ranges. To load these weapons at a canter was something of a feat but the commandos, Dutchman and Hottentot alike, showed that it could be done. Van Jaarsveld had made the pattern and in this fashion battles would be won on the veld for many years to come, the greatest of them all being Blood River nearly sixty years later.

The First Kaffir War was over, a demonstrable victory for the Company's servants over the rising power of the black men. More than 5,000 head of cattle were retaken, van Jaarsveld parcelling them out among his men to the fury of their former owners. The council, having little choice, approved van Jaarsveld's action but added warningly that it was not to be taken as a precedent.

Other things than Kaffirs were troubling the council at this moment for it seemed that the Company might at last have to think about its defence from the sea. Relations with the English had always been good and at times, such as during the Marlborough Wars, had been positively cordial. The American War, however, brought a change and on 31 March, 1781, the French frigate *Silphide* arrived with despatches from the Dutch ambassador in Paris informing the Governor that his country, in alliance with the French, had been at war with England for the last three months. The Governor was also advised that there was no immediate cause for alarm as M de la Motte, a French spy in London, was keeping Paris reliably informed about any plans the English might have for a descent on the Cape. Just over a fortnight later a British squadron under Commodore Johnstone arrived in Porto Praya roads in the Cape Verde islands. There it was surprised by the French admiral, the Bailli de Suffren, who had sources of intelligence other than M de la Motte. Johnstone, though caught at anchor, fought Suffren off and limped in pursuit of him. The French admiral, however, had too long a start and was able to land at Table Bay the troops he had brought to reinforce the almost defenceless colony. Johnstone in his turn surprised Suffren in the Bay but wisely came to the conclusion that the assault of the place was beyond his powers and sailed away. The rest of the war left the Cape untroubled.

For a long time the Company had been trading in South Africa at a loss and its financial difficulties were now becoming acute. The Directors in Amsterdam set their faces doggedly against anything which would make the place self-supporting even to the extent of forbidding the making of blankets from local wool on existing local looms at a time of great shortage. The officers of the Company were not always of the quality of the pioneers and corruption was rife. Holland had long ceased to be the great power she had been in the seventeenth century and the Company was rotting away. The consequence of this can be seen in the peculiar conduct of the Second Kaffir War which began in March, 1789.

This time it was a long-drawn-out and, from the Company's point of view, thoroughly unsatisfactory business. The First War had shown that the commandos had the will and the ability to defeat their enemy in the field. The Second was an exercise in the use of Danegeld with precisely the same results that King Ethelred had experienced. It began at a moment particularly embarrassing for the Company. The province of Graaf Reinet was in the process of formation and this brought the farmers into a confrontation with the Bushmen of a kind far more serious than anything which had gone before. The Bushmen were being pushed steadily northwards and obviously felt that the process had gone on long enough. Raids on the farmers' cattle took place with monotonous regularity and were followed up by the murder by poisoned arrow of any European or Hottentot servant who might happen to be away from help. As the Spaniards had found in the sixteenth century, the Dutch are a brave and tenacious people who do not easily give up that for which they have laboured long and hard. Though a man had to carry out his work with his weapons always at hand the farmers clung grimly to their steadings. Murder was followed by reprisal and torture was regularly practised by the Bushmen on those unfortunate enough to fall living into their hands. The farmers, understandably, were not gentle with what they held to be venomous reptiles. The manhood of most of the districts not abutting on the eastern frontier was fully occupied in keeping the Bushmen down and there were no reserves to carry on simultaneous war in the Fish River bush.

The Xosa at this time were in a state of confusion following on the death of Rarabe in a fight with the Tembus. His Great Son had died in Rarabe's lifetime leaving a child, now ten years old, who was named Gaika. Some clans had already crossed the Kei before Rarabe was killed and their chiefs announced that by leaving tribal territory they had shaken off their allegiance to the infant heir though they acknowledged the suzerainty of the paramount chief Galeka. Rarabe's council appointed another son, Ndlambe, to act as regent during the infancy of Gaika but the legality of this was questioned by some.

As a result there was jealousy and feuding among the Xosa chieftains sufficient, as most people thought, to distract them from making another concerted invasion.

All the same, the situation was uneasy. The Kaffirs knew perfectly well that the Dutch had their hands full with the Bushmen; many Kaffirs were working on the farms well inside the frontier and would constitute a valuable Fifth Column. In addition to these many more were engaged in illicit cattle trading with the Europeans and could see their weakness.

In March, 1789, the invasion came; a large body of Kaffirs under several chieflets swarmed across the river and poured over the entire Zuuiveld. They moved at such speed that the farmers had to abandon their cattle and ride westward for their lives. A demand for help was galloped to Cape Town and the burgher captain, Kuhne, called out the commandos that were left. The Council, however, decided that war must be avoided on any account as if it were some kind of commercial undertaking in which both sides have an equal voice. They appointed a commission of two men to negotiate with the Kaffirs and to buy peace at any price. Their names were Wagener and Maynier and their memories are still execrated. The Kaffirs had expected a walk-over but as Kuhne's commando came nearer they began to remember what had happened when they had tried conclusions with the mounted burghers before. Most of them vanished into the Fish River bush wishing nothing more than to get safely back to their own lands before the terrible lopers tore into them. To their consternation they found the river to be in flood and impassable. Kuhne and his men arrived and were plainly preparing to charge. The Kaffirs, or many of them, abandoned hope. However, not a shot was fired and the commandos were seen to be moving away. The Council's order had arrived; the Kaffirs were not to be molested, no attempt must be made to recapture the stolen cattle and the commando was to disband immediately. The men were near mutiny but in the end the orders were obeyed. Kuhne pointed out the awful consequence of showing weakness in the face of a savage enemy but it was to no avail. The sullen commando rode home while the Kaffirs exulted in their incredible good fortune.

Mr Maynier arrived and sent a courteous message to the chief

Tchaka that he would be glad if he called. Tchaka, uncertain what to believe, replied that he was not well enough to make the journey but sent emissaries. Mr Maynier enquired mildly whether they did not recognize the Fish River frontier. They answered that this was not in question but the Xosa had bought all the land between the Fish and Kowie rivers from a Hottentot named Ruiter. There may have been a grain of truth in this for Ruiter was a notable blackguard but the Xosa knew better than to believe that he could have any title to this large parcel of country. Maynier remarked that all the chiefs now west of the river were men who had acknowledged the frontier and he offered to refund whatever Ruiter had been given. The emissaries refused. They were willing, they said, to pay as tribute the same as the farmers had been paying in rent, not adding that if the Company wanted to collect it it had better come gun in hand, but they refused to move. Mr Maynier went back to Graaf Reinet and the Kaffirs endured a moment of panic when a rumour that the farmers were laagering up sent them scampering into the Amatola Mountains. In the end Maynier proclaimed that the Kaffirs might remain in possession of the land said to have been bought from Ruiter 'during the pleasure of the Government'. Everybody knew what that meant.

The burghers of Graaf Reinet were appalled at the betrayal. Those who still had farms continued to work them though almost in siege conditions, enduring sporadic warfare with Bushmen to the north and Kaffirs to the east. The feeling amongst them was that they no longer owed anything to so feeble a government and that one day they would saddle up and take back what had been theirs, no matter how much blood might flow.

This threatening situation continued until May of 1793, when the farmers were horrified to learn of the selection of Maynier as the new landdrost of Graaf Reinet. If this were not calamity enough, drought struck the frontier lands and killed off the cattle; the Kaffirs stole the reserve stores of grain and the position of all of them became desperate. The farmers decided that the time had come when they must fight or perish. Without reference to Landdrost Maynier, the commando of Graaf Reinet was embodied and moved to attack. They received an unexpected recruit—Ndlambe. He assured them that the men they were about to destroy were bad men and were his enemies. The commando recovered about 800 cattle but within a few days full-scale war had erupted. Some 6,000 Kaffirs poured across the river, burning and killing as they went; this was more than large-scale cattle lifting for every European or Hottentot upon whom they could get their hands was murdered after torture, although it is right to say that women and children were allowed to go free. Of 120 farms between the Kowie and the Zwartkop only 4 escaped destruction. The strutting Kaffirs drove off more than 65,000 head of cattle, 11,000 sheep and 200 horses.

Maynier hurried up with offers of more and better presents if only they would go home. Some chiefs virtuously pointed out that they had already withdrawn behind the frontier, ignoring the fact that they had done so only to dispose of their enormous quantity of loot. Others agreed to go back provided they were allowed to keep their takings. The farmers were quite certain that, for all his protestations to the contrary, Ndlambe was at the bottom of the invasion and that the differences within the Xosa ranks had somehow been resolved. Even Maynier could not accept terms such as these and he made his way back to Graaf Reinet to seek instructions. When he arrived there he learnt that another foray was at that moment taking place. The council had already sent orders to the landdrost of Swellendam to get his commando under arms and to ride to the scene of the devastation with all speed. He was to drive the Kaffirs back across the river and to release the stolen cattle but on no account was any punishment to be inflicted. Maynier, hearing of this, summoned the commando of Graaf Reinet but such was the contempt in which he was held that most of its officers refused to serve under him. The two commandos met up early in September where the town of Grahamstown now stands and between them they numbered about 600 men. Maynier, quite unabashed, insisted on his legal right to the command which the Swellendam men had grudgingly to concede. He announced his intention of leading the greater part of the force across the river to pursue such Kaffirs as had withdrawn and ordered the remainder to stay in reserve and wait upon events.

Maynier's force crossed at Trompetter's Drift and managed to recapture a few cattle. They passed the next ten days riding up and down looking for a ford across the next river, the Keiskamma, and being unsuccessful had to make their way to its mouth where they crossed over a sand bar. This gave the Kaffirs comfortable time in which to take the stolen cattle far beyond Maynier's reach and to double back to the Zuurveld also by way of Trompetter's Drift. Maynier's commando fought a sharp action on the Buffalo river where they killed 40 Kaffirs and picked up about 7,000 cattle but that was the sum of their achievements. The constant riding to and fro had worn out his horses, the drought had made forage hard to find and he was obliged to fall back to the Keiskamma losing most of the cattle by the way. There he met Ndlambe who was at pains to assure the landdrost that this war was not of his making. True he was accompanied by a large herd of cattle bearing colonial markings but this was entirely fortuitous. He was, in fact, on his way to restore them to their rightful owners having with great difficulty retaken them from wicked men who had stolen them. Mr Maynier found this very satisfactory.

As the commando wearily approached the Fish River word came in that the Kaffirs were holding the ford in some force. A brave Hottentot swam over to the other bank and made his way to the farm where the Swellendam burghers were still kicking their heels. They rode at the crossing place, the Kaffirs scattered and Maynier's riders came over unmolested. The combined force then spent three weeks riding aimlessly about the Zuurveld trying to bring to battle Kaffirs who disappeared at their approach only to surface as soon as they had ridden on. The campaign was without form and it was plain that there were only two courses open to the Government. Either they must make it known that any Kaffir found west of the river would pay for his trespass with his life and find the force which could carry this out or they must come to terms. They decided on the latter choice; Maynier attended a meeting of chiefs who explained blandly that they were quite willing to end hostilities but the restoration of the cattle was an impossibility; they had all either been eaten or had died from the drought. Maynier expressed himself to be content with this account of the matter;

the Kaffirs remained in possession of all they had taken and of the greater part of the Zuurveld.

Before the Swellendam commando had reached home they had news of the murders of two more farmers and of a Dutch woman. Maynier wrote a whining despatch to the Government exculpating the Kaffirs from all blame and asserting that the war had been caused by the misconduct of certain farmers. He was, for a time, regarded as the man who had brought to an end a most inconvenient war and his authority at Cape Town was greatly strengthened. So ended the Second Kaffir War with all the fruits of victory in Kaffir hands and the farmers almost in open rebellion against the Company.

When the war with revolutionary France began in Europe, the Government at Cape Town was on the verge of disintegration. Its chronic insolvency coupled with the unbending refusal by the Directors in Amsterdam to allow the burghers any voice in their affairs and the ignominious way in which the Second Kaffir War had ended made it plain that things could not go on like this for much longer. Some burghers, the Prinsloos amongst them, refused to swear allegiance to the new Governor, Sluysken, who was powerless to do anything about it. Many people had Jacobin sympathies although their home country was in alliance with England.

It was common knowledge that this state of affairs was precarious as the pro-French party in Holland was strong and not likely to remain idle. A change of sides at any moment was perfectly possible. In Cape Town there was a battalion of regular mercenary troops, by no means all of them Dutch, and a small corps of Dutch gunners in the Company's service. The mercenaries would probably rather serve with the French than against them but the gunners could be relied upon if there were to be a recurrence of the events of 1781.

Nothing happened until 12 June, 1795, when a Mr Hercules Ross, secretary to Major-General Sir James Craig, arrived in a Dutch ship and brought with him letters for the Governor from his General and from Admiral Elphinstone. These were found to contain an invitation to the Governor and his military commander, a Scotch soldier of fortune named Colonel Gordon, to visit the senders in the Admiral's flagship just over the horizon.

Sluysken declined the invitation but said that he was willing to be represented in order to hear what these gentlemen wished to say to him. In reply there came Captain Hardy, R.N., and Colonel Mackenzie of the 78th (The Ross-shire Buffs), accompanied by Ross, who spoke Dutch, as interpreter. They handed over a letter from the Prince of Orange written from Kew on 7 February ordering his Governor to admit the troops of his ally the King of England to defend the Cape against the French. A covering letter from Elphinstone honestly informed the Governor that his country had been overrun and his Prince was a fugitive but expressed the opinion that British arms would put this right before too long.

The Council, hastily summoned, decided that in the circumstances the Prince's order must be treated as a nullity but they agreed to supply provisions to the fleet on the usual commercial terms and to allow small parties ashore for recreation. It was, of course, intended only to gain time in the hope that other instructions might arrive. On 18 June the General appeared before the Council and told them bluntly that he intended to carry out his orders to enter the colony and put it into a state of defence, giving his word that at the end of the war it would be handed back and that there would in the meantime be no interference with the administration beyond anything that military necessity might demand. The Council gave their reply in writing; the Governor's oath of office did not permit him to comply and any attempt at a landing would be resisted. A short while afterwards supplies to the fleet were cut off.

For a month Elphinstone and Craig did all they could to accomplish their purpose without having to resort to force. The anti-British and pro-Jacobin sentiments of the Colonists were strong but not universal, for the House of Orange had many supporters. *Ad hoc* forces of various kinds were raised though their qualities and allegiances were frequently uncertain. No orders came from the Batavian Republic. The fleet could not stay on station for ever; on 14 July 350 Marines and 450 men of the 78th landed and occupied Simon's Town without resistance, Sluysken having ordered that nobody should fire on them, and were later reinforced. On 7 August English ships sailed past Muizenburg, the main defended position, and fired a few broad-

47

sides. At the first shot the mercenary infantry fled into Cape Town. A column of 1,600 British troops (the 78th, Marines and a Naval Brigade) began to march from Simon's Town along the sea-shore towards the capital. The Dutch gunners and some others offered resistance but they did not stand against a sharp charge by the 78th. There was a little scrappy fighting over the next few days, the bluejackets of the Naval Brigade crossing the marsh at times up to their armpits in wet sand, but as more troops (84th [The York and Lancaster Regiment], 95th and 98th [both subsequently disbanded] with some guns) arrived from St Helena it became obvious that resistance would be futile. Craig again tried to persuade the Government that it should face up to reality and avoid pointless killing. The Council, to make things look better for posterity, issued a defiantly worded refusal to surrender (two signatories being J. Smuts and de Wet) and, after a decent interval, capitulated. British casualties were 3 killed and 37 wounded.

The Council closed its books, Governor Sluysken went home, Colonel Gordon shot himself; the Bushmen and the Kaffirs continued their depredations, unaware of what had happened. The caretakers, as the British commanders regarded themselves, accepted without enthusiasm the task of restoring solvency and of establishing a régime of freedom under the law. The individual burgher had to decide for himself whether, in the absence of any other constituted authority, he would give his temporary allegiance to King George or remain in a vacuum. As the existence of the majority depended upon the regular receipt of an official salary many, especially in the capital, found the decision made for them. The Provinces were less of one mind.

CHAPTER 3
The Coming of the Redcoats

On 16 September, 1795, the British force took possession of Cape Town and the powers of the former Governor were assumed by Admiral Elphinstone, General Craig and General Alured Clarke, acting jointly, with Hercules Ross as their secretary and interpreter. They accepted without hypocrisy the fact that their presence amounted only to that of temporary custodians but they determined that as long as they remained in office the country should be administered for the benefit of those who lived in it and no longer as a commercial proposition. Many of the functionaries of the Company were willing enough to remain in office, for their continued existence and that of their families depended upon the receipt of regular salaries; they duly took the oath of allegiance to King George for 'so long a time as His Majesty shall remain in possession of this colony'.

The new men did their best to conciliate the Dutch 'population by the creation of a burgher senate, still nominated rather than elected, and by freeing trade, reducing taxes and abrogating the old laws that forbade a man to come and go and to sell his wares as seemed best to him. Nevertheless, the new régime could not have been called in any sense a popular one. Many of the burghers cherished an ill-digested idea of some sort of Jacobin republic and the French were still the most favoured nation after their own. The presence of the troops of that country during the American war had raised the tone of Cape Town from 'the tavern of the seas' to 'Little Paris' and it is undeniable that if occupation by a power other than Holland had to be accepted the great majority would have preferred to see the Regiment of Luxembourg back again rather than the 84th Foot.

Within two months both Elphinstone and Clarke had left the Colony and Craig was formally appointed Governor, his troops being reduced to less than 3,000 men. He was in no position to provoke a crisis, even had he wished it, for the disbanded forces of the Company had only gone home and might easily have been organized for another trial of strength whenever they chose. Stellenbosch and Swellendam submitted tractably enough but the nearer one came to the frontier the more turbulent was the temper of the people. Trouble flared up in Graaf Reinet, the latest organized province, when Craig appointed a new *landdrost* to replace the present holder of the office who had not taken the oath. The new man, Mr Bresler, had once been an officer in the French service but was stoutly attached to the House of Orange; he was given firm instructions to do everything possible to improve the conditions of the farmers, 'to study their welfare and to protect them against their enemies'.

When Bresler arrived to take up his duties he was bluntly told that his authority would not be recognized until a meeting of 'representatives of the people' had been held to decide the attitude Graaf Reinet should adopt. Bresler waited patiently for a fortnight and then, by invitation, presented himself at the meeting which included the *heemraden*, the militia officers and three gentlemen holding no offices who were the 'representatives'. On being asked the reason for his presence in Graaf Reinet, Bresler firmly read out his commission and stated that he would preside over a meeting of the *heemraden* that afternoon. In answer to a question, he said that he could not acknowledge that the representatives had any standing.

At the time he had appointed, Bresler rang the bell of the *drostdy* and hoisted the Union flag. A crowd, headed by Marthinus Prinsloo and his friends, collected round him and demanded that the flag be hauled down at once. Bresler, alone and unfriended, refused. He was thrust aside and the flag lowered by three men, two bearing the ominous names of Joubert and Kruger, who informed the *landdrost* that Prinsloo had been elected 'protector of the voice of the people', that the taking of the oath of allegiance was forbidden and that another meeting would be held in a month's time at which a final decision would be taken. Bresler sensibly decided to await its outcome rather than to call on Craig for troops, for he had good reason to hope that moderate and sensible men, of whom there were plenty, would make their voices heard above those of Prinsloo and the other malcontents. This might well have happened but for the arrival just before the meeting of a man named Woyer, the former district surgeon and a notable agitator against the British. Woyer spoke eloquently for independence and in the end Adriaan van Jaarsveld, the son of the man of the same name who had trounced the Kaffirs in 1779, announced that those present were resolved to set up their own government and would only agree to terms which he wished written down. These were:

1. That the people of Graaf Reinet were willing to take to Cape Town for sale such articles as their land produced, according to the ancient custom.

2. That they would observe all reasonable orders and laws, provided the English governor would furnish them with powder, lead, clothing and such other articles as they needed.

Another speaker, Hendrik Krugel, added two more:

3. That the people of Graaf Reinet would not draw the sword against the English.

4. That their only reason for refusing to take the oath required was that when the States General of the Netherlands should retake the country they would not be able to justify themselves if they did so.

Mr Krugel was undoubtedly being what the Boers call 'slim', but the proposal was carried by acclaim. One must sympathize with the feelings of people who were cut off from the world and who could not understand that the business of government cannot be carried on in this unworldly way. Bresler did his best to explain what must be the consequence of a rebellion, no matter how elevated the sentiments which caused it, but no one would listen to him. Three days later he left for the capital. He reported the situation to Craig who sadly accepted that his duty could be done in only one way, but he had no intention of being hurried into a show of force which might set the whole colony ablaze.

One event over which he had no control occurred soon afterwards and gave him cause to hope that force would not be needed after all. A squadron of warships under the new flag of the French puppet state called the Batavian Republic was sent to sea to take reinforcements to the former possessions of the Company in the east for fear that they might fall into British hands. News of Sluysken's surrender had arrived before it sailed but the Admiral was given no orders other than to use his own discretion. He anchored in Saldanha Bay early in August expecting help from his countrymen but none came. Instead, Admiral Elphinstone returned with his fleet, Craig moved every soldier he possessed to the shore and the Dutch squadron surrendered. Their crews, having seen something of revolutionary France at first hand, were loyal to the House of Orange and were in a temper near to mutiny. The troops, mostly Germans unwillingly impressed into service, shared their feelings and the majority were only too glad to change sides. Eight fine ships of the line, three frigates and two minor vessels passed into British service together with many prime seamen. The transports sailed on to India with most of the original passengers in British uniforms. As the news spread inland all hope of foreign intervention vanished.

The disaffected party at Graaf Reinet met again on 22 August but this time the men most vociferous for independence kept away. The former *landdrost*, Gerotz, and his secretary, Oertel, spoke up firmly in favour of accepting the temporary authority of the British. This time he was listened to and a letter signed by all the most prominent burghers, including van Jaarsveld, was despatched to Cape Town announcing the climb-down. It was only just in time, for the Governor had already assembled a military force to over-awe the secessionists. Five companies of light infantry, drawn mostly from the 84th and 98th Regiments, two hundred cavalry from the 8th Light Dragoons, 150 locally enlisted irregular horse and three field guns had been placed under command of Major King of the 84th at Groenkloof together with a corps of Hottentots.

The Hottentots had originally been in the service of the Company and had dribbled in to the camp at Stellenbosch where they had been found work as cooks and followers. Major King had been impressed by their quality and obtained leave to organize them in a regular fashion and to have them issued with arms. Their first commander was John Campbell, a subaltern in the 98th, and officers and British N.C.O.s were attached from the regiments already in the Colony. All the Hottentots were expert horsemen and a proportion were mounted to do duty as guides and orderlies. From this nucleus there grew up the Corps which was to be called the Cape Mounted Rifles. When the authority of Holland was restored after the Treaty of Amiens the regiment remained intact in the Dutch service and after the final occupation of 1806 the majority volunteered to return to their founders.

Craig agreed that Gerotz, in consideration of his services, should remain in office for the time being and proclaimed an amnesty for everybody except Woyer, who had left the country to seek help abroad. The wild men of the Prinsloo faction retired to the Boschberg breathing threats of marching on Swellendam but when the news of the surrender of the Dutch fleet penetrated to their fastness they grudgingly accepted the situation. An attempt was made by the Governor of Batavia to run a supply of arms ashore for them but, after many adventures, his ship was taken by H.M.S. *Hope* in Delagoa Bay.

An uneasy peace lay over the Colony. In November, 1797, the new, civilian, Governor arrived to take over from General Craig, and Major-General Francis Dundas (not to be confused with his uncle Henry Dundas, later Lord Melville, the Secretary of State for War) was appointed commander of the forces. Lord Macartney, by birth an Irish squireen, had risen high in the diplomatic service by his own merits; in turn he had been envoy to the Court of Catherine the Great, Governor of the Caribees, Governor of Madras during the war with Haider Ali (in consequence of which he had fought a duel with a General in Hyde Park and been wounded), and he had only recently returned from a particularly unrewarding mission to the Emperor of China. He was a high Tory and one method of teaching a gentle lesson to crypto-Jacobin landowners which he revived from a forgotten past was the billeting on them of dragoons. It was not

Macartney's fault that he knew nothing of the hinterland of Cape Town for no maps worth the name were to be had. 'We are shamefully ignorant of the geography of the country. I neither know nor can I learn where this Graaf Reinet is, whether it is 500 or 1,000 miles from Cape Town.'

Bresler, who did know, was sent back to take up his duties again and with him went the Governor's secretary, John Barrow, who had been with Macartney in China. The two men set off with three wagons to cover the 500 miles and Barrow, who had had some scientific education, took with him instruments for map-making. It took them a month to complete the journey. Barrow started with a prejudice against the Dutch, for he had written to Dundas in April that most of the rebels were 'buried in the forests of brushwood near the mouth of the Kareege which is a most dismal den or that they have taken themselves into Kaffreland'.

Their reception at Graaf Reinet was friendly and Gerotz gladly handed over his duties. Barrow's opinion of the 'Boors' was not raised by his hearing a conversation between two young men who were, quite without boasting, comparing the number of Bushmen they had recently shot. Barrow was outraged and not in the least mollified when these questions were put to him: How often had he seen farmers murdered with poisoned arrows when at work on their own land? How many cattle had he seen wantonly mutilated? Mr Barrow had seen none, but the 'Boors' remained his villains, cruel, idle, drunken, cowardly and ravishers of female Hottentots.

Nor did he like their dorp: 'It [Graaf Reinet] consists of an assemblage of huts placed at some distance from each other, in two lines, forming a kind of street. At the upper end stands the house of the *landdrost*, built also of mud, and a few miserable hovels that were intended as offices for the transaction of public business; most of these have tumbled in and the rest are in a ruinous condition and not habitable. The jail is composed of mud walls roofed with thatch and so little tenable that an English deserter who had been shut up in it for amusing the country people with an account of a conversation with French officers, made his escape the first night through the thatch. The mud walls of all the buildings are excavated and the floors under-

mined by a species of termes or white ant which destroys everything that falls in its way except wood: and the bats that lodge
in the thatch come forth at night in such numbers as to extin-
guish the candles and make it impossible to remain in any room
where there is a light. The village is chiefly inhabited by
mechanics and such as hold some petty employment under the
landdrost. Its appearance is more miserable than that of the
poorest villages in England. The necessaries of life are with
difficulty procured in it for though there be plenty of land few
are found industrious enough to cultivate it. No milk, no butter,
no cheese, no vegetables of any kind are to be had on any terms.
There is no butcher, no chandler, no grocer, no baker . . . they
have neither wine nor beer . . . It would be difficult to say what
the motives could have been that induced the choice of this
place for the residence of the *landdrost*.' The last few words
explain Barrow's perplexity; Graaf Reinet was not a village in
the way the word was understood in Barrow's native Lancashire;
it was the *landdrost*'s wagon-laager, come to rest and with its
wheels removed.

Bresler and Barrow moved on, the latter having quickly
exhausted the joys of civilization; their task was to see all the
chiefs in the Zuurveld and try to persuade them to go home,
but Barrow's presence made it a reconnaissance for the Governor's benefit. The Secretary was a man of prodigious energy
and could not understand that others, especially in Africa, might
not want to live at such a pace. He castigated in his book the
idleness of Boer and Hottentot, saying of the latter that it was
to them like a disease. Like an earlier Cobbett, he rode dis-
approvingly on. Only when the Great Fish River lay behind did
Mr Barrow meet men he could observe with enthusiasm: 'The
finest specimens of the human figure I ever beheld. They
possessed a firmness of carriage and an open manly demeanour
which, added to the good nature which illuminated their features,
declared them to be equally unconscious of fear, suspicion or
treachery . . . a young man about 20 of six feet ten inches
high was one of the finest figures that perhaps was ever created.
He was a perfect Hercules.' Mr Barrow had met the Xosa. He
approved of the chiefs he met, even going to the length of trying
to find a pair of breeches for Tuli who had set his heart on

having some. None were big enough. Once the chiefs were on terms with him, Barrow got their story from them. They were all, so they said, not merely willing but anxious to return but Gaika had now come of age and they feared his anger. Some said openly that Ndlambe was a much wronged man and that they would be glad to see him made chief in Gaika's place.

Mr Barrow and the *landdrost* rode on to the Keiskamma where Gaika came to greet them. He arrived at full gallop on a racing ox accompanied by half a dozen similarly mounted friends. At 20 Gaika may have been an attractive personality and certainly Barrow found him 'possessed in a superior degree [of] a solid understanding and a clear head' [*sic*]. This was a fair assessment but it did not take into account the fact that Gaika had debauched the wife of his uncle Ndlambe and on that score alone was unacceptable as chief to a majority of the Xosa. Mr Barrow, at any rate during his dealings with the Kaffirs, seems always to have cast his vote for the person with whom he last spoke, provided that he was not a 'Boor'.*

Gaika took the line that his war with Ndlambe was over as the latter was his prisoner. The tribes in the Zuurveld were rebels against his authority but he would be willing to receive them back without reprisals if they wanted to come. He wished only to live in amity with the Europeans of the Colony and readily agreed that there should be no intercourse between the two peoples originating from his side of the border unless it was sanctioned by him. In addition to this he would send regular communications on matters of interest to the *landdrost* at Graaf Reinet, his messenger being identified by a staff, on the brass head of which were engraved the arms of England. Gaika was a far-sighted man who had no wish to see his tenure of the

* Barrow was still at heart a simple soul, and relied too much on first impressions, a thing particularly dangerous in Africa where the best is easily discernible but the worst takes time to show itself. His book swings from near prurience in his investigations of the intimate life of the elephant to the reverse in his description of Hottentot dress. A cod-piece of jackal-skin worn hairy side out, was 'one of the most immodest objects in such a situation as he places it that could have been contrived'. He was sufficiently taken by Gaika to write from Graaf Reinet to Lady Anne Barnard on 12 October, 1797, that 'He seems to be the adored divinity of his people and they know no other'. *Lady Anne Barnard at the Cape of Good Hope*, Dorothea Fairbridge, O.U.P., 1924.

chieftaincy marked by continuous warfare with the formidable Boers.

As Bresler and Barrow made their way back it became clear that, whatever Gaika may have said, the tribes in the Zuurveld had no intention of budging. The *landdrost* of Swellendam was informed of this and messages were sent to Ndlambe's subordinates telling them that if they did not return they would be put out by force. Nothing, however, was done to put the threat into operation, for no British troops were to be had and the official view of the commandos was that they were not capable of dealing with the Kaffirs on their own. Barnard, the Colonial Secretary and husband of the ebullient Lady Anne who was doing more to make the British popular than any man could hope to do, wrote to Dundas that 'night is the time [the Kaffirs] choose for their attacks, no enemy whatever is to be seen by daylight although they see you and watch all your movements; it was at one time thought that the farmers, if they had powder would have been sufficiently strong to have subdued them but it was proved in an action that 300 farmers had against 150 Caffres and Hottentots in which the Boors [*sic*] were beaten, 5 of them killed and 104 horses taken from them that if they were left to fight their own battles the district of Graaf Reinet would soon change its inhabitants.' Lord Macartney was of opinion that more could be made of the Hottentots, for he wrote to the same addressee that 'There is no doubt that the Hottentot is capable of a much greater degree of civilization than is generally recognized and perhaps the converting him into a soldier may be one of the best steps towards it'. Nevertheless the fact remained that the Government was not strong enough to translate aspirations into action and for the time being the liberation of the Zuurveld must wait.

The frontier continued to simmer while Macartney was absorbed by troubles nearer home, including a Naval mutiny on the pattern of Spithead and the Nore. At the end of 1798 he retired but continued to be maintained by the Colony to the tune of £2,000 a year for life. Dundas replaced him at the head of affairs and had hardly taken the oath of office when he was faced by rebellion. The farmers of Graaf Reinet had never accepted the new order with enthusiasm and they were becoming increasingly angry at the continued Kaffir presence in the Zuurveld in defiance of the order of the government. The Boers were well aware that the garrison at Cape Town was at its lowest level since the occupation, for the salted and experienced 86th (subsequently The Royal Ulster Rifles) Regiment had been sent to India being replaced by two weak units, the 61st (The Gloucestershire Regt.) and 81st (The Loyal Regt.). Both of these, in addition to being well under establishment, were made up of very young soldiers who sickened quickly and easily. On top of this, a disastrous fire, started by the burning wad from the morning gun igniting a thatched roof, had destroyed the cavalry barracks, burned to death 130 horses and consumed most of the military stores in the Colony.

Before a shot was fired there happened an event which provided some sort of respectable *casus belli*. Adriaan van Jaarsveld was arrested for forgery. He owed the orphan chamber £733 for the payment of which he had given a bond secured on his farm. No interest had been paid since 1791 but when seven years later a demand for it was made he produced a receipt on which '1791' had been altered to '1794'. He had ignored a summons to appear before the Court in consequence of which orders were sent to Bresler to have him arrested. This Bresler did when van Jaarsveld paid his next visit to him at the *drostdy* and, protesting his ignorance of the order, he was driven off in a wagon under escort of a sergeant and two troopers. This was too much for Prinsloo to bear and, as soon as the news reached him, he mustered a private commando of forty armed burghers and set off in pursuit. They overtook the party and compelled the soldiers to give up their prisoner. Other malcontents joined them and the whole body, numbering about 150, made camp near the *drostdy*. Prinsloo and three others, guns in hand, marched into the building and informed Bresler, rather improbably, that they were all in fear of being arrested as van Jaarsveld had been. They refused to accept Bresler's explanation that he had been arrested because he had not obeyed a lawful summons but insisted that the *landdrost* had acted not out of duty but from spite because of the man's past behaviour.

Prinsloo and his friends expected this to be the opening of a general insurrection but, to their chagrin, they got neither help nor sympathy from the more sober farmers. The commando broke camp and reassembled later at Prinsloo's farm. Here they were joined by two very rough customers, Jan Botha and Coenraad du Buis who eked out a savage existence amongst the Kaffirs. Du Buis, indeed, enjoyed a special relationship with Gaika whose widowed mother had become his concubine. Thirty men had been left at Graaf Reinet to watch the *drostdy* and they were heard talking openly of kidnapping Bresler and carrying him off to the Kaffirs as a hostage. The *landdrost* managed to get a letter through to the Governor and the knowledge of this together with the firm conduct of Sergeant Irwin of the 8th Light Dragoons, commanding the small guard of 8 troopers, and the persuasion of the local *predikant* decided the besiegers to disperse. This time they had left it too late, for the letter had reached Dundas on 16 February and on the following day he sent Brigadier-General Vandeleur overland with a strong detachment of the 8th and a squadron of irregular horse. Two companies of the 91st (The Argyll and Sutherland Highlanders) were shipped also to Algoa Bay. Vandeleur was standing no nonsense. He gave it out as he passed that the burghers must remain on their farms until he had finished his business and that any found away from them without excellent reason would be treated as traitors. His march was a considerable feat for troops with little African experience but he found himself able to write to Dundas on 26 February that 'The whole detachment, mounted and dismounted dragoons, and Hottentots as well, and the horses, considering the length of the march, have kept up their condition wonderfully, not a single sore back or lame horse. I intend going on without a halt until we pass Attiguas Cloof, where we shall arrive about daylight on Thursday morning, a march of 58 Dutch hours on horseback or 348 English miles in 12 days.' It was not until 19 March that the two parts of his force had joined up and entered Graaf Reinet. There 53 local farmers joined him but there was no sign of Prinsloo's army. His son, however, came into the camp bearing a petition for pardon from the insurgents. The General replied that they must lay down their arms and that any who had a mind to surrender should meet him at a designated farm in the Boschberg on 6 April.

Vandeleur and Bresler (whose brave conduct had been mentioned by Sergeant Maxwell in his report) marched there with the whole force except for a small guard left at the *drostdy*, arresting van Jaarsveld and his son without resistance on the way. Prinsloo with more than a hundred men rode in and they formally laid down their arms. Ninety-four were mulcted of small fines on the spot and sent home; the rest, the more deeply involved, were sent to Cape Town for trial. More came in later but the small hard core, including the ring-leaders Botha and du Buis, made their way into Kaffir country where they were turned back by the Tembu but received by Gaika. The records show that nine of Vandeleur's men deserted and accompanied them but it is not clear whether these were British soldiers or Hottentots. The latter would seem to be the more likely.

Dundas showed his gratitude to the loyal burghers by sending them presents, the three Field Cornets in particular receiving a gift that must have delighted their hearts, ' a double-barrelled gun with second sight, a very large bore calculated for killing elephants, long and strengthened at the stock with a thin plate of iron, packed in a neat case with cleaning rod etc. and a brass plate on each case with the name of the Commandant to whom it belongs and the following inscription "Given by Major-General Dundas as a reward for Services done to the British Government" '. The Kaffirs were not overlooked, their chiefs receiving 'a few dozen of handsome copper breast-plates with the British arms engraven on them' and lesser fry getting coloured beads, cases of 'coarse knives', tinder-boxes and flints and small looking-glasses.

The end of Prinsloo's rebellion, however, brought no peace and it was the fortuitous presence of Vandeleur's little force that first brought the British army into hostilities with the Kaffirs.

The Third Kaffir War had begun almost at the same moment as the rescue of van Jaarsveld was being carried out. Its causes were complex but the most important single one was the old feud between Ndlambe and Gaika which had flamed up from a quarrel over a woman. The Briseis of the war was a maiden named Tutula, said to be the most beautiful in all Kaffirland, and she belonged to the older man. Gaika, in contravention of tribal law and custom, as he and the girl were related, took her from his prisoner. By some means Ndlambe contrived to escape and crossed the Fish River where he was joined by most of the tribes there. The only exception was the Gunukwebe under a chief named Cungwa who maintained his fealty to Gaika. Ndlambe's people marched westwards killing and destroying everything in their path and Gaika had the bloody lion's tail swiftly sent to his adherents as his order for battle. At the same time Vandeleur's column, their business at Graaf Reinet done, was making its way back to Algoa Bay, taking no part in the hostilities. When they reached the Sunday River Cungwa's men hurled themselves at the red-coats from ambush preceded by a shower of assegais. Vandeleur had not allowed the fact that he was not at war to cause him to neglect the usual military precautions and a few volleys stretched enough of the Gunukwebe on the ground to force the remainder to take to their heels. The most probable explanation of the attack is that Cungwa had been persuaded by du Buis and Botha (who had tried hard to make Gaika join forces with the Graaf Reinet rebels) that the British had come to drive them back over the Fish River. There is ground for believing that Dingiswayo, who became the founder of the Zulu military empire many years later, was present in Cungwa's ranks. Vandeleur made no attempt to retaliate, for the lesson had been a sharp one and he did not want a full-scale war.

On 5 May, 1799, Vandeleur sent off an officer's patrol of 27 men of the 81st under Lieutenant John Chamney to reconnoitre the country towards the sea whilst the main body fell back to the Bushman's River on which they were to rendezvous. What happened to them is told by Barrow, the Governor's secretary. 'This officer had been detached and was returning to camp when he was surprised among the thickets by a large body of Kaffirs, who attacked them hand to hand with the iron part of their Hassagais, the wooden shaft being previously broken off. This young officer defended himself bravely until 16 of his party were killed. The remaining 4 with a Dutch boer got into a wagon that accompanied the detachment safe at the camp. Poor Chamney [*sic!*] was on horseback and when the wagon set out had 3 Hassagais sticking in his body. Finding himself mortally wounded, and perceiving that the whole aim of the enemy was directed towards him, he made a sign to the wagon to drive off, and, turning his horse, he set off in a contrary direction pursued by the whole body of Kaffirs affording thus an opportunity for the small remains of his party to save their lives by flight.' Chamney was almost certainly taken alive and the details of his death were never known. The first British officer to fall in this long sequence of colonial wars behaved with great gallantry but there was, of course, no award then existing by which his memory could be further honoured.

Fired by their success against a small party, the Kaffirs had one more try at attacking Vandeleur's camp. Again they were driven off by coolly delivered musketry but this time Vandeleur pursued them nearly to the Fish River and recovered many stolen cattle in the process. Cungwa lost heart and sent in envoys to treat for peace. Two of them were dressed in parts of Chamney's uniform and were fortunate to escape with their lives. The march continued to the point on Algoa Bay where Port Elizabeth now stands and there Vandeleur built a block house, the first military work, seaward defences apart, in the colony. It is still there. The flank companies of the 61st and 81st were left behind whilst the rest of the column was shipped back to Cape Town against the background of a war which dragged on for years. It was only an incident but it was the Army's introduction to a form of campaigning with which it was to become painfully familiar.

Vandeleur was not unwilling to fight even though his orders did not then sanction the use of British troops. He summoned the commandos of Swellendam and Graaf Reinet to take the field and went with them. Eighteen burghers who should have been there were missing; they were languishing in cells in the castle at Cape Town where they were to be confined for the next year and a quarter awaiting trial. Prinsloo, van Jaarsveld and the others may have been, technically, traitors but such treatment of men who had lived all their lives on the limitless veldt with the smell of wood-smoke and blood in their nostrils and who had daily felt the little wind that blows before dawn was inhuman.

The commandos were larger than had been usual in the past for there had been some unfortunate instances of small, over-confident parties having come to grief and this time the Xosa were not alone. Since the beginning of hostilities many Hottentots had, of necessity, abandoned employers who could no longer look after them. As they were without any other means of subsistence they gathered into bands, roaming the countryside and raiding desolate and unguarded farmsteads. These masterless parties were always a terror to the farmers in time of war for when the men went away on commando their women and children were left to fend for themselves; it could not have been otherwise in a thinly populated country but even in areas well into the Colony there was danger from such as these and it was one of the reasons why the commando system could not stand the strain of long absence on campaign. The settlers were grateful for the chain of posts which Vandeleur left from Algoa Bay back to Cape Town by way of Graaf Reinet.

'From the thorough knowledge the 8th Dragoons had by experience acquired of all the roads, passes over the mountains, fords through the rivers, their address in swimming those with or without their horses, and their knowledge of the Dutch dialect spoken in the Colony . . . farmers trusted these men to such a degree as to leave their houses and cattle in their charge when they set out with their families and products to Cape Town; but nowhere were they more welcome guests than in the farms managed by widows; the activity and courage of the relay dragoons protected their houses from the runaway slaves, their cattle from beasts of prey which the dragoons delighted in hunting down and repressed the insolence of the slaves and Hottentots employed.'

These last, however, were becoming a serious problem; the wandering gangs numbered many hundreds and a lot of them were hanging around the British camp, at no pains to conceal the fire-arms they had stolen from their employers. Vandeleur would not permit this and gave orders that any man who wished to remain a camp-follower must be disarmed. The troops relieved many Hottentots of their guns and the word went swiftly round that Vandeleur was going to betray them to their enemies. The Hottentots at once formed into three groups under elected 'Captains' (the customary word for a Hottentot leader since they had no chiefs) named Stuurman, Boesak and Trompetter who marched them off to join with their old persecutors, the Xosa.

63

They were received as allies and set themselves to work to give proof of their value by burning and pillaging far and wide and by butchering any Europeans who could not escape them in time.

The commandos, out for retribution, assembled at the Bushman's River early in June. They were carrying not only the usual three days' ration of biltong and rusks but were provisioned for a campaign that could last for two months. They had brave and experienced leaders in Commandant Tjaart van der Walt of Swellendam and Hendrik van Rensburg of Graaf Reinet, both of whom had received presentation rifles from Dundas which they were eager to try out. Vandeleur was in overall command. His orders from Dundas were to drive the tribes back over the Fish River but to stop there. Once they were back where they belonged Vandeleur was, by ambassadors, presents and promises, 'to endeavour to impress the king or great chief of the Kaffir nation with confidence that the Government wished to maintain peace.'

The sentiments were unexceptionable but those who advised Dundas failed inexplicably to realize that there was no such thing as a Kaffir nation and that, in any event, they were treating with the wrong man. The tribes in the Zuurveld and now beyond were, of course, led by Ndlambe (though the real chief was Kawuta) and they were in a state of something like war with Gaika. It was to Gaika, however, that the emissaries of General Vandeleur were sent and not surprisingly they were away for a long time.

The commandos, to their fury, were kept doing nothing and 'nix maak' is anathema to the Boer. The spirit went out of them as their store of rations dwindled and the Xosa concluded that the white men were afraid to attack them. In consequence of this more and more Xosa clans reinforced by renegade Hottentots and doubtless guided by them swept far beyond any previous tide-line. They crossed the Gamtoos River, far to the west of Graaf Reinet, killing and looting as was now customary, and by the end of July Bresler had to report that the whole District of Graaf Reinet was occupied and an attack on the village itself was expected at any time.

Gaika was still not showing his hand. Everybody knew that

he was getting his due proportion of the stolen cattle from all but the hard core of Ndlambe's people but still he refrained from open war. The British administration refused to believe that its favourite chief could be guilty of such duplicity. On 7 August Dundas went personally to assume command taking with him some British troops (50 Dragoons and a company apiece from the 61st and 81st) and, as his political adviser, the not-forgotten Mr Maynier. Dundas held to the view that hostilities were to be deplored for the races had somehow to live cheek by jowl and that a *modus vivendi* must be found. He had not been much taken by what he had seen of the frontiersmen. In a letter to the Governor dated 'Fort Frederick, Algoa Bay, 6 January, 1800', he expressed his opinion of the situation he had found.

'To the habits of licentiousness, injustice and cruelty of the white inhabitants with the system of oppression under which the native Hottentots of the Colony have lived and the injuries the Caffres have sometimes sustained many of the evils of insurrection have to be ascribed. Having made peace with the Hottentots and having also established a military post at Algoa Bay [named Fort Frederick in honour of H.R.H. the Duke of York] I hope by the presence of troops to awe the Dutch inhabitants'.

Maynier could always be relied upon to demonstrate that, no matter what were the facts in issue, the black men were right and the white men wrong. He began to practise his diplomatic art in his now customary way. He made a bargain with Ndlambe that he and his Hottentot friends would not trespass beyond the Zuurveld (in which they were already adjudged trespassers) and, in consideration of such high-mindedness, richer gifts than ever should be given. It was hardly a secret that the undertaking was given simply because the Kaffirs and their allies had so ruined the country beyond the Bushman's River that it was valueless until nature had been allowed a chance to restore it to fertility, assisted by farmers who would be thrown out as soon as it suited the Kaffirs to come back. This state of affairs was described by Mr Maynier as 'peace' and he was appointed as a reward for his services and superior philosophy a Judge of the High Court and 'bookkeeper of the loan Bank'.

The men of the commandos returned to their farms, those who still had farms, in despair. The enemy had secured their base for the next move forward and the caretaker Government was leaving them on their own to hold on to their land as best they could. Prinsloo and the others who had shed no blood of any man were being held in horrible conditions awaiting trial for their lives. Hottentots who had revolted against their employers, murdering, torturing and destroying, were not punished but rewarded. One can hardly be surprised that the South African Dutch were not taken by the vaunted excellence of the English legal system. On Christmas Day, 1799, Mr Maynier's horn was exalted further. He became 'Resident Commissioner and Superintendent of Public Affairs within the Districts of Swellendam and Graaf Reinet with power and authority to issue such orders and directions as might appear requisite for the good government of the said districts and for the proper administration of justice therein'. The heart of the farmers sank almost to a point of no return.

From Downing Street came instructions. 'In fact it appears to me that the proper system of policy to observe towards these Persons would be to interfere as little as possible in their domestic concerns and interior economy and to consider them rather as distant Tribes dependent upon His Majesty's Government than as subjects necessarily amenable to all the laws and regulations established within the immediate precincts of that Government.' In less stilted language, it meant that there was little or nothing to choose between the Boers and the Kaffirs and both should be left to stew in their own juice.

Lord Macartney's successor as Governor was Sir George Yonge, one of the few 'bad' British Governors, but under him the trial of the Graaf Reinet insurgents took place at Cape Town in August, 1800. Their judges, all Dutchmen, sentenced Prinsloo and van Jaarsveld to death, eight others to be 'struck over the head with a sword and banished from the Colony for life' while banishments and prison sentences of varying degrees were imposed on the remainder.

Yonge was sent home in merited disgrace over matters of a financial nature the following spring and Dundas did what he could to mitigate the savagery of the punishments. Van Jaarsveld and Prinsloo were saved by the Treaty of Amiens and the amnesty which followed the Dutch resumption of sovereignty, but the memories of English justice were embalmed in Dutch minds with the permanence of a fly embedded in amber.

Dundas was determined so far as possible to hand back a flourishing Colony and not something resembling Bavaria after the Thirty Years War. Maynier was continuing to send in his regular reports praising the behaviour of Xosa and Hottentot while execrating that of the farmers.

The day came when these traduced people cried 'Enough'. They appeared in arms under Commandant van Rensburg and camped outside Graaf Reinet. Dundas with his usual promptitude sent a small British force towards Graaf Reinet but he was persuaded that the rebels were those who represented all that was best in the District. Maynier was recalled, his place being taken again by Bresler and a commission of three British officers was charged with temporary authority and ordered to enquire into what had gone wrong. Major Sherlock of the 8th Light Dragoons, a commissioner, was particularly energetic and rode many hundreds of miles to pursue his enquiries of the farmers. He saw for himself the desert that existed between Graaf Reinet and Algoa Bay where roving bands of Hottentots were still murdering such farmers and their families as remained. All those to whom Sherlock spoke told him the same thing. This was not a rebellion against the Government, but Maynier must go. When they were assured that he had already gone they gladly said that they would give no more trouble. Maynier was tried on a multiplicity of charges and honourably acquitted of them all but, although he was paid £1,000 to cover his expenses and restored to his two oddly juxtaposed offices at Cape Town, the frontier did not see him again. Lynch law continued to provide such order as prevailed in the midst of the marauding bands.

The two commandos were again called out but few men reported for duty. Commandant van der Walt with sixty men stormed a fortified village at Roodewal, across the Sunday River, on 13 February, 1802 (his son being killed in the assault) and fought a drawn battle with Stuurman's gang of Hottentots a few days later. With so few men he could do no more and they went back to their farms.

Dundas decided on one more effort before handing back the Colony. In June, Stuurman having refused his terms, he attacked the Xosa and Hottentot gangs on the Sunday River with both commandos which had remustered under the stimulus of a promised battle and the provision of rations. Skirmishing between small parties went on for two months in the thick bush, which always clothes the river banks in the Colony; it was moderately satisfactory for more than 200 corpses were counted on the ground and 13,000 cattle recovered.

On 8 August, 1802, Commandant van der Walt was shot dead in a scrimmage at Baviaan's Kloof. It was worse for the Europeans than the similar death of Stonewall Jackson at Chancellorsville. All the heart went out of the farmers for only the brave old Commandant had kept despairing men together and no other leader of his quality was at hand. Again the farmers dispersed. The British troops were being withdrawn in preparation for the hand-over and the Kaffirs and Hottentots were complete masters of the old colony for as far west from the Fish River as they might choose to go. In January, 1803, as the hand-over was proceeding, the burghers took the field again. There was no fighting but as the price of their not attacking, the Xosa and Hottentots again agreed to behave themselves and not to venture beyond the Zuurveld.

In March, 1802, the Treaty came into effect and General Janssens of the Batavian Republic's service marched his troops into Cape Town on Christmas Eve. The Third Kaffir War, officially ended by the agreement made in February, passed into history. Hottentot and Xosa set to and quarrelled furiously over the loot. The Boers licked their wounds and bided their time in the hope that the new administrators would be men like themselves who knew what must be done and did not lack the firmness to do it. The next war, however, was not to take place until after the British had come back again. From this point the Kaffir Wars, so far barely coming within the four corners of Fortescue's definition, would begin the process known to the present generation by the unpleasing name of 'escalation'.

CHAPTER 4
Batavian Republic

IT was to a Holland very different from the old money-grubbing Company that the Cape was returned early in 1803. The two men sent to personify the power and authority of France's ally, the Batavian Republic, were no Amsterdam merchant princes. Jacob de Mist was a young lawyer well indoctrinated with the radical principles of the French Revolution. Many men in all countries could still look upon these with approval for General Buonaparte was not yet Emperor and the casting-off of the yoke of centuries of feudalism was looked at askance only by those who stood to lose by it.

De Mist had been appointed Commissioner-General with the task of acquainting himself with everything that was to be known about the Colony and then of submitting a draft Charter to the States-General which would, when approved, be the future Constitution. His companion was General Jan Willem, a professional soldier who was formally appointed Governor on 1 March, a day of general thanksgiving for deliverance. The superiority of British institutions had not so imprinted itself upon the colonists that they had any misgivings about their reversion to the mother country.

De Mist and Janssens began by proclaiming a general amnesty for all political prisoners who had been confined or banished by the late administration, but for one man the release had already come. Adriaan van Jaarsveld died in prison just before the new Governor arrived.

After a month spent in re-organizing the machinery of government in Cape Town, Janssens set out for the frontier. First he set himself to win back the Hottentots and in this he was successful. Stuurman and Boesak with their bands were now living in abject poverty for they had never taken thought for the morrow and their loot had long been consumed. The Stuurman clan was bought off by a grant of land on the Gamtoos river; Boesak's people gradually dispersed. The Hottentot levies formerly in British service were incorporated in the forces of the Colony and a number of recruits from these two communities joined them. Two Dutch farmers, whose savagery to the Hottentots had made them more than ordinarily obnoxious, were removed to places far away.

Having achieved this important end so satisfactorily, the Governor moved on to try and settle things with the Kaffirs. Though the news was not to reach him for some considerable time, war had started again in Europe just as he was setting out, an extraneous circumstance which was eventually to cause all the fruits of his careful and wise diplomacy to fall to the ground. The sea-power of England put the Cape at her mercy whenever she wished to seize it.

Janssens, however, continued his visitation, calling first upon Ndlambe, still in the Zuurveld and as troublesome as ever. Ndlambe, Cungwa and some minor chiefs met the Governor by arrangement on the bank of the Sunday River during the last days of May. Janssens took the precaution of having as his escort all the troops he could collect, the garrison of Fort Frederick and a strong burgher force under Commandant van Rensburg. All the chiefs spoke with one voice on the things that mattered most. They were anxious, so they said, to be friends with the colonists and understood perfectly that the frontier was marked by the Fish River; they were willing to hand over all runaway slaves and deserters, for their quarrel was still only with Gaika, against whom they were at that moment preparing an onslaught. If they beat him, they would withdraw into their own country but if Gaika were victorious, their return must wait for a more propitious moment. Janssens tried hard to persuade them to give up the idea of another internecine war and succeeded in winning over all except Ndlambe whom nothing would induce to live at peace with his hated nephew. Janssens moved on in order to find out what Gaika had to say about it, having first issued a proclamation forbidding the farmers to engage Kaffir labour and enjoining the dismissal of all who had not served the same master for more than a year.

Janssens met Gaika on the Kat River and could not fail to see that his favourite counsellor was the renegade Dutchman du Buis. The atmosphere was cordial enough but Janssens was firm about the first condition. He would do no business with du Buis or with any other of the white ruffians who hung around Gaika's court. Gaika, who had found them to be a mixed blessing, readily agreed to dismiss them and was as good as his word. He told the Governor quite plainly that he would make no difficulty about re-admitting the tribes in the Zuurveld to their own country with the exception of Ndlambe and his people. His quarrel with his uncle went too deep to be susceptible of settlement by arbitration. With this Janssens had to be content. He continued to beat the bounds of his Governorship, riding round to the north to find out how things were going in the interminable conflicts with the Bushmen, and then returned to Cape Town. The first piece of news that greeted him was that an order had arrived requiring him to send his best regiment of regulars to Java. To make good the deficiency he expanded his force of Hottentots. His greatest worry now was the risk of another sea-borne landing, so the frontier must be left to take care of itself.

Trade was almost at a standstill and when De Mist returned home in January, 1804 he was compelled to travel in an American ship, for only under a neutral flag would he be safe from the ubiquitous Royal Navy. He too had perambulated the border regions and his conclusions were the same as those of Janssens but the many administrative reforms, long overdue, had been De Mist's special charge. He established a new district between Algoa Bay and Graaf Reinet which Janssens named Uitenhage, an old family name of the Commissioner-General, and he appointed Andries Stockenstroom its first *landdrost*. Both he and Janssens realized the disastrous consequences of the mistake made so long ago in importing slaves and they prohibited the practice from then onwards.

De Mist dreamt of a future in which, long after he was dead, the blacks already in the colony, and their descendants, would have their own separate province while the greater part of the country would be inhabited solely by white men. The present policy of separate development was thus envisaged well over a century and a half ago by a very liberal disciple of the French Revolution.

On Christmas Day, 1805, the French privateer *Napoleon* was run ashore at Hout Bay by H.M.S. *Narcissus*, her crew making their way to Cape Town with the tale that a great fleet under English colours was on its way.

The story was true. Though still under threat of invasion, Britain, as in 1940, had despatched a powerful force from her scanty reserves to operate in Africa. It was a brave decision by Castlereagh for the troops had embarked and sailed while Lord Nelson was still trailing Villeneuve to the West Indies. Six and a half thousand troops under the veteran Sir David Baird, escorted by three ships of the line and six frigates commanded by Commodore Home Popham, sixty-one sail in all, were only a week away. Baird had already served in the Cape under Dundas and, rather unusually, many officers who also knew the country and its defences were with him. On 5 January, 1806, disembarkation began, not this time to the south but in Saldanha Bay only a few miles north of the capital. There was no opposition but the crashing surf rolled over one of the ship's boats drowning 36 men of the 93rd Highlanders. The Highland brigade of Brigadier-General Ferguson scrambled ashore, wet but in good order, and covered the landing of three more regiments and a few guns. Only one company of burgher militia, led by Commandant Linde, attempted to interfere with the landing and they were smartly driven off at the price of one Highlander killed and four wounded.

Janssens did all that a brave officer could with the heterogeneous force of about 2,000 men which was all that he could muster. He had two regular regiments, Dutch by courtesy only, the Waldeck-Rousseau battalion of German mercenaries, a hundred and fifty dragoons and sixteen guns, manned partly by Dutch artillerymen and partly by Javanese. The crews of the *Napoleon* and of another French privateer also joined him, together with a miscellany of Hottentots and slaves.

At three o'clock in the morning of Wednesday, 8 January, 1806, Janssens marched out to do his duty. He found himself confronted by two columns marching down the slope of the Blaauwberg towards the capital. On the left were the red-coats of the 24th (South Wales Borderers), 59th (The East Lancashire Regt.) and 83rd (The Royal Ulster Rifles) under command of Baird's brother and on the right the tossing plumes, bare knees and bagpipes of the 71st (The Highland Light Infantry), 72nd (The Seaforth Highlanders) and 93rd (The Argyll and Sutherland Highlanders). The sight of the scarlet columns, beautifully ordered and with an ominously sparkling line of steel surmounting them, was too much for the Waldeck Regiment. At the arrival of the first cannon balls they turned about and quitted the field, followed, as soon as the muskets of the Highland column came down to the 'Charge Bayonets', by the remainder.

The only ones to stand their ground were the burghers, the gunners and the French privateersmen, but even they could not remain where they were for long. As the Highlanders swept on with claymore and bayonet Janssens withdrew his army, being himself the last to leave in company with a battery of Dutch horse-artillery. He marched his men over the mountains into the hinterland around Hottentots Holland where the small garrison of Simon's Town joined him after spiking their guns.

Baird entered Cape Town without further opposition and Colonel von Prophalow, the senior officer left there, signed a formal capitulation of the town on the Friday afternoon. Janssens, for want of provisions, could achieve nothing and surrendered a few days later with the honours of war. The Dutch troops, having undertaken not to bear arms again for the enemies of King George, were sent home; the Frenchmen, who had fought most gallantly, were treated as prisoners of war. The Hottentots, for the most part, changed sides once more and for the last time.

Lord Castlereagh was inflexibly determined that the short reign of the Batavian Republic should be ended and that, when the time should come for a general settlement, the future of the Cape would not be negotiable. The vulnerability of India had been demonstrated by Bonaparte's expedition to Egypt and if at some future time this enterprise were to be repeated it was by no means certain that a Nelson or an Abercrombie would be on hand to repel it. The greatest maritime power in the world would have need of secure sea routes to the East and van Riebeeck's refreshment station could not be suffered to remain in hands that might not always be friendly.

One of the incumbrances to go with the Colony was to be a succession of the most arduous and difficult colonial wars the British army would ever be called on to fight.

CHAPTER 5

The Frontiers Move Out

THOUGH the colonists could not have been expected to show much enthusiasm for becoming subjects of the British Crown once again, the resentment was not nearly as great as it had been ten years earlier. There were several reasons; in the first place disenchantment with the example of France, where the dictatorship of Napoleon had replaced the glorious dawn of the age of equality, had long set in. Secondly, it was plain to see that if the Colony was not to become stagnant a good deal of aid from somewhere abroad would be needed. The Company had never parted with a solitary gulden if it could be avoided, the Batavian Republic was a helpless captive and only Britain, the mistress of the sea, had the ability to provide it. Lastly, a closer acquaintance by the frontier people with the British soldier had led, as usual, to an understanding of his good nature and there was no dislike of the red-coat.

The Government at home had been careful, with the example of Sir George Yonge in mind, to select as Governors men of the highest quality. The first was the Earl of Caledon, head of the famous Irish family of Alexander and an ancestor of the Field Marshal of our day. A contemporary description could apply equally well to either man; 'He was upright and amiable, in disposition good tempered, courteous and benevolent, though when occasion required firmness no man could be more resolute than he'.

For three years there was peace on the frontier, which was as well since the bulk of the garrison was taken away, soon after the occupation, for the imbecile descent, inspired by Home Popham, on the Spanish colony of Buenos Aires. Caledon sent out surveying parties to map the Colony, much of which was still unexplored except by hunting parties, and he also examined the works of the various kinds of missionary. A number of different denominations had sent out people to save the souls of Hottentots and Bantu. The Moravian mission station at Genadendal, not far from Cape Town, was a model of what such places should be. The proselytes were clean, industrious, contented and well taught in useful arts apart from learning also the message of Christ. The London Missionary Society's establishment at Bethelsdorp, however, was quite a different proposition. The Rev Mr Vanderkemp had concluded that in order to understand the Hottentots he must become one. He dressed, behaved and smelt like a Hottentot and his brand of evangelization could equally well have been called sedition. When a report on it reached the Governor he took advice from the judges and military officers who were unanimously of the view that the place was a public menace and should be closed down. Unfortunately Vanderkemp made such a nuisance of himself that this wise move was never carried out.

In 1809, Lord Caledon sent out a party under Colonel Collins to 'explore the country to the north-east of the Colony and ascertain the condition of the various branches of the Xosa tribe'. They set out at the end of January, north from Graaf Reinet to the Orange River, where they were the first Europeans to record the existence of a great river which flows from the north. They named it the Caledon. From there they journeyed south-eastwards through unknown and sparsely inhabited lands until they reached the great outcrop of the Amatolas where peaks rise sharply to more than 6,000 feet. After threading their way through this range without molestation, they turned north-east and crossed the Kei just below its junction with the Kaboosie. Shortly after this the explorers found themselves among men who figure prominently in the frontier wars for some years to come. First they visited the right-hand son of Kawuta, Buku, chief of a substantial section of the Galekas and then they rode to the kraal of the great son of the same chief, Hintza. Hintza was legally paramount chief of all the Xosa but, as a result of a quarrel with Gaika, he had been driven out of his former kraal on the west bank of the Kei and was in close alliance with the neighbouring Tembu. They noted that his council included two Europeans, a deserter from the British army named MacDaniel and a Boer named Lochberg. After leaving Hintza, of whom much more will be heard, they went on to the upper Keiskamma to interview Gaika himself. His fortunes had fallen very low since his enemies, the friends of Ndlambe, had for a long time past been raiding his cattle and little was now left to him. Once again, all the country between the Kei and the Fish Rivers had been almost completely denuded of its former inhabitants.

The last call was on Ndlambe in the Zuurveld; he and his son Umhala, another name of ill-omen, were intractable. They cared nothing for what might have been said by Gaika, Hintza or anybody else. They would only quit the Zuurveld if they were turned out by force of arms, openly asserting now that they held the land by right of conquest.

Colonel Collins went back to write his report for the Governor. He had no doubt at all about what its contents must be; this great and fertile land, potentially the finest farm land in the colony, could not be left to waste, inhabited only by poverty-stricken gangs of marauders. The Xosa, who had no possible right to be there, must be expelled by force if they would not go of their own accord. A payment should be made to them by way of compensation so that a long-term grievance might not be created and with it they could stock their own farms within their own territories. New magistracies, near to the frontier, should be established in order to protect the Kaffirs from the baser type of European, of whom there were already too many, and to restrict intercourse between the races to essentials.

Caledon could not see his way to accepting the proposals at that time though he recognized their soundness and equity. The expeditionary force in Spain (the battle of Talavera had been fought whilst Collins was on his trek) demanded every available British soldier and requests for the troops which would be needed to ensure the success of the operation would not be enthusiastically received by the Cabinet. No action was taken and Caledon, who had been very much occupied with reform of other kinds, went home in 1811. To replace him there came Lt.-General Sir John Cradock who had commanded the army in the Peninsula during the period between Sir John Moore's force evacuating the country and the return of Sir Arthur Wellesley.

Cradock found that conditions in the Zuurveld were not far removed from anarchy. Soon after he had assumed office he read Collins' report and came to the conclusion that only by putting its recommendations into effect could the Colony be saved from creeping back into barbarism. Caledon had come to the same conclusion during his last days in office and General Grey, who had been Acting Governor during the brief interregnum, had no doubts about it at all. The situation had rapidly deteriorated during recent months for the *landdrost* of Uitenhage had reported that only one farm east of his *drostdy* still remained occupied. Grey, lacking authority to begin active warfare, had gone as far as he felt himself able by authorizing Major Cuyler, a British officer who was *landdrost* of Uitenhage, to assemble a commando and to call upon the small garrison of Fort Frederick for any help he might need. This was purely a defensive operation designed to prevent further infiltration but Cradock, as soon as he had acquainted himself with the situation, recognized that it was not nearly sufficient.

On 8 October, 1811, while Wellington was making his careful preparations to storm Ciudad Rodrigo and carry the European war into Spain, Cradock ordered out the commandos of Swellendam, George (a new District just founded), Uitenhage and Graaf Reinet. Colonel Graham, late of the 93rd Highlanders but now commanding the 600 Hottentots known as the Cape Corps, was placed in command. So shrunken was the British garrison after satisfying the demands made upon it for troops to be employed elsewhere that the only additional men the Governor could give him were 49 gunners, 166 troopers of the 21st Light Dragoons, 221 soldiers of the 83rd and 3 of his own Highlanders. Graham, who was to be the first of many British officers to leave his name permanently on the map of South Africa, was given strict orders. He must do all he could to send the Kaffirs back across the Fish

River by peaceful persuasion. If he failed in this, he was to fight. So began the Fourth Kaffir War and the first to be a British responsibility.

CHAPTER 6
Grahamstown

THIS would be a convenient moment to break with the mere cataloguing of events, of which Sir Edward Hamley so strongly disapproves, and give what he calls 'some of the philosophy of the business'. In spite of the events of 1806, the Cape was still *de facto* and, until after the Congress of Vienna, *de jure*, a dependency of the Netherlands and the Prince of Orange was at that very moment a member of Lord Wellington's staff. Nonetheless, it was clear that the colony could only be held by a Power which commanded the sea routes and this settled its destiny. The men of the commandos were exercised only in making the place safe for themselves and their families against the bands of Kaffir marauders and they were whole-heartedly willing to serve alongside British troops for that purpose. On the frontier the feeling, if feeling there was, amounted simply to getting this menace removed and wondering about future government later. These gangs of masterless men, much like those who plagued England during the Middle Ages, were to be one of the greatest curses of the country, after drought and locusts, until recent times; a main factor inducing the Boers, by no means totally defeated, to end the war with Britain in 1902 was that they had resurrected themselves and were again raiding farms occupied only by women and children whose men were on commando.

The first task of the commander of any army in the field is

not to defeat his enemy; it is to arrange matters by careful preparation and good staff work so that his command shall continue to exist for as long as it is needed. A campaign, particularly in a vast land deficient in roads and bridges, is a protracted and gigantic picnic. The ruined Zuurveld produced no food on which an European army could live; neither was there forage for their horses. The commandos, by long tradition, paraded with three days' supply of biltong and mealie-rusks, but as soon as these were exhausted they must turn to their friends for supplies to keep them alive.

The country transport was, of course, the ox-wagon with its great, billowing canvas tilt and its span of sixteen cattle, the driver almost invariably being a Hottentot. Their capacity was considerable but their speed dreadfully slow. The ox is a patient and hard-working beast but he has his idiosyncracies and they must be respected. He will not be hurried, he must be allowed to chew the cud after feeding, he cannot work with the full sun on his back nor is he insensitive to cold and rain. Disregard these limitations and he will die. Something of the same kind could be said about soldiers, especially those from a relatively urban society experiencing their first campaign under African conditions.

Having made his arrangements for the picnic, the commander must next decide how and where he can hit his enemy to hurt him enough to make him give in. In Europe the answer is obvious —you must beat his armies in the field and occupy at least some of his principal towns. This had not held good in the war of 1812 in the eastern states of America, for the burning of Washington had achieved no recognizable military advantage and had merely stiffened resistance. The Xosa had no regularly formed armies to be beaten in a stand-up fight nor towns to be occupied —though war against them was less exasperating than war against the Bushmen, which was like fighting smoke. With a preponderance of troops and secure communications the school solution is to march up to your enemy, create for yourself a secure position and wait. He must then either attack you, in which case your superior weapons will beat him, or he must go away. If the resources available do not permit this and the time available is limited by the picnic factor, the only course is to harry the life out of him by constant and pugnacious patrolling, which will thin his numbers by casualties and desertions, and to destroy his crops and seize his cattle in the hope that you will thereby make him go hungry before you do. Once he has cleared off, if you wish to keep him from returning, you must fortify your frontier with a line of garrisoned posts—forts in 1811, block-houses in 1900—maintain a reserve at not too great a distance and establish a system of communications that will not break down as soon as the sun goes in.

For defenders in the position of the Kaffirs in 1811 there is only one course. Anything in the nature of a pitched battle in the open or a fire-fight must be avoided. (Thanks to men like Du Buis they had a good number of muskets but they were poor shots.) First they must lay in stocks of food in places accessible to them and not to their enemies, and then these enemies must be lured into thick bush or savage mountains which will tire them out and where their firearms will avail them little. After a steady trickle of casualties from sickness and poisoned arrows the enemy can then be swamped by numbers of athletic savages immune from disease and thoroughly familiar with the country. If they are delayed long enough to consume all their supplies even without battle the time must come when they have to quit the field. This process can be accelerated by continued attacks, even feint attacks, on their vulnerable wagon trains, which will cause dispersal of troops through the necessity of leaving strong baggage guards. With a little luck, the drivers may be persuaded by bribes or threats to run away and leave them stranded.

The attackers in bush warfare require arms different from those used in more regular fighting. Speed of fire and stopping power are more needed than accuracy and a weapon for hand-to-hand fighting is essential. The commandos never dismounted if they could help it and their *roers* loaded with large slugs (one captured by the British is said to have carried half a pound of shot in each barrel) were the best weapons of the day. If a man were unhorsed he had to fight it out with his *herneuker*, the great hunting knife used for killing zebra at the gallop. The British and Hottentot troops carried the single-barrelled smooth-bore musket which fired a ball weighing an ounce and a quarter.

It was effective to drop the most ferocious Kaffir in his tracks but was very slow to re-load and far too long to be handy. When the chance of a long shot came it was of little use, for at ranges of more than a hundred yards it threw very wide of the mark.

With superior mobility in the bush, the ability to exist on very little and far greater resistance to fatigue and sickness on their side, the Kaffirs were by no means out-matched. If they did not have Czar Alexander's Generals January and February they had instead General Bush and General Fever. Townborn men take some time to become accustomed to bush and jungle, especially to the strange nocturnal noises, but the British soldier has always shown an unexpected aptitude, generation after generation, in eventually making the place his home.

We must now go back and see what happened. The burghers were the first to take the field, the commandos of Swellendam, George and Uitenhage meeting at the mouth of the Sunday River. The Graaf Reinet men alone, under command of *Land-drost* Stockenstroom, took ground to the north of the Zuurberg range. For the Swellendam men this involved a ride of something like 400 miles while the Graaf Reinet commando had to travel less than half that distance. Nevertheless, the former were the happier men for they were able to leave their farms un-manned without serious risk to their families while for the latter there was no knowing what might happen as soon as the dust of their hooves had settled.

Graham was a thoroughly sound officer and was not so conceited as to believe that only British troops and British officers were to be relied upon. He respected Cuyler's local knowledge and experience and settled upon him as the man most likely to be able to come to terms with Ndlambe, for he would be able to read signs that would have no message for newcomers. Accordingly Cuyler was sent ahead with an escort of burghers to cross the Sunday River and to beard Ndlambe in his lair. The mission nearly cost Cuyler his life for Ndlambe was equally determined on war and was waiting for him. As he passed through the bush which encumbered the river bank a shower of assegais was hurled at his men and one was wounded. Cuyler, undaunted, rode hard for the kraal of Cungwa which he knew to be not far off and reached it in safety. The first thing he noticed there was that the men were all wearing the blue crane feathers which clearly meant war. Cungwa himself did not put in an appearance but on the following day there arrived Ndlambe, plainly in a fighting mood. He walked alone to where Cuyler and his escort were waiting, stamped his foot and shouted angrily for all to hear, 'Here is no honey; I will eat honey and to procure it will cross the rivers Sunday, Koega and Zwartkop. This country is mine. I won it in war and I will maintain it.' He shook his assegai, and blew a single blast on a horn. Two or three hundred of his warriors rushed from concealment upon Cuyler's little party, bellowing their war cries and intent on killing. Cuyler, ever distrustful of Kaffir chieftains, had kept his men in the saddle and the fleetness of their horses alone saved them from massacre.

Ndlambe and Cungwa now began to have second and less passionate thoughts about the wisdom of what they had done and instead of carrying immediate war into the colony, they hid their warriors in the country to the east of the Sunday which was then called the Rietbergen. This was a land of hills and thick bush, about forty miles long by a dozen in breadth, where a determined defender could make a stronghold of every kopje and thicket and where an enemy could be forced to get off his horse and go on foot into the bush. 'To follow the enemy vigorously to his haunts and lurking-places requires a perfect knowledge of the service in all its branches and an intrepidity and recklessness of danger, which, while they become the soldier, prove the courage of the man', Sir Harry Smith said of it and Ndlambe was no less aware of the fact.

The Fourth Kaffir War opened with disaster for the colonists. In the last days of December Graham got a message through to Stockenstroom, *landdrost* of Graaf Reinet who was still lying with his commando in the hills of the Bruintjes Hoogte to the north of the Zuurveld, telling him to make a sweep down through the Zuurveld and across the Rietbergen to join forces with Cuyler. Stockenstroom had misgivings about the wisdom of this course, for it would leave Graaf Reinet and all its farms defenceless before raiders from tribes other than those of Cungwa and Ndlambe. Brought up in the tradition that an order was more a basis for negotiation than something to be obeyed without question, Stockenstroom set off with an escort of 24 burghers to seek out Graham and to explain his point of view. About half-way across the Zuurveld he happened across a party of Xosa of the Imidange tribe and, against the advice of the burghers, engaged them in conversation. The tone was friendly enough and for half an hour Stockenstroom sought to persuade the Kaffirs of the wisdom of returning to their proper place; well versed though he was in Africa and its ways he failed to see that all the time more and more men were creeping through the bush, completely encircling his little party. At a signal they erupted from their hiding places and flung themselves at the Boers. Stockenstroom, eight farmers and a Hottentot interpreter were stabbed to death in an instant; four more were wounded but managed to fight their way out on horseback together with the rest of the escort, shooting and cutting down half a dozen of the murderers as they went. As soon as the survivors reached the camp at Bruintjes Hoogte and told their story Stockenstroom's son, also named Andries and an Ensign in the Cape Regiment, set off with eighteen other mounted men to take retribution. Within a matter of hours he tracked down the killers and slew sixteen of them. There could be no question about their identity for young Stockenstroom and his men also recovered all the horses of the victims.

Graham remained persuaded that his plan was the correct one. Two companies of Hottentots of the Cape Regiment had already been sent to join the Graaf Reinet men and Major Fraser of that corps was ordered to carry out the sweep originally demanded of Stockenstroom. Fifty farmers under Field-Cornet Pretorius agreed to go with him and the combined force moved south. Their route lay through broken country and they were obliged to march through many defiles. In one of these they came under a determined attack by large forces of Xosa who were thrice driven off at a cost to them of about 20 killed. There were no casualties amongst Fraser's men for no assegai could reach them and the Kaffirs were not allowed to come to close quarters.

Cuyler, meanwhile, was busy harrying the Kaffirs in the Zuurveld. The farmers, enraged by the murders and encouraged by the fact that the Government really seemed to mean business, put their backs into the task. Six columns, each of 50 farmers and 20 Hottentot soldiers, went into the Rietbergen to flush out the Gunukwebe. Graham says that the Boers were 'orderly, obedient, and undertook with cheerfulness and alacrity the fatiguing and arduous duties allotted to them'. The Kaffirs prudently avoided coming face to face with the Boers but adopted the tactics of the bush-cow which, when hunted, moves slowly in a circle so that it becomes difficult to distinguish between pursuer and pursued. The first half of January, 1812, was taken up with a score of petty fights in which the Kaffirs incurred a number of losses—exactitude is impossible—in men and cattle. Only one European was killed. The Kaffir casualties should be reckoned in tens rather than in hundreds but they included Cungwa. About 3,000 of the scrawny, long-horned cattle which spelt wealth in Africa, were repossessed. The Graaf Reinet men recovered the bodies of Stockenstroom and his companions but remained to the north of the Zuurveld with a not unreasonable concern for what might be going on behind their backs. As things fell out, nothing eventful took place there at all. Gaika, no longer with the advantage of the advice of Du Buis, made no move. News travels fast and mysteriously in Africa and Gaika was certainly aware of the punishment being meted out to his hated uncle. This was no time to quarrel with the men who were hammering Ndlambe; a prudent and impover-ished chief would do far better to remain their friend.

Cungwa, in fact, had been fighting a rear-guard action to enable Ndlambe to get away. In the middle of January the latter was across the Fish River with what remained of his herds and his tribe. Pato, who had succeeded Cungwa, led the Gunukwebe the same way before the month was out and they settled them-selves along the lower reaches of the Keiskamma. February was spent in winkling out small groups which had escaped the original combing and in these operations two hundred men of the newly arrived 60th Rifles were given their introduction to bush warfare. By the end of the month not a Kaffir was to be seen west of the Great Fish River. Although it had achieved this useful result, the campaign had, from the colonist's point of view, been almost bloodless. Only Cornelis Jacob Swart, burgher of Swellendam, had been killed in action.

The Xosa were firmly told that if they remained in the land which they had won they would be left in peace. As something like 20,000 of them had been uprooted from their squatterdom, presents were sent of seed-corn and cattle to prevent their lapsing into poverty and Gaika came in for a reward of 500 of the best beasts. A further six hundred were kept in reserve to be given to the Kaffirs as soon as they gave proof of good behaviour.

The Fourth War, the first to be declared as a deliberate act of policy by the colonial government, was concluded and the result was, for a change, satisfactory. The burden had been borne almost entirely by the Boers and the Hottentots; it was now necessary to do something to enable the commandos to stay at home.

By the end of the campaign 800 burghers and 1,252 British and Hottentot soldiers were in the field but to collect such a force had taken time. It was the duty of the Government to make the frontier secure against any attempt by the Kaffirs to come back again and much thought was devoted to this. The possibility was by no means far-fetched for already news was coming in of increased pressure on the Kaffirs from the north where a new nation was coming into existence under the leadership of Dingiswayo and still known as the Amatetwa. They were steadily gobbling up their weaker neighbours and might well decide to expand southwards. In that case, the Xosa, the Tembu and the others would certainly prefer war with the colonists, who ended their battles with gifts of corn and cattle, to war with Dingiswayo whose methods were different.

A substantial permanent army was out of the question for this was 1812. Ciudad Rodrigo had fallen while the war was in progress and not a single man would be spared for a remote and relatively unimportant conflict. The British troops already in the field were recalled and only the 60th and a few dragoons for orderly duties remained.

The alternative was to fortify the Fish River area in some fashion. It was bound to be an unsatisfactory business for thick bush extended for several miles on either bank and a sizeable force could be collected under the noses of the garrisons without their knowing anything about it. A line of 22 small posts from the sea to the mountains of Bruintjes Hoogte, manned in part by burghers and in part by soldiers, came into existence, their base being upon a new village. It was to be built on 'a farm once occupied by a man named Lucas Meyer', 25 miles from the sea and on a spur of the Zuurberg which rose to 2,000 feet above sea level. The choice was made simply because the place was the centre of the semi-circle of posts all of which could be reached from it in one day's march. Work began on the village in August. It was named Grahamstown.

CHAPTER 7
Zulu Hinterland

LEAVING the inhabitants of the Colony to build their new town and to keep up their intermittent patrols of Hottentot levies through the Fish River bush, we should consider what was happening away to the north. The herdsmen of what we call Natal were, at the beginning of the nineteenth century, very much like their brethren of the Xosa, the Tembu and their neighbours. There was, however, rising to the north the star of a man who was to build from these comparatively harmless pastoralists the greatest military power ever to exist in black Africa and which would in time drive the weaker tribes willy-nilly into conflict with the men from Europe.

Dingiswayo, it will be remembered, had possibly been present at the ambush in which the Kaffirs had first set eyes on the disciplined men who wore the red coat of King George. It is known for certain that at that time and under another name he had wandered about southern Africa having been cast out of his tribe by the chief, Jobe, against whom he had probably been conspiring. When death eventually overtook the old man in 1809 the outcast returned, took the name of Dingiswayo ('The Wanderer') and assumed, legitimately, the chieftaincy of the Mtetwa.

He started his reign by translating into action the military ideas which his exile had impressed on him and began the organization of his people into regular regiments. Of these the most formidable was the Izi-Cwe, the sardonically named Bushmen regiment. Among the young men conscripted into it was a 22-year-old of outstanding physique named Chaka, standing over 6 feet 3 inches and already with a considerable reputation for bravery and hardihood. With the regimental dress of white ox-tails at wrists and ankles, the kilt made from strips of fur, and black feathers of the widow-bird streaming from a skin cap, Chaka was a figure of terror; within a year, consequent upon his prowess in a tribal war, he had risen to a captain's command and was largely responsible for the training of the regiment.

Dingiswayo was no Genghis Khan for, although he set himself to make of the insignificant Mtetwa a great nation he was not the savage and blood-thirsty butcher that his successor was to become. He knew something of the ways of the white men having, during his hegira, met up with an expedition sent out by Lord Caledon to explore the interior. One man in particular with whom he became acquainted was Dr Cowan, one of the party, to whom he had acted as guide and whose horse and gun he inherited on Cowan's death. From Cowan he learnt much of the world outside the changeless cattle lands and he found out that civilized men were not always minded to remain cooped up in the small communities from which they had come. Cowan probably was the inspiration for Dingiswayo's essay at empire-building but he had never, one imagines, appreciated that his audience would soon try to do for the black races what the elder Pitt had done for his own people.

As the Mtetwa people were the nucleus around which the Zulu empire was to cluster, and the tribes which were to be added to them were not so very different in character, they deserve some scrutiny. Physically they were fine specimens of manhood and the description given in Chapter 1 of the typical Bantu fits them well. Their organization, both tribal and family, was rigid and the passage of centuries had done little to alter it. In their life as cattle-men and hunters in a forgotten Africa which teemed with wild beasts ranging from great herds of elephant down through the lion and the leopard to the humbler buck in all its many varieties and the disgusting hyaena, they were brought up from earliest childhood to be strong and brave. During the good years their diet was plentiful and healthy, being based on the products of their herds and their agriculture, rudi-

mentary though the latter was. Milk-curds and meat supple-
mented by maize and the vegetables that Africa yields so
generously and for so little effort were their staples and the
ordinary Nguni, the generic name for all the tribes akin to the
Zulu, fared far better than did his contemporary in the slums
of the cities of Europe.

The distribution of duties was traditional and well understood;
the boys from a very early age were packed off at sunrise to
watch over the herds upon which the life of the tribe depended
both in summer and in winter. (The seasons are, roughly speaking, reversed in South Africa where winter sets in at the beginning of July.) It was their business to protect the herds from
predators, of which there were many, and as they remained at
this duty until about the age of 16, they grew up strong, self-
reliant and trained to arms. Like all black African people, their
personal cleanliness was of an order far superior to that of most
other races even if they were a little careless about the disposal
of excreta.

It was the business of the women and girls to tend the houses
and cultivate the fields, for husbandry was a task beneath the
dignity of the warrior. The girl-children were put to work helping their mothers as soon as they could toddle to the fields, and
as they grew older they were taught the essential art of pounding
maize in a mortar with a long pole to produce the mash from
which beer was brewed.

The grown men were not exactly overworked, for in time of
peace their duties were limited to the repair of the houses, the
mending of fences, the manufacture and cleaning of their
weapons and the begetting of children. The father within his
family possessed the right of what medieval Europe called the
high justice, the middle and the low and there was no appeal.
The family would ordinarily meet twice a day in the hut for
meals, the first about mid-day and the last before sundown. The
precise place occupied by each member for eating and sleeping
was strictly regulated by custom and meals were taken with
decorum and after washing.

The only art known to them was in connection with the sexual
act and to this intensive study had been devoted by succeeding
generations with a creditable singleness of purpose. From earliest

childhood the young Nguni, boy and girl alike, was painstakingly
schooled by the appropriate parent into making this sometimes
rather routine business into an experience mutually rewarding to
both participants. Chastity, of a sort, was strictly enforced but
to avoid the necessity for maintaining psychiatrists a form of
modified sexual intercouse known as *uku-hlobonga* was permis-
sible. Those wishing to be better informed about the matter will
find it clinically described in the diaries of Henry Fynn. If the
participants became over-animated and pregnancy resulted, the
man was mulcted of a fine of 3 cows, payable to the girl's father.
There were also times when intercourse became mandatory, for
after the warrior had killed his man in battle he was obliged to
copulate with the nearest available woman since until he had
done so, he was unclean and could take no part in communal
life. It would have been a sad breach of etiquette for any woman
solicited for this patriotic purpose to decline to participate, but
the practice did not encourage prolonged campaigns.

The army was undergoing radical changes under the rule of
Dingiswayo and the greatest innovator was Chaka. First he con-
temptuously rejected the feeble throwing assegai, rightly divining
that the power of a horde of muscular and disciplined men lay
in its ability to get quickly to grips with its enemy and to destroy
him utterly with edged weapons. He first experimented with
various kinds of hunting-spear but found none to his satisfaction.
In the end he designed his own; a heavy, leaf-shaped blade made
of a metal which approximated to steel by reason of the charcoal
used in its smelting, sharpened all round and firmly fixed to the
hard-wood shaft by a glue made of the juice of roots; finally it
was held in position by the skin of the tail of an ox being shrunk
over the join. This well-balanced thrusting spear, named Ixwa
after the sound produced by it being drawn from the entrails of
its victim, was the tool that was to make empty deserts of whole
tribal areas; it probably slew more people than ever did the
invention of Sir Hiram Maxim.

Dingiswayo's army consisted of infantry alone. To propel
such a force upon its foe and to gain the maximum shock effect,
the second need was for speed of movement. Oddly enough,
the Nguni went about their business shod with sandals, well
made from another main product of their herds. These Chaka

scorned as being not merely effeminate but a hindrance to fleetness and he issued an order that henceforth the soldiers should march and fight bare-foot. To give point to the order, he ordained that a dance be held on a floor carpeted with thorn bush. Any warrior who allowed himself to miss a step because of what Chaka judged to be excessive tenderness was at once put to death. The speed of the regiments over the ground increased very materially and with it their manœuvreability.

In place of the former tactics of the football crowd, Chaka introduced serious battle drills. His army was divided into the anatomically but accurately named 'chest', 'horns' and 'loins'. Starting their battle *en masse*, when the commander deemed the moment to have come he gave the signal at which the 'horns' separated themselves from the main body, reaching swiftly far out to right and left with the object of encircling the inert mass opposed to them, while the 'chest' closed in on the centre and the 'loins' remained in reserve to be used when and where the situation demanded it.

With these weapons and revolutionary methods of warfare, tribe after tribe was taken over. Dingiswayo did not, as a rule, erase the vanquished from the earth but followed Rome and Napoleon by pressing them into service as allies and auxiliaries. Nothing in Africa could stand against his regiments and there was no knowing how much wider the bounds of the Zulu might be set. As the first sods of Grahamstown were being turned, Dingiswayo promoted Chaka to the rank of regimental commander and earmarked him as his heir presumptive. Part of the advice the older man gave him was that the white men had weapons which killed infallibly from a great distance and that, whatever Chaka might venture against other black tribes, it would be better not to try conclusions with these wizards. Chaka never did, but the result of his conquests was a steady migration of broken clans southwards towards the Drakensbergs. The Great Trek had begun, but in the wrong direction.

CHAPTER 8

Slachter's Nek

I N the lands to the south of the mountain passes, nothing was known of the slowly growing menace that lay beyond. The frontier was, for the first time, under some sort of regular surveillance, a burgher force being kept permanently in existence with the aid of a subvention from other farmers more happily situated, and the posts maintained their tiny garrisons. They were in no sense fortified places but from them went out intermittent patrols mostly made up of Hottentots (now officially designated 'The Cape Regiment') as they were far more efficient in searching the bush than any others. The posts in rear were manned by burghers, and by 1812 a battalion of the 60th Rifles, most of them Germans, was added, together with a troop of dragoons for maintaining communications. Though the little force could not have achieved much against a determined comeback by the Kaffirs, it did at least provide a fairly efficient distant early-warning system.

Civilization crawled on leaden feet towards the debatable lands. Young Stockenstroom was appointed deputy *landdrost* of Graaf Reinet and directed to set up a court-house on the bank of the Great Fish River itself. He chose as its site 'a loan farm in the occupation of Jacob van Heerden' whose lease was cancelled with compensation. The village which grew up around the building manifesting the existence of a government was christened 'at the request of the inhabitants of that part of the country'

by the name of the man whose firmness had called it into existence and, on 21 January, 1814, the *Gazette* officially named it
Cradock. At the same time Major Fraser of the Cape Regiment
was made deputy *landdrost* of Uitenhage and took up his duties
at Grahamstown.

Following the English tradition, judges were sent out on
circuit from Cape Town as far afield as Graaf Reinet and Uitenhage in order to make sure that injustices brought about by
prejudice or ineptitude of the local *landdrosts* should not be
allowed to remain unchallenged. Also, inevitably, arrived the
missionaries. Many of these gentlemen came to the wilderness
with the entirely honourable intention of bettering the lot of the
subject races but it was not uncommon for them to allow their
zeal to outrun their discretion when dealing with peoples as
alien to everything they had ever known as would have been
the dwellers in some strange planet. The philosophy of the
frontier Boer drew very clear distinctions between the places in
the scheme of things to be occupied by themselves and the
remainder who, in varying degrees, were subject to them. Their
attitude to their servants would, no doubt, have been deemed
illiberal by a baron of King Stephen's reign but that had been
the situation now for the better part of two centuries and men's
hearts were not to be changed simply because a new government ruled in distant Cape Town. The raucous complaints of
the mission stations reached the ears of Mr Wilberforce in
London and orders were transmitted to the Governor to enquire
thoroughly into their truth. Major Cuyler, *landdrost* of Uitenhage since its foundation, was the first target and no worse a
choice could have been made. He was a man of complete
integrity and humanity whose father had been a rich merchant
in New York. When the American War began, Cuyler senior
had sided with the Loyalists and in consequence of this had
been driven from his country when hostilities ended. His son
had bought a commission in the 59th Regiment and had been
seconded from the Army to take up his appointment which was,
of course, a combination of a civil and a military one. Cuyler had
not only been an active and successful officer during the war but
had played a conspicuous part, to some extent on the strength
of his own antecedents, in persuading some of the more unbridled

of the farmers that they must not treat Hottentots and Kaffirs as they would never have treated their cattle. This did not prevent the Rev. Mr Read of the London Missionary Society and Mr Vanderkemp from bringing the most outrageous charges against him. It was alleged that more than a hundred murders had been committed in the District of Uitenhage alone and that Cuyler had winked at them all. Cuyler, outraged at so baseless an attack on his personal honour, demanded an investigation. Two judges were sent out and the enquiry was both thorough and fair; the end of it was that one Dutch woman and six men were found guilty of minor offences and punished while all the gravest charges were found to be complete fabrications. The judges observed in their report with an understandable bitterness that 'if Messrs Vanderkemp and Read had taken the trouble to have gone into a summary and impartial investigation of the different stories related to them, many of those complaints which have made such a noise, as well in as without the Colony, must have been considered by themselves as existing in imagination only, and consequently neither the Government nor the Court of Justice would have been troubled with them.' Cuyler was completely cleared of all the allegations against him and the Boers began to entertain respect for the judiciary.

This may seem of doubtful relevance to the story of the wars on the frontier but it is not. For every Mary Kingsley or David Livingstone who came to Africa in the nineteenth century there were half-a-hundred Vanderkemps and Reads. Their influence was, on balance, wholly mischievous as will be seen when the history of the later and greater conflicts comes to be told. A sense of vocation is a praiseworthy thing but when it is coupled with an absence of a sense of proportion and a complete incapacity to reject obvious untruth it can become a public danger. With all his excellent qualities, the black African has never found a strict regard for the truth to be a necessary part of his equipment and there must be something in the air of what men then called the Dark Continent that nourishes the eccentricities of evangelists. From the time of the Cuyler enquiry onwards, missionary (the L.M.S. brand in particular) was synonymous on the frontier with gullible fool and incorrigible trouble-maker.

Under Cradock reforms were carried out which should have

made it clear that henceforth this was to be a British Colony. The most important of these to affect the frontier was land reform. The old Company's loan-farm system had long outlived such usefulness as it might have had. Tenure was insecure, a flat rate of payment was demanded for all farms alike and boundaries were as nebulous as could be expected. Worst of all, a farmer had nothing to leave on his death, for if he had more than one child the farm must be sold and the proceeds divided. The system may have served to keep the Company's servants on a tight rein but it did not make for families letting their roots down into the soil. In August, 1813, this was transformed into a new sort of tenure whereby each farmer had to accept a sensible rent and to have his farm surveyed in order to decide what it should be. No farm, except with the specific permission of the Governor in freak cases, should exceed 6,000 acres; the Government reserved to itself certain mineral rights and the power of making roads across it, but the farmer could now devise it by will to whomsoever he pleased. The Boers, being both farmers and innately cantankerous, grumbled. What about the great tracts of Africa that were not parts of the Colony? Why should they not just occupy these as in the past? And what of those parts of the Colony itself that were, for one reason or another, still empty? However, all new grants adopted Cradock's system and Cape Colony can claim, if it wishes, that its scheme of land registration by compulsion ante-dates that in England by nearly a century and a half. The Zuurveld now disappeared from history only to re-appear under the name of Albany, in honour of Cuyler's birthplace.

In October, 1813, the Governor decided on a tour of inspection and was pleased with what he found, though he could not fail to see that the Colony was by no means an European reserve. Many bands of Xosa were still wandering about begging and stealing but their numbers were not alarming. 'His Excellency has had the further satisfaction to approve of the good and unoffending conduct of the inhabitants of the frontier towards the Kaffir tribes, the faithless and unrelenting disturbers of the peace and prosperity of this Colony', said the *Gazette*.

The reforms were good and necessary but they did not, could not, touch the Colony's overmastering difficulty. The war in

Europe was nearly over and the Cape was not going to be handed back to a ruined Holland. All the same, it was still a Dutch settlement in everything but name and that state of affairs could not for ever endure. Many more white men were needed to secure and develop it and they showed no signs of coming. Colonel Graham knew of the wholesale depopulation that was going on in his native highlands and wanted to bring ship-loads of Campbells and MacDonalds to Albany. It is a pity he was not allowed to have his way for these were just the kind of people the Colony needed and they would certainly have found it congenial. Instead of that they enriched Canada and the United States. The history of South Africa, more than almost anywhere else, abounds with 'might have been'.

In April, 1814, the long war ended with the abdication of Bonaparte and a British army in the south-west of France. Cradock, who had seen the unpromising beginning of it all, went home and in his place came another eponymous Governor, Lt-General Lord Charles Somerset. With the bluest of blood, the highest of connections (his younger brother was a Major-General with the Duke and one younger still was Fitzroy, the great man's Military Secretary and the future Lord Raglan), the highest of Tory principles and an utter inability to see any point of view but his own, he did not seem the ideal choice for His Majesty's vice-gerent in this barbarian wilderness. He was to remain in office for twelve years and it was within a few months of his arrival, on 13 August, 1814, that the Government of the Netherlands ceded to the Crown of Great Britain, in exchange for a substantial cash grant, 'the Cape Colony, and the settlements of Demerara, Essequibo and Berbice in South America'. Anyone who wished to retain his Dutch nationality was free to dispose of all his property and to sail for home within six years. Of the entire population of the Colony, only the brother of the Dutch Ambassador to London and the secretary of the High Court chose to do so.

Lord Charles, as befitted a son of the great house of Beaufort, regarded the Colony as a run-down estate that stood in need of improvement and he knew a good deal about farming. An attempt to grow more and better tobacco was a failure—the Boers were going to have to wait a long time for their Magaliesberg—but the production of quantities of grain far above the usual and designed for the food of the garrison soon followed upon his practical advice and example. It goes without saying that an English nobleman of the Regency worshipped the horse and thanks to judicious imports of blood-stock, the Cape was within a few years providing numbers of excellent chargers for the army in India.

The farmers on the frontier paid little attention to all these things, for, provided only that it left them alone, the kind of government at Cape Town was a matter of indifference to them. They still had their grievances; as the Kaffirs were quiet, the existence of a corps of the inferior beings known as 'Totties' on the frontier, armed, clothed and paid by the Government, was a standing affront to them. Somerset, who regarded Hottentot soldiers as something even more despicable than some of the Duke's curious auxiliaries in Spain, took the same view and wanted to disband them. The Government at home had no troops with which to replace them and their sudden disappearance would have been too great a temptation to Ndlambe, so it could not be done at once. This small circumstance was the production of another of the great 'if only's, for a single British battalion might have averted another and very ugly incident which was about to take place.

In 1815 there lived on a farm at Baviaan's Kloof in the wildest part of the Colony and on the border of Kaffirland an old backveld Boer named Frederik Bezuidenhout. He was a man of the same kind as the Prinsloos and van Jaarsvelds, ignorant, uncouth and living in a world of utter isolation, than which he had known no other. Both his heredity and his environment had made of him a hard and self-reliant man to whom the use of his *roer* for protection against wild beasts and wilder men was a daily occurrence. He knew nothing of Governments, whether in London or in Cape Town, except that they were now and then a minor irritant to him but as the journey from the nearest *drostdy* was through more than thirty miles of roadless bush and veld, they did not bother him much. He was, as one would expect, harsh with his servants though not to the extent of making him notorious for cruelty. Two years previously a Hottentot in his employment, no doubt learning of the Cuyler business, filed a complaint against his master with the *landdrost* at Graaf Reinet. The *landdrost*, in a regular manner, summoned the defendant more than once to appear before the Court at Graaf Reinet to answer the charges but Bezuidenhout, though there could be no doubt that the summonses had been properly served on him, did not obey, nor did he offer any explanation for his contempt. The *landdrost*, having no choice, laid the matter before the judges on circuit, one of whom was Bresler.

Everybody, the Dutch judges not least, understood the hardship that the summons would cause. Bezuidenhout's farm was in a remote spot on the Baviaan's River and was much exposed to raids from both Bushman and Kaffir. He had himself fought the wilderness for it and he had twice seen the home which he had built with his own hands burnt and sacked. His wife had been killed by Kaffirs and her body lay in the little cemetery which, as in every Boer farm, was fenced off in its curtilage. If he were compelled to undertake the long journey to Graaf Reinet in order to answer a charge which was stale and possibly only vexatious, he must leave all he possessed in the charge of his few slaves. As soon as the dust raised by the iron wheels of his wagon had subsided, the news would have passed that the Baas was away; it would not be surprising if on his return he would be greeted by the mutilated corpses of his retainers, the bodies of his poisoned dogs and the smoke rising from his house and crops. His flocks and herds and all else he owned would be gone. The law could not be defied for ever but one cannot but feel that this was not the way to treat a Christian. Certainly that represented the general feeling on the Border shortly afterwards, and it seems that the spirit of the directive from Downing Street regarding the treatment of frontier farmers had been either overlooked or forgotten.

Bezuidenhout, again taking no notice of a summons served upon him by the highest tribunal in the land, was sentenced to a month's imprisonment, as he would have been in any civilized country. The *landdrost* of Graaf Reinet was Stockenstroom, who had been promoted from his lesser post at Uitenhage, and he, when the order of the judges reached him, set about the arrangements for Bezuidenhout's arrest. He directed his under-sheriff to apply to Field Cornet Olivier for assistance and also furnished him with a letter to Captain Andrews, commanding the nearest post, requiring him to afford his aid should the under-sheriff request it. The Field Cornet refused point blank to help. Bezuidenhout, he explained, was a dangerous man who would certainly offer violence and he had no wish to be hurt. It is much more likely that the 'kith and kin' argument influenced him rather than cowardice.

Andrews was troubled with no such inhibitions; he at once sent a subaltern with a dozen Hottentot soldiers (he had no others) to take the prisoner. They reached the farm on 16 October but Bezuidenhout was not there. His gun was missing. Soon Rousseau, the officer in charge of the party, learnt the reason. Together with his servant Hans, a young man named Labuschagne who lived with him and another called Erasmus, Bezuidenhout was awaiting their arrival. A few shots were fired at the troops, deliberately aimed wide in the hope of scaring them off, but the Hottentots fired back and Bezuidenhout, Hans and Erasmus ran into two small caves by the river, Erasmus having one to himself. Bezuidenhout's cave was ten feet above the ground and could not be rushed; Rousseau attempted to parley with him and indeed is said to have spent three or four hours trying to persuade Bezuidenhout to give himself up; all he got for an answer was that he would never be taken alive. After giving him generous warning, Rousseau ordered his men to attack the cave and seize him. Bezuidenhout fired one shot which missed and as he was loading his spare gun (one cannot easily understand why it was not loaded already if he really meant to make a stand) he exposed part of his body and was shot dead. The other two promptly gave themselves up. (Both were acquitted at their subsequent trials on grounds of duress; the judges seem wisely to have strained the law a little.)

Bezuidenhout's funeral next day was a political event. His brother swore dramatically that he would have the lives of Rousseau, Stockenstroom and others whom he suspected of having had some hand in Frederik's death and that he would not rest until the Hottentot corps had been driven from the frontier. This won widespread and noisy approval; the meeting adjourned to another farm where, as on a previous occasion, it was determined to ask help from Gaika. This, of course, was the one thing that would alienate the sympathy of all but the maddest of extremists, for an invitation to black men to wage war on white could not be forgiven.

During the next month there was much toing and froing and it will come as no surprise to learn that one of the conspirators was Hendrik Prinsloo.* He had the ill luck to be taken prisoner by Captain Andrews on his way to a conspirators' meeting at which, incidentally, it was announced that Gaika had been offered the whole of the old Zuurveld and all the cattle of the Cape Regiment in exchange for the help of his warriors in wiping out the hated Hottentots. Gaika sat firmly on his fence, probably much amused. He could see plainly that the cat could only jump in one direction. An economy of truth is not a Kaffir monopoly, for one loud-mouthed plotter named Botma made it his business to go from house to house announcing that Gaika had agreed to come in and that all who would not join in the rebellion could expect no more than to be left to the mercy of the Kaffirs. It says much for the courage of the farmers, and of the Boer women in particular, that the threat did not frighten them into unwanted revolt.

The deputy *landdrost*, Van de Graaf, called out a small armed body of farmers who, having been harangued by Bezuidenhout, promptly changed sides. The whole body, about 60 in all, marched to Andrews' post and demanded that Prinsloo be handed over to them. They arrived too late, for there had come before them a party of British dragoons and a burgher force under Commandant Nel. Major Fraser of the Cape Corps was now in command. Bezuidenhout tried hard to suborn Nel but had no success with him; the conspirators had to be satisfied with delivering a letter to Fraser announcing blood-curdlingly that he had better not part with Prinsloo as they would be back in four days; they took a theatrical oath of fidelity to their cause and went away. For some days they sought vainly for proselytes but without much success; their alliance with Gaika was too much for most Boers to swallow.

On 17 November, 1815, the insurgent bands met at Slachter's

* Hendrik, the son of Marthinus, was one of those imprisoned with van Jaarsveld in consequence of which he was known as 'Kasteel Hendrik'.

Nek, where the Baviaan's River joins the Fish. There, next day, they were confronted by a force commanded by Cuyler, recently made Lieutenant-Colonel, with whom was Nel. He had with him 30 burghers and 40 dragoons under Fraser, a small enough force with which to attack determined men behind cover, but Cuyler was a brave and skilful soldier. Even so, he was Dutchman enough not to want to spill the blood of decent men who appeared to have taken momentary leave of their senses. There were affecting scenes as brothers and friends went amongst the rebels trying to reason with them but it achieved little. To back down now in the face of Cuyler's small force would be the act of a coward and nobody had ever called the Bezuidenhouts and Prinsloos that.

Cuyler was on the point of attacking when horsemen were seen riding towards them; the emissaries to Gaika and other potential allies were coming back to report dismal failure and the drifting away of those who had been supporters. Krugel, one of the ring-leaders, called out 'In God's name, let me go down and receive my punishment'. Eighteen men walked to where Cuyler was sternly waiting and laid down their arms. Jan Bezuidenhout was not of their number. With some others he fled to Kaffirland, hoping for the protection of Gaika; Nel with 22 burghers and Fraser with a hundred Hottentots were soon after them. Fraser broke an arm when thrown from his horse but his subaltern, McInnes, cut in ahead of Bezuidenhout who was encumbered with his wagons and ambushed them. Jan Bezuidenhout was not a man whom one instinctively either admires or even likes, but about his death there was something Roman. To ask his life of the hated and despised Totties was something he could not do; the summons to surrender was answered by a shot; Marthe Bezuidenhout coolly reloaded for him as he took up his second gun and his son, Gerrit, fired also. It did not last long; he was twice hit and died from loss of blood on the bed of his wagon. One Hottentot soldier he took with him. Marthe and Gerrit, who was not yet 12 years old, still had to be overcome by force.

Thirty-nine prisoners were brought to trial at Uitenhage where Colonel Cuyler, in his civil capacity as *landdrost*, prosecuted. All of them admitted their guilt; the order of the Court was that

103

Marthe Bezuidenhout be released but that all the others be taken back to the farm at Slachter's Nek where six of them, including Prinsloo and Krugel should be hanged. The remainder, after witnessing the hanging, were to be fined or imprisoned for different periods according to the degree of their guilt.

It fell now to Lord Charles Somerset to decide whether or not to exercise the prerogative of mercy. This was not a duty for which all his previous experience and background had prepared him. The Boers had a very clear recollection of the fate of the earlier Graaf Reinet rebels but this was outside Somerset's recollection. On the legalistic view there was nothing that could be said in favour of the rebels. They had appeared in arms against lawful authority and had done their best to bring the Kaffirs back to kill and pillage amongst their own people. It was no thanks to any of them that the farms in the west were not now in flames, the bodies of their former occupiers being picked by the hyaenas and vultures while their cattle were driven back across the drifts. Manifestly, they deserved death.

There were, however, other considerations which would weigh heavily with the Boer community. In the first place, they had not actually shed any blood; this invites the answer that it was only because they had not had the chance. Second, they were white men, brothers and cousins of those who had stayed loyal, and the Colony was not so rich in men like these that it could afford to take their lives to demonstrate an abstract principle. Five widows and twenty orphans, five farms deprived of their masters ought not to be the price of imbecility. Lastly, it would have been one thing to have shot them down in open combat but the rope and the tree were quite another matter. Nothing like this had ever happened before and none could say what effect it would have on the minds of Hottentots and Kaffirs. Would they think to themselves, 'See what a wonderful thing is the justice of the English. It is so refined that they will kill their own kind when they have not even taken a single life'? Or would it be, 'See what a curious thing is this English justice. They kill our masters for the most trivial of reasons and they spare us. We have, therefore, nothing to fear from the Boers any longer. A trumped-up charge of murder supported by some very expert lying and the English will kill them all for us and we shall have their farms'? It was anybody's guess, but there was a strong probability that the second interpretation would have its adherents.

Somerset had no difficulty in coming to his decision. After twenty years of war and with the smoke of Waterloo hardly blown away, life to him was cheap. A labourer in England who had stolen a fowl because his family was starving would expect to hang. For a crime of this proportion, who but a madman could expect a sentence other than death? There could be no question of a reprieve.

The execution was carried out with the same incompetence as the rebellion. The condemned men and their friends sang a hymn together and the drop fell. Four of the ropes broke and the men picked themselves up unhurt. The crowd saw the hand of God in it and cried out to Cuyler, in command of the 300 troops there to keep order, that the victims should not have to go through the ordeal again. Cuyler, whatever his private feelings may have been, had no power to do anything and the grisly business was repeated, this time effectively. Somerset, having made his example, was merciful with the remainder. One was banished for life from the Colony (he was a deserter from the Batavian army), seven were banished for life from Graaf Reinet, Uitenhage and George only, ten were sentenced to short periods of imprisonment with the option of a fine in place of their earlier and more severe sentences. The other sixteen, after witnessing the execution, were set free.

It is easy to see now that the executions were a political mistake. In justice they were undoubtedly correct and one should not be too swift to speak harshly of Lord Charles Somerset for being a man of his generation. The effect of them was, however, a disaster for as time moved on and men forgot, or grew up without knowing, the crimes that had been not so much committed as attempted, the villains became martyrs. Slachter's Nek has joined in folklore other imaginary acts of brutal oppression like the Boston Massacre, Tonypandy and the Jallianwala Bagh at Amritsar. They never happened, at least not in the fashion in which people are now firmly convinced that they happened, but that does not matter. They are noble rallying cries for those who think that they ought to have happened so that they can justify their charges of massacre and oppression. In the 1850's Judge Cloete was told by farmers in Natal that they 'could never forget Slachter's Nek' and 30 years later the same witless cry was thrown at Sir Bartle Frere. You can still hear it today if you steer the conversation in the right direction.

CHAPTER 9
Debatable Land

His refusal of clemency to the Slachter's Nek rebels marked the beginning of the unpopularity of Lord Charles Somerset in all quarters. Boers who had had little enough sympathy with the Bezuidenhouts at the outset found themselves instinctively outraged by the taking of the lives of their own people on the part of an alien power. Certain of the missionaries took great care to ensure that their versions of the affair, none of them conspicuous for accuracy or dispassionate judgment, found their way back to London and even some of the few British found themselves unable to express approval of what had been done.

All this coincided with progressive reductions in the numbers of British troops in the Colony which was only to be expected at the end of more than twenty years of war. For some years a substantial garrison was maintained in St Helena to guard against the possibility of an attempt to rescue Bonaparte and the troops there (who had, incidentally, taken over the island of Tristan da Cunha from its independent proprietor for fear that it might serve as a base for such an attempt) would be available for duty in the Colony at short notice if it became necessary. With the passage of time it became reasonably safe to assume that the Emperor's star had indeed sizzled out in the inhospitable ocean and these troops dwindled in strength also as the British government displayed its customary indecent haste to pare all military establishments to the bone as soon as the immediate need of them seemed less obvious.

The effect on the Colony was considerable. Only a substantial accretion of numbers of settlers of the right kind, Kipling's men, who could shoot and ride, would provide a sure shield for the Zuurveld and no sign appeared that any were likely to come. For the next two or three years the only new settlers were, to all intents and purposes, more missionaries and these could hardly be counted on in a crisis.

Only the Hottentots remained and Lord Charles did not come within miles of sharing Lord Macartney's feeling about these much humbugged people; the Boers hated to see them in arms and, after Slachter's Nek, the tide was running strongly against their continued existence as the main permanent force in the Colony. They could not be disbanded completely, for that would have only produced more bands of vagabonds trained to the use of arms, but in 1817 their establishment was reduced to a Major's command of six companies, each of 3 sergeants, 2 corporals and 50 men. This minimal force was the only one in permanent residence on the long frontier to be watched and guarded. Cattle reiving, of course, had never quite stopped and one foray into Kaffirland had been carried out in 1816 when two hundred men of the Cape Corps had crossed the frontier and brought back a thousand cattle.

The 72nd Highlanders, who had been mercilessly shuttled about between the Cape, Mauritius and India for the last five years, arrived in the Colony at the end of the same year to relieve the 21st Light Dragoons who were sent on to India. The only other reinforcement was the Royal African Corps which, for all its resonant name, was nothing more than a penal battalion designed originally for service on the island of Goree off Senegal, whose climate and living conditions were so vile that even the War Office was unwilling to furnish a garrison of British soldiers. The members of the Royal African Corps were recruited almost entirely at the gaol gates and contained some of the roughest characters that Regency England could produce. The sins of their officers must have been many to demand such atonement and the Colonists were far from sure whether they would not need more protection from their protectors than from their enemies.

These latter, in the unaccountable way of Africa which everybody who has lived there knows but none can explain, were entirely aware of the defenceless condition to which the Colony had been reduced; it was only thanks to the bitter hatred between Gaika and Ndlambe which the passage of time had strengthened that they did not choose this most propitious of moments to return to the Zuurveld. The woman Tutula who had been the original cause of it (and who was still alive in 1873 to tell George Theal with pride how much dissension she had created) should be reckoned one of the greatest benefactresses the Colony has known.

The Governor, thoroughly alive to his weakness, issued orders to the posts: 'It is to be clearly understood that no provocation is to be given to the Kaffirs in their own territory. No cattle belonging to any inhabitant or farmer are, upon any account, to be permitted to stray or graze over into the Kaffir territory; neither is any Kaffir to be molested when within his own boundary, nor is any soldier, or other person, permitted to cross the Great Fish River, except when tracing depredations, or in the pursuit of stolen property. It will be a primary object to capture any Kaffirs trespassing within the limits of the colony, and his Lordship anxiously hopes that this may be effected without bloodshed. Should cattle be traced, the party tracing them will, if it consider itself strong enough and if commanded by an officer, follow until it shall retake them. In order to encourage the men employed upon this duty, his Lordship has directed a reward to be given to the party making a capture, of five rix-dollars for each Kaffir not wounded, and one rix-dollar for each head of cattle retaken, and for each head afterwards restored from a Kaffir Kraal, in lieu of that which shall have been traced to it. Any Kaffir who is captured is to be well secured and to be conducted from post to post to the *Drostdy* at Uitenhage'.

The first part of the order was directed at men like Du Buis who were conducting a thriving though illicit trade across the frontier, bartering trade goods and sometimes firearms for cattle. The terms of it, however, show how much less strong the Governor felt than when his predecessor's order had gone out four years earlier to the then Commandant to 'try to do something that would prove to the savages and unceasing robbers that His

Majesty's government would no longer be trifled with or suffer the property of the colonists to be destroyed'. It was quite safe to trifle with it now.

Cradock had tried to induce settlers to move into the Zuurveld by offering them farms at very low rents but the scheme was not a success. By the beginning of 1817 ninety of the 145 families who had accepted were gone, partly because the farms were too small to be viable but basically because the rate of cattle-lifting had become so great that it was not possible to continue. Within the previous 18 months 3,600 head of cattle had been carried off; it is a little difficult for even the most devout farmer to love his neighbour as himself in these circumstances. The only way to bring this situation to an end would have been the despatch of a strong punitive expedition into Kaffirland but the means of doing this did not exist. Lord Charles did the only other thing possible; with a fairly imposing escort he went to visit Gaika who was popularly though erroneously supposed to wield supreme authority over the Xosa. Gaika, anxious as ever not to involve himself in the quarrels of others and probably with an uneasy conscience over the matter of some of the cattle, was not minded to receive his Lordship. It took all the diplomacy of Cuyler, Stockenstroom and Fraser to persuade him to attend a meeting on the bank of the Kat River a little above the place where Fort Beaufort was to be erected in six years' time.

Gaika arrived attended by a retinue befitting his presumed importance and in which was included his right-hand son Macomo of whom more will be heard. Ndlambe, equally impressively attended, came also. He had little to contribute but was determined that his enemy should not gain some advantage behind his back. Gaika began, as was his custom, by asserting that he wished as much as the Governor to bring the cattle-raiding to an end and that he would put to death all culprits apprehended. However, doubtless with a sidelong look at Ndlambe, he was not answerable for refractory clans which would not recognize his lawful authority. Somerset said flatly that he would not treat with any chief but Gaika. In the end an agreement was reached; the colonists might follow the spoor of stolen cattle into Kaffirland and, if the spoor led to a kraal, the people there should pay for the loss. There was nothing new about this as it merely followed ancient tribal law. In exchange, parties of Kaffirs, suitably identified, might travel twice yearly by a specified route to Grahamstown for purposes of trade. There was no talk of war but Lord Charles went home by way of the posts, now 14 along the Fish River and 12 more in rear, and inspected the garrisons, approving especially the newly installed system of signalling between the Fish and Sunday River districts.

The first Kaffir trading party to visit Grahamstown in April, 1817, the treaty being not yet a month old, could not resist the opportunity to pick up a few cattle, which belonged only to Hottentots. Their indignation was great when a company of the 83rd under Lieutenant Vereker chased them and a scrimmage followed in which 5 of their number were killed before the cattle were restored. Two months later the 83rd had gone to Ceylon and the Hottentot corps was reduced even more, a miserable 78 cavalry and 169 infantry being all that the Treasury would allow. The 400 gaol-birds of the Royal African Corps alone replaced them despite the Governor's representations to London.

It was plain to see that war on the frontier must come again soon and in the year 1818 the first light winds began to blow. The eternal Gaika/Ndlambe feud started it all. The latter had been rather in eclipse since his expulsion from the Zuurveld but suddenly the sun began to shine on him again. One of his sons, Dushane, had long ago succeeded Ndlambe's half-brother Cebo, right-hand son of Rarabe, as chief of Cebo's clan. As the quarrel was between members of the Great House of Rarabe, Dushane had very properly remained aloof from it. Over the years his clan, the Imidushane, had increased until early in 1818 Ndlambe began to work upon Dushane's filial duty and in the end father and son decided to make common cause against Gaika.

It so happened that at the same moment there appeared on the scene an unusually accomplished witch-doctor, Makana by name, who had lived for a time at the mission station of the Rev Doctor Vanderkemp. Makana had listened intently to the interminable sermons of the missionary and had been particularly intrigued by one on the subject of the resurrection. Though he only partially understood what he had heard, Makana was

111

greatly taken by the idea, not wholly foreign to the Kaffir, of a life after death and he took himself off from Bethelsdorp back to his own people. There he announced that he was in direct and regular communication with the spirit world and offered to give tangible proof to any who had the hardihood to doubt him. The scoffers were told to go at a prescribed time to the mouth of the Buffalo River where the waves make strange noises, breaking against and sucking through a hollow rock called Gompo. There he would join them and so would their dead relatives. All went well except for the fact that the departed ones failed to put in an appearance, but this detracted only slightly from the prestige which the mere attempt bestowed on the necromancer. Being so mighty a seer, common men might not pronounce his true name and he became known by the Xosa as Nxele, the left-handed one. By way of the Dutch 'Linksch', it reached the Cape archives in the anglicized if rather misleading form of 'Lynx'.

Makana was not an evil man and, indeed, brought about a number of improvements in Xosa behaviour, one of them being the sepulture of the dead rather than the casual leaving of their disposal to the fauna. By 1816 he was living at no great distance from Gaika's then kraal in the lovely Tyumie valley at the southern side of the Amatolas. The highest point of this beautiful range, still bearing the name Gaika's Kop, rises more than 6,000 feet above sea-level and in July and August is often capped with snow. The Tyumie River leaps in cascades from one of the thick forests covering the deep kloofs of the mountain and runs through fertile land, great fields of corn covering the valley in season until it flows into the Keiskamma after many other streams have added their waters to swell it. There could be no more beautiful place for Makana to have made his magic.

Like almost everybody except the British officials, he was no friend to Gaika and adhered to Ndlambe because in him he saw the best hope of uniting again the sons of Rarabe. To achieve this, the allies must first get rid of Gaika. Makana's was the brain that devised the strategem which would achieve this and it was a clever one. He sent out a party to steal some cattle from one of Gaika's subordinates and to fall back with them slowly towards the east. Gaika's war council agreed that the insult must be wiped out, all save one who advised otherwise. Ntsikana was a kind of Christian, which explains the wording of his message 'Listen, son of Umlawu, to the words of the servant of God and do not cross the Keiskamma. I see the Gaikas scattered on the mountains. I see their heads devoured by ants. The enemy is watching there and defeat awaits your plumed ones'. Gaika hesitated, but a thinly-veiled suggestion that he was reluctant to face Ndlambe with arms in his hand settled the question. He set off with his people downstream and swung eastward around the end of the mountains. From Debe Nek under the peak of Intaba-na-Ndoda (Mount McDonald) Gaika saw what seemed to be all the warriors of the Amandlambe mustered for war and resembling patches of red flowers on the plain below him. Mankoyi, Gaika's best captain, let out a yell of 'Huku, today we have them' and had to be restrained from rushing headlong at them.

It was as well that he was prevented from having his way for the wily Makana had spread his second-rate troops thinly on the ground as bait and his 'plumed ones'—the veterans—were concealed near by. To clinch matters, a substantial reserve of Galekas was kept in hand three miles further east still ready to exploit the victory. As Gaika did not oblige by setting in motion the usual unorganized rush, Ndlambe sent his young soldiers—called 'round-heads' for the same reason as the word was used in our own civil war—to attack him, knowing that they must be broken by Gaika and that he would then pursue them, which is exactly what happened. As Gaika's yelling and uncohesive masses reached the plain driving the 'round-heads' before them, Ndlambe's plumed ones rose up. From noon until sunset, says Xosa tradition, the battle swayed back and forth. Macomo, odious brute though he later became, fought like a hero and with his father and the Praetorians, returned again and again to the charge. In the end, however, the Gaikas broke and fled, Ndlambe's men pursuing them westwards and spearing them as they ran. When the pursuit ended with the dark, they returned to the killing-ground and by the light of fires kindled for the purpose they sought out the wounded and slowly killed them. No battle like this had ever been fought before between Kaffir tribes south of the Drakensbergs. Europeans call the place Kommtje flats, from the saucer-like depressions that cover the plain. In Xosa these are called amalinde and in tribal lore

Amalinde is the name by which the battle is called. 'No such wailing as that of the women had ever before been heard in Kaffir country'.

Gaika managed to reach one of the Governor's military posts around the spot where the treaty had been settled; with a skill all his own, he contrived in spite of his Homeric defeat, to cling on to a good proportion of his herds. His demands for aid and retribution arrived at a fairly good moment, for Somerset had managed to trade some of the blackguard soldiers of the Royal African Corps for several hundred of the 60th Rifles who did not want to return to England with the regiment. They were, for the most part, locally enlisted men who had deserted from the Regiment of Waldeck-Rousseau. By good fortune he had also the 38th (The South Staffordshire Regiment) 775 strong and with their Peninsular laurels still unwithered.

The British insistence on loyalty has often, in its colonial history, produced odd results. Colonial governments or quasi-governments had a habit of picking their champion on slender evidence of form and then sticking to him regardless of everything. Mir Jaffir, Shah Sujah, and a dozen others are cases in point. In Cape Colony, their man was Gaika; he was not the lawful paramount chief (that was Hintza), he was loathed and despised by most of his people but it mattered not. He was H.M.G.'s choice and must be upheld. The commandos were embodied, the 38th marched to Grahamstown and Colonel Brereton of the Royal African Corps was put in command of the frontier. With a force mainly consisting of burghers and followed by a mob of vengeful Gaikas, he crossed the Fish River in December, 1818, and attacked Ndlambe's victorious horde. The Kaffirs had not sought this extension of hostilities and withdrew smartly, taking most of their loot with them. Brereton burnt a few kraals but Gaika's people became completely out of hand. Murder, pillage and every form of beastliness were visited on the now victims and Brereton turned from his allies in disgust. Even though he had the misfortune to hold no command better than that of the Royal Africans, he was a soldier and not a hired butcher. He left the tribes to fight it out and re-crossed the Fish with 23,000 head of cattle. Gaika came in for 9,000 of these, for the British are always generous to their favourite chiefs and not less so when it costs them nothing. Of the remainder, some were given to the farmers, from whom they had been stolen in the first place, and the rest were sold to defray the cost of the expedition. The commandos were sent home.

It would have been much better if Brereton could have done the business more thoroughly but he was not equipped or provided for more than a swift raid. As soon as he had disappeared over the river Ndlambe revived remarkably, fell again upon Gaika and poured his men back into the colony. In the empty, or nearly empty, Zuurveld there were none to withstand them and those who could not get away to the posts laagered up and waited. There was the usual tale of murders and one killing is recorded in the manuscript records of the 72nd Highlanders in these words: 'This year [1819] the regiment had to regret the loss of Capt Gethin, who, with one sergeant and a private, was killed on 3 February near the post of De Bruin's Drift, on an excursion against the Kaffirs. It appears those savages had entered the colony and taken off some cattle belonging to a Boer in the neighbourhood of his post. On the circumstance being reported, he instantly set out with a patrol in pursuit, and, lighting upon their traces, pushed forward in advance with some of the men and Boers who were mounted and came up with the cattle in a thick bush. Depending on the support of the Boers (who were well armed) in the event of an attack, he, with the few men that had accompanied him, fearlessly entered, and were proceeding to drive the cattle out, when they were attacked and surrounded by the Kaffirs; and though the cowardly Boers were within hearing (and among them the owner of the cattle), not one had spirit enough to render the least assistance. The party behaved with the greatest bravery, fully determined to sell their lives as dear as possible. Capt Gethin defended himself with the butt end of his gun, till, overpowered by numbers and exertion, he fell. His body was found afterwards, pierced with 32 wounds. By this unfortunate affair was lost to the regiment a highly-respected and valuable member, and to the service a brave and intelligent officer, whose gallant conduct in the Peninsula, particularly at the capture of St Sebastian, had been rewarded by promotion'.

One would like to have heard the Boers' account of the

matter. Whatever their faults, cowardice is an accusation seldom levelled at them. The Boer did not look upon warfare through the eyes of the soldier. Military glory meant nothing to him and he found himself in the field for two purposes only; one of these was to kill Kaffirs but the other, no less important, was to avoid getting himself killed. For the soldier, death in battle was an occupational hazard; if he were to fall, somebody else would take over from where he had left off and in any event it would be better that he should sacrifice his life than that people might suspect that the ranks of the Umpteenth harboured a poltroon. To the Boer, it was necessary that, if at all possible, he should come through with a whole skin for if he were assegaied there was nobody else who would look after his farm and family. If this meant that he must now and then pass up the opportunity of shooting a Kaffir or two or even that he might leave the soldiers to extract themselves from the scrape into which they had managed to get, he could bear it with composure. His friends and neighbours all knew what manner of man Oom Piet or Young Cornelis was and no demonstration of senseless valour would weigh with them very much.

Another officer's patrol under Ensign Hunt was attacked in the open at night; the Kaffirs were beaten off but Hunt was stabbed to death. An attempt was made on the London Missionary Society's station at Theopolis which the Hottentot residents beat off, but obviously there was no unanimity amongst them as nine of their race were killed by the inmates of the rival Moravian mission at Enon before it was evacuated. Colonel Cuyler, having no military command, sent wagons and oxen to as many unprotected places as he could and brought many people into Uitenhage but cattle to the number of about 11,000 and horses and sheep uncounted were once more covering the plain and travelling east.

Makana, alias Lynx, was the directing brain behind it all and he was trying desperately hard to bring in other branches of the Xosa which so far had hung back. He was without doubt an orator of power for he managed to rally more fighting men than ever before and those under his own eye displayed a disdain for death and wounds more recognizable in Chaka's impis than in the Amaxosa. He rightly decided that speed and audacity were required if a decisive blow was to be delivered against the colonists and he chose the object of it.

Grahamstown was not a fortified place but it was the *place d'armes* of the frontier. A half-breed named Hendrik Nutka, recently a spy for Gaika but now turned enemy, had furnished information about the garrison and an attack seemed a feasible operation. The Graaf Reinet commando had been ordered to arms but horse-sickness was holding them up and none were near the town. Only the Light company of the 38th, 135 of the Royal African Corps and about 120 Hottentots of the Cape Corps were there to hold it.

The commander was a Major Willshere of the 38th and, although the information would have meant little to Nutka, he had learnt his trade in Portugal and Spain under the Duke. Willshere made the best dispositions he could, heartening his men by his example and even putting fire into the bellies of the Royal Africans, to the memory of whose previous glories an appeal did not lie. He had been born into the 38th, the son of a Q.M., and had seen his first service at Montevideo and Walcheren before he fought in seven major battles in Spain and France. His fire-eating nature had won him the nickname of 'Tiger Tom'. Whatever the odds against him, he was not the man to be frightened out of his position; he had two small field pieces, ex-Dutch, and these he confided to Captain Trappes. The African Corps was left to defend the barracks while the company of the 38th was drawn up just outside the town and the other infantrymen took advantage of such cover as could be found between the houses.

Soon after the sun rose on 22 April, 1819, the men in Grahamstown could see silhouetted against it a great army of Kaffirs drawing themselves up in battle formation, streaked with ochre and dosed with 'mouti' to make them invulnerable. A party was observed moving off to block the road to Blaaukranz, along which the commandos might be expected to come, while the remainder sorted itself into 3 columns. Willshere did not have to wait for long; drumming and yelling, the three columns rushed forwards more or less together. The 38th, in square, stood perfectly still and quiet, as they had done so often in Spain, though this was a far more nerve-racking business. When two

117

columns directed at his men arrived within range Willshere gave the order to fire. A hundred Tower muskets crashed and the heavy lead balls tore into the attackers, lead flattening on bone and throwing the men violently back on those who followed. There was a short exercise in fire discipline and the columns recoiled; the third one, however, under Makana himself, had forced a way into the barracks and were face to face with the Royal Africans. For all their ordinary unsoldierliness, these fought like tigers and showed that they too could shoot, for over 100 black corpses lay on the square before the survivors drew off. The first two columns, however, had only retired to shake themselves out and were coming back again. Willshere and his men with the guns firing grape were doing well but the outcome was still uncertain when there rode in a company of Hottentot hunters under their captain Boesak. These men were excellent shots and had the advantage of being able to recognize which of the Kaffirs opposed to them was the most useful target. Old Boesak and his men picked off the leaders, the 38th continued to ply them with musketry and before long the Kaffirs broke.

Three British soldiers had been killed and 5 wounded. The Kaffir losses cannot be even guessed with any pretence to accuracy. An eye-witness named Captain Stretch in a letter to the *Cape Monthly* in 1876 wrote that 'about 2,000 Kaffir bodies were strewn around', while Captain Harding gives his estimate as 1,300. Certainly more than 500 bodies were counted on the field, but the mathematics of the business are unimportant. What mattered was that a tiny force of which the backbone was red-coats had broken and driven off a vastly more numerous Kaffir force and an attempted *coup-de-main* had failed. Three of Ndlambe's minor sons had been shot dead, probably by Boesak's people, and Hendrik Nutka had fallen wounded into the hands of the Royal African Corps who shot him as he deserved. Now was the time, if the troops could only be found, to give the Kaffirs the sharpest possible lesson.

From the point of view of Cape Town, however, this was more easily planned than executed for the 54th regiment (The Dorsetshire Regt.) were still somewhere on the sea. They had sailed from Portsmouth on 1 February but calms and baffling head-winds were delaying them and there was no means of knowing when the look-outs would spy the topsails of the transports. An entire month went by before they were seen gliding slowly into the Bay and it was not until 31 May that disembarkation began. Five companies (half the battalion in terms of the then organization) did not go ashore at all but were ordered to carry on their journey to Algoa Bay. They disembarked in the shadow of Fort Frederick five days later and, in spite of their soft condition after more than four months at sea, they were immediately formed up and marched off towards the frontier. Their timely arrival brought the field force up to a respectable total but there is a lack of unanimity about exactly what it was. Sir John Fortescue makes the total 1,100 British troops drawn from the 38th and 72nd with 220 Cape Corps and 150 Hottentot levies. He ignores the presence of the 54th whose historian, the very experienced Captain C. T. Atkinson, reckons it as being 1,700 regulars while Theal puts the figure at 1,900. Atkinson is the most likely to be right. All agree that the burgher force numbered about 1,800, a figure which must include the many servants without whom no commando ever travelled.

Willshere formed his motley force into three columns. The northernmost was given to *Landdrost* Stockenstroom and consisted entirely of mounted burghers, mostly Graaf Reinet men. These set out from there on 22 July to move by the west and south sides of the Winterberg through the familiar country of Bruintjes Hoogte and the Boschberg reaching the Fish River near its confluence with the Baviaan. On the 31st the centre column under Willshere's own command marched out from Grahamstown to make the crossing at De Bruin's Drift, and Major Fraser of the Cape Corps led the right-hand column, the five companies of the 54th, and a part of the Hottentot levies to act as guides and trackers. Their crossing-place was near the sea, between two points later known as Fort Dacre and Wellington. For Stockenstroom's men the experience was one devoid of novelty and they set to work in their accustomed fashion, methodically clearing out each kloof and ravine by the process of picketing the heights with their most renowned marksmen while the remainder moved in to drive the Kaffirs, if there were any, on to the guns. Time and again the process was repeated, usually with no result, for the tribesmen no longer had any stomach for a fight and had vanished.

Much the same duties fell to Willshere's column, made up about equally of burghers and regulars, but the hardest time of all was endured by the 54th. They were not confronted by any substantial body of Kaffirs but the conditions of climate and geography were dreadful for men so long cooped up in slow sailing ships. May and June are the worst months of the South African winter and the cold at night was, to many, reminiscent of the conditions they had endured in the Pyrenees. The rain too was something quite outside their experience for rain in Africa does not fall in drops; it has been well described as like being under a lake from which the bottom has been suddenly removed. It washed the powder from the pans of their flintlocks, reducing their weapons to ill-balanced and unhandy pikes.*

The Fish River bush has been mentioned before. It is at its most formidable along the lower reaches where the thickets are dense and extensive; they cannot be penetrated except by the slow and laborious process of cutting for which a matchet or some similar tool is indispensable. The triangular bayonet of the day was completely useless for the purpose and the 54th, dressed and equipped for European warfare, were at a serious disadvantage. The only tracks were those made by elephants, still abundant in 1819, but it was not wise to linger on these as the elephant has firm views on his rights of way and will tolerate no obstruction of them. Luckily the bush was untenanted other than by game and the 54th eventually emerged into the open. The movements of the columns, once they were clear, were co-ordinated by the messages sent by the mounted orderlies of the Cape Corps without whose work Willshere could have done no more than grope blindly forward with each column completely cut off from his headquarters and from its neighbours. 'This was hard and difficult work', says the 54th's historian, 'the weather was cold and wet and ravines and kloofs in the hills provided splendid cover of which the Kaffirs made skilful use.

* In August, 1970, the *Daily Telegraph* published reports that more than 20 inches of rain had fallen in East London within 4 days drowning at least 6 people. A few days before, the same newspaper had written of drought a little further west causing the death of many cattle and the abandonment of farms.

There was little fighting and hardly any casualties but eventually the Kaffirs were driven across the Keiskamma behind which and its tributary the Tyumie they now agreed to remain'.

The campaign, known as the Fifth Kaffir War, lasted only a fortnight for on 15 August, Makana, aghast at the disaster he had brought upon his tribe, came in to surrender to Stockenstroom. His motives were entirely creditable for, had he wished it, he could easily have made his escape deeper into Kaffirland where his reputation was as high as ever. His explanation, perfectly sincere, was that his people were starving and he hoped by giving himself up to gain good treatment for them, A few days later, when Stockenstroom was at Willshere's camp reporting his capture, a party of Kaffirs was seen on the edge of the bush making signs to show that they wished to talk. Stockenstroom, for all the manner of his father's death, went with Willshere and another officer alone and unarmed to parley. Two of the men were councillors, one of Ndlambe and the other of Makana, of whose surrender they were ignorant. Makana's man made a short speech which Stockenstroom took down in writing: 'We wish for peace; we wish to rest in our huts, we wish to get milk for our children, our wives wish to till the land. But your troops cover the plains and swarm in the thickets, where they cannot distinguish the man from the woman, and shoot all. You want us to submit to Gaika. That man's face is fair to you, but his heart is insincere. Leave him to himself. Make peace with us. Let him fight for himself and we will not call on you for help. Set Makana free and Ndlambe, Kobe and the others will come to you any time you fix. But if you will still make war, you may indeed kill the last man of us; but Gaika shall not rule over the followers of those who think him a woman.'

There was something in what the councillor said. More than 30,000 head of cattle had been seized, an unknown but substantial number of casualties had been inflicted and every piece of Kaffir property down to the last clay pot had been destroyed. Ndlambe's power had been broken and his warriors were destitute fugitives.

Willshere sent a swift messenger to Cape Town and the Governor announced his intention of coming to dictate terms of peace. Makana, meanwhile, was sent under escort to Cape Town where he was incarcerated on Robben Island while a decision on what was to be done with him was discussed. He solved the problem himself by attempting to escape in a stolen boat but, being no sailor, he capsized it in the surf and was drowned. His body was never found and for more than half a century he retained amongst his people the legendary existence shared by the Emperor Barbarossa, Holger Dansk, King Arthur, Charlemagne and Lord Kitchener. Somewhere in a cave Makana was waiting for the hour to strike when he would return to his people. His mat and ornaments were carefully preserved until 1873 and the proverb 'Kukuza kuka Nxele—the coming of Nxele' was synonymous with the Greek Kalends. His brief encounter with the missionaries eventually bore fruit for his grandson, Galada, received Deacon's Orders in the 1880's as the Rev John William Gawler.

The Governor arrived at the future Fort Beaufort on 15 October where he was attended by Gaika and such of the surviving chiefs as could be persuaded to come, the principals being Eno, Botumane, Pato (whose people occupied an important strategic position in the hinterland of Algoa Bay adjacent to the sea), Habana and Gasela. Ndlambe was believed to be still in flight, far away.

Lord Charles came straight to the point; the Fish River bush created an impossible boundary for, to those who knew it intimately, it contained hiding places for thieves and for stolen cattle which could only be found, if they could be found at all, by disproportionate effort and the use of large bodies of troops. It also provided the most perfect forming-up place for any future attack on the Colony where large bodies could gather without their existence being even suspected by the patrols. This could not go on. The obvious frontier was the Keiskamma, 15 miles to the east where it entered the sea but tapering westwards further inland. The banks were more open and the length was less for the Keiskamma rises in the mountains nearer to the sea and which already formed the inland frontier. This mesopotamian land belonged by tradition to the Gunukwebe whose killing of Lt Chamney had been the event that had begun the long confrontation. The Governor, who still refused to do business with anyone but Gaika, made his proposition. If Gaika would cede this land to the Colonial Government an undertaking would be given in exchange that it would not be settled but kept empty and only entered by regular military patrols. The Gunukwebe had shown themselves to be enemies of the Colony and should not complain that the fortunes of war deprived them of it. Gaika did not like the idea at all, for the concept of cession of land to a power outside Kaffirdom was something never contemplated by tribal law. Nevertheless, he was in no position to argue the point. He expressed himself in agreement provided that he was left in undisturbed possession of the Tyumie valley where, he explained disarmingly, he had been born. Not even the colony's favourite Kaffir could expect that to pass unchallenged and it was pointed out that at the date of his birth the valley had been occupied only by wandering Bushmen. Gaika, never at a loss, explained that he had not meant this so literally; he had been taken to the valley as a boy and wished to leave his bones there.

Lord Charles agreed. Gaika should keep his valley and the frontier should henceforth be 'the ridge of hills branching off from the Winterberg range and forming the watershed between the Kat and Tyumie rivers, the Tyumie to the Keiskamma and the Keiskamma to the sea'. Incredibly, this was never even put in writing, let alone surveyed or mapped. The other chiefs then present were invited to acknowledge Gaika as their overlord and to confirm what he had just done.* They reluctantly agreed but their consent can hardly be regarded as a free one. For ever afterwards throughout the colony's history they regarded the land as wrenched from them by force and spoke of the British as 'omasiza imbulala'—the 'people who rescue and kill'.

The Boers, of course, were not satisfied. The commandos had lost many horses through sickness during the campaign and a preponderance of the liberated cattle had belonged to them. When these were again sold by auction to defray the cost of the war instead of being returned or others given in compensation, they sulked angrily.

Five years later a small boy named Paul Kruger was born on

---

* Gaika replied that 'he was much obliged to his Lordship for conferring on him the honour and title of chief of his nation and begged that His Excellency would accept the same compliment from himself'. C. Grant (Lord Glenelg) *The Wrongs of the Caffre Nation,* (1837) p. 71.

a farm near Colesberg. The first thing he remembered learning from his father was that the English were a wicked people. They had freed all the Boer's slaves in the middle of a harvest leaving the farmers to starve in the midst of plenty and had only paid contemptuous compensation; next they had murdered the Martyrs of Slachter's Nek; finally they auctioned their cattle, all of which, he was assured, had been retaken by the commandos unaided.

The arrangement obviously could not last for long. Quarrels brought about by shortage of land can hardly be resolved by depriving both parties of it and leaving instead a vacuum of irresistible temptation. It can be argued that Lord Charles had no more power to annex land to the Crown than Gaika possessed to give it away and indeed future Governors were to find themselves in trouble with the authorities at home for so doing. It may have been memories of Torres Vedras and the ruined land deliberately put in the way of Massena that provoked the idea but the longer-headed men realized that it was the seed-time for a harvest of trouble.

CHAPTER 10
The Settlers

NOBODY had any illusions about the current situation. It went by the name of peace as it had done after Mr Maynier's disastrous attempt at diplomacy, but the empty tract of fertile land now created could not be other than Tom Tiddler's Ground. The Armstrongs and Elliotts, the Kers and Kinmont Willies would not be deterred from carrying on their illicit trading and raiding simply because authority on both sides of the empty zone forbade it and they continued exactly as they had done before. The Hottentots of the Cape Corps did their best but they were far too few in numbers to police so large and unorganized an area.

Two things were plainly needed if the frontier was to be made secure—men and military works. The Regular army was receiving its customary reward for winning a great war and only the Duke's policy of 'hiding it in the Colonies' kept an army in being at all. It was made very clear to Lord Charles Somerset that the Cape was a useful place for staging on the journey to or from India and that regiments might find it convenient to recuperate there but he must not expect the luxury of a large, permanent garrison.

As long ago as 24 April, 1817, the Governor had written to Lord Bathurst, the Colonial Secretary, that the population of Albany should become 'sufficiently numerous to afford itself protection from its own body, its peculiar interests should be entrusted to itself without calling in regular troops'. The only recruits the Colony had received, however, were two hundred young men from the south of Scotland brought out by an entrepreneur named Mr Moodie. About 150 of them were craftsmen and Mr Moodie made quite a handsome profit by having them all indentured to him for a term of 3 years. Their passages cost him about £20 apiece and, as they were all single men, he had no great difficulty in selling the indentures soon after their arrival for sums considerably in excess of that. Mr Moodie's borderers were men of excellent quality and soon settled into useful niches but the same cannot be said of the protégés of a fellow-countryman named Mr Gosling. Fired by Mr Moodie's example but lacking his capital, this gentleman 'got out 12 boys from a charitable institution termed the Refuge for the Destitute, but his expectations of success were not realized, and some of the lads with criminal instincts turned out badly'. Mr Tait brought out 'seven Scotch labourers'. They attached themselves to farmers around George where they throve. Mr Tait did less well for, with the advances he had received for their passage money and that of others who never came, he bought himself a farm. Three bad harvests in succession ruined him and he went home. The only other addition was about 700 men who, nominally, belonged to the 60th Rifles and took their discharges in the Cape. As they were the leavings, after all the other foreigners which that famous regiment had had to accept had been posted to the Royal African Corps, it is no surprise to learn that they did more harm than good.

Lord Charles, however, was not content to leave the manning of the border in such hands. Lord Bathurst was in sympathy with him and their correspondence continued throughout the second half of 1817. The enthusiastic description of the Zuur-veld was, perhaps, better than it merited for Lord Charles asserted that the climate was delicious, the soil fertile and the land in every way apt for the cultivation of wool, cotton, corn and tobacco all of them fit for export. It was a misrepresentation but not a fraudulent one. Lord Charles had seen the Zuurveld at its smiling best; its worst could only be learnt by experience. His plan was to despatch organized parties, each under a recog-nized leader who would be answerable to the Government for their solvency and who would be their commander when the farms to be granted to them came under attack.

The moment for producing such leaders was a lucky one for many ex-officers of both services found themselves unable to settle to a commercial and civilian way of life. Many had already taken service with Simon Bolivar in Venezuela or with other less admirable liberators as the only form of adventure open to men who had marched from Lisbon to Bordeaux. These were the kind of people who were admirably adapted to become small marcher lords but few of them had the necessary money. In 1819 the Government in London decided, for a variety of reasons, that it would be expedient to empty the country of what the *Annual Register* called its 'redundant population'. Parliament voted with alacrity that £50,000 be appropriated from public funds for the purpose, and, for the first time, official advertisements appeared in the newspapers. Applications were sought from potential party leaders upon strict terms. On the part of the Governments at Westminster and Cape Town it was promised that free passages would be provided and that for every man over 18 there would be a grant as soon as he arrived of a farm of 100 acres. At the end of three years the leader would be given a further hundred acres for each man who remained in the party. The first ten years would be free of all taxes and after that the annual rent would not exceed £2 for each hundred acres. The corresponding obligation of the settlers was to pay a deposit, the leaders being responsible for collecting and handing it over before they sailed. A man with a wife and two children paid £10, a single man over 18 the same, and another £5 was required for every additional child over 14 or pair of children under that age. One third of the deposit was to be refunded when the party landed, the next third when they took possession of their land and the rest three months after that. Seed corn and tools, together with rations for a short but undefined period, would be made available at cost.

To many unemployed labourers and mechanics thrown out of work by the post-war depression it sounded like paradise. The owner of a farm of 100 acres was a man of some parts in Kent or Worcestershire; nobody told them that some of the land was more like Connemara. It seems hard to imagine how the green and pleasant England of George IV could have assumed the aspect of an over-crowded island with no future but to many it appeared exactly that.

The response was overwhelming, there being over 90,000 applications, and only one-twentieth of those who applied were accepted. In the end 57 leaders were appointed and between them they undertook to muster 1,035 Englishmen, 412 Scotchmen, 174 Irishmen and 42 Welshmen. About two-thirds of them were accompanied by families.

Though the leaders were picked men, mostly officers who could not make ends meet on half-pay, the followers were a mixed lot. For every industrious artisan bent on carving out a better future for his family and himself, there was at least one other who had got a girl into trouble or made such a nuisance of himself in other ways that his parish had joyfully passed round the hat to collect his £10 in shillings and coppers.

Only a minority were men who had made their living on the land, for the long wars had given impetus to the Industrial Revolution and many of the adventurers had been town-dwellers whose ordinary vocations had included the making of locks for the muskets of Wellington or saddlery for his horsemen. Some were seafaring men, including a company of hardy fisher folk trom Deal where for twenty years the trade of 'hovelling' among the ships of the Navy and the merchantmen in the Downs had provided an adequate, if not a comfortable income. With the outbreak of peace they found themselves with too many galleys in pursuit of too few ships and there was very real distress in the little town. Mr Charles Gurney collected together a party of the bolder, or more desperate, spirits numbering 13 men, 3 women and 8 children who, on arrival, set themselves to ply their old trade of fishing. At the mouth of the Zwartkop river they established their tiny settlement to which they gave the name of their old home. The place is now called Port Elizabeth, whose northern and southern districts are called respectively Deal Party and Walmer, much as they are in Kent.

Between December, 1819, and March, 1820, sixteen transports brought 1,079 men, 632 women and 1,064 children from English ports into Table Bay. A further 126 men, 73 women and 150 children came from Cork.

Lord Charles was not there to welcome them, for the warship carrying him home on leave passed them somewhere off the Guinea Coast. His office had devolved, entirely by accident, on another Peninsular General, who had the good fortune, if such it was for him, to be passing through Cape Town on his way home from India. Sir Rufane Shawe Donkin had not been the Duke's brightest officer, for he had commanded a brigade at Talavera which had been, quite literally, caught napping and lost 150 men without firing a shot. Not surprisingly, little had been heard of him since. He did not come from the higher reaches of the nobility and was rather nearer to what are now called the grass roots than Somerset had ever been. The latter was under something of a cloud locally for he had lived in the princely fashion which came naturally to him but was not understood by the colonists. He had quarrelled with local democrats and had been accused, quite unfairly, of approving an increase in the Cape Corps in order to create a command for his son Henry.

It was for Donkin to decide where the parties should go and it was unfortunate that his complete lack of local knowledge led him astray. His first mistake was to send all the Irish to Clanwilliam; it was one of those many places in South Africa that looks splendid in fine weather; it was left for the newcomers to discover that it was uninhabitable. They were unlucky in their choice of leader for Mr Parker was firmly under the impression that he had been promised land on the Knysna and he had unimaginable schemes for founding a city with factories, fisheries, cathedral and all.* He picked a fierce quarrel with the Colonial Secretary, Colonel Bird, whom he accused of conspiring to encompass his ruin and then went home.

The destitute families at Clanwilliam were moved to Albany where the English were already looking around and wondering where to start. Disenchantment with the lovely land was swift to come. True, it looked, for the most part, like an English park but much of it was fit only for rough grazing and was so stony that it could not be ploughed, even by those who knew how to do it. Relations with the Dutch settlers were, on the whole, better

* This land, in fact, had long been granted to George Rex, said to be the natural son of George III and Hannah Lightfoot. His estate was by far the finest in the Colony.

than might have been expected. Each community was puzzled at first by the aspect of the other; to the Boers the clean-shaven chins of the English verged on blasphemy for if that had been what the Almighty had intended he would not have endowed men with beards. The hill-billy appearance of the Boers, huge circular felt hats, tangled whiskers and queer leather garments, amused the English but they had to respect these veterans and to acknowledge themselves to be recruits by comparison. The Boers, not sorry to see more muskets in the hands of old soldiers, treated them kindly and helped out with their own stores when the settlers' supplies began to run low. In all, the frontier garrison was strengthened by about 4,000 men, women and children.

John Philipps, one of the most literate of the new settlers, was quite firm about it; 'I like them much, it appears they have been extremely wronged and misrepresented.' Judging from comments made in his letters home he appears to have spoken with the voice of nearly all the new arrivals. This was more than they felt about some of their own countrymen who were placed in authority over them. Captain Trappes, who for some time acted as *landdrost* of Albany, was one of the less popular of Donkin's appointment for after a visit to Lampeter, Philipps' farm, his host wrote of him that 'He is detested . . . a bachelor of 50 to 60, a sensualist, a Scoffer of Religion and the biggest misanthrope I ever was acquainted with'.

Africa treated the new settlers in much the same fashion as it had welcomed van Riebeeck's company long ago. Many of them had the advantage, if such it were, of being allotted old, abandoned farms and were able to build up the walls, clear out the shrubbery which had grown up inside and replace the burnt thatch without too much difficulty whereas others had to start completely from scratch. Here and there they found old crops well on their way to going back to nature but more often it was a matter of getting down to it with their few slaves and clearing the bush by hand before they could even see their inheritance. The same predators quickly appeared and no sooner were the first pitiful crops showing themselves than rain, flood and a new corn disease akin to rust obliterated them. As the first flocks and herds began to appear the Kaffirs again interested themselves and a raid by Nambili, one of Ndlambe's former captains, ended with the murder of an English boy who tried bravely to save his father's stock. Ndlambe, who was now quite an old man and had had enough of war, sent in the murderers for punishment. The Hottentot corps was a broken reed; many of them deserted to the Kaffirs taking their firearms with them and Philipps speaks scathingly of them as 'the infamous Cape Hottentot Regiment'.

To compensate for their unreliability a Volunteer Force was formed of 600 men under the command of the *landdrost*, Mr Rivers. It seems to have been of dubious value for, according to Philipps, it never mustered for training and its Adjutant was 'a creature of the *landdrost* who had been at home an uphol-sterer'. The experienced 72nd were moved on to India and were replaced by the 6th (The Royal Warwickshire Regt.), good troops but quite unused to Africa. One of the officers, Captain Foley, was, however, an artist and his sketches show very well the conditions in the early days of what is now called the Settlers Country.

By 1822 Grahamstown had grown into a neat village of about 25 houses but it was entirely without means of defence. New villages came into being at Bathurst, the first English community in South Africa, and around Fort Frederick. Here there grew up a regular harbour which was named in memory of Donkin's recently deceased wife, Port Elizabeth. The Acting Governor modestly contented himself by leaving as his memorial the stream named the Rufane River, famous now for its oysters. This was not much of a barrier against unknown black Africa, for rumours were already filtering down of the desolation that Chaka's impis were making of Natal and of the lands on either side of it. Nevertheless, the faint-hearts had been weeded out and the border had some sort of a garrison.

Lord Charles had clearly seen the need for a strong place in the north and, before going on leave, he had given orders for the construction of a regular military work on the west bank of the Keiskamma below its confluence with the Tyumie River. Fort Willshere, as it was to be called, was designed as a 'strong, pentagonal fort', to be built of stone and fit to stand a siege. Donkin, as soon as the Governor had gone, decided that it was too expensive. The 72nd, who had already made a start, were ordered to stop work and to build instead a cheap barrack. An old picture in Cape Town by the settler artist Edward Turvey shows it soon after completion as a collection of small thatched buildings with not so much as a wall around them. It is just as well that it never had to stand assault for the Kaffirs were slowly learning new methods of warfare. 'Fire is their grand weapon, and they affix a firebrand to their assegais which they throw at the thatch with unerring aim at 70 to 100 yards distance', wrote John Philipps. The misnamed Fort would have stood little chance against this. To make certain that the Kaffir warriors should be familiar with every detail of it, Fort Willshere was designated a market to which, periodically, the Kaffirs might come in order to sell their wares and buy European goods. They took full advantage of it.

Apart from the raid just mentioned, there was no activity on a large scale by the Kaffirs between the ending of the last war and 1824. Lord Charles Somerset returned from leave at the end of 1821 and was well briefed by his son about what had gone on during his absence. He brought with him a new bride— the first Lady Charles had died in Cape Town soon after their arrival—but her presence did nothing to soften the quarrel with Donkin. The acting Governor had been 'absolutely deranged by the death of his wife' and there can be no denying that since that melancholy event he had done some very odd things. He had allowed discharged men of the Royal African Corps to take up some land to the east of the Great Fish River in flat disobedience of his orders from Lord Charles and the fact that Gaika had given a grudging consent was no excuse. He had weakened Fort Willshere so that it could not fulfil its planned purpose and, worst of all in the Governor's eyes, he had used his temporary authority to bear down on Henry Somerset. Henry was a Captain aged 27 when his father had gone home and, from all accounts, he was a popular figure. There was a school of thought which held that Lord Charles had only had the establishment of the Cape Regiment increased so that Henry could thereby get a step in rank not otherwise open to him without leaving the Colony. As no other troops were forthcoming from home it is hard to find much justice in this and Henry, as his subsequent performances were to show (except upon one occasion), was a thoroughly competent professional officer. Donkin had insulted him, threatened him with court-martial and finally forbidden him to show his face in Cape Town. The reasons for his attitude are not clear but undoubtedly he had been egged on by the Colonial Secretary, Colonel Bird.

Bird is one of the least attractive figures in colonial history; he was a dedicated trouble-maker without a scintilla of loyalty to his chief and he hated all Somersets. Most of the troubles which brought about the cloudy end to Lord Charles Somerset's period of office are to be traced to his senior official who made it his business to issue unpopular orders in the name of his chief of which the latter was quite unaware and then, by back-stairs channels, to ensure that the Governor received the blame. Be that as it may, the anger which Lord Charles felt against his *locum tenens* was so furious that he refused to meet him for the customary handing-over. Lord Charles entered Government House by the front door; Sir Rufane left by the back, to continue to receive in England regular bulletins from Bird setting out everything that could be useful to hurt Somerset.

He had troubles enough at Cape Town without looking at the frontier. Lord Charles was no liberal reformer and found him-self, partly as a result of Bird's assiduity, engaged in quarrels with the Church, with those who wished to establish newspapers and with his own council. The settlers had mixed feelings about him; Stockenstroom regarded him as devious and swore eternal hatred. Philipps took Stockenstroom's part, describing him as 'so popular and upright', but some of Stockenstroom's own activities a few years later make one doubt the rightness of his judgment. A description of Lord Charles at one of the rustic race-meetings which were held now and then at Grahamstown says that he rode in a veil, carrying a parasol and looking like an old lady of 70 going for a ride in Hyde Park. The writer adds kindly that the new Lady Charles had done well to produce three children in 32 months.

It is the fashion now to blame Lord Charles for everything that went wrong during his long tenure of office but this does him far less than justice. He was certainly a die-hard reactionary but that is not always a bad thing in a Governor much plagued by fools, knaves or men who might be either honest or qualified for one of these categories. He is blamed for having a huge and well-stocked farm which was the envy of all others but no allowance is made for the fact that it was also a most successful agricultural college. Possibly there were other men of the Regency who might have made better Governors but it demanded all the authority and prestige available to get action from an uninterested government to send out the settlers. Fort Beaufort (erected 1823), Somerset East and Worcester are worthy memorials.

CHAPTER 11

Lord Charles Somerset

I⊤ was in the decade which began in 1820 that the future course of South Africa was plotted. During the long negotiations, mainly between Palmerston and Talleyrand, that led to the creation of an independent Belgium carved out of the Kingdom of the Netherlands, it had been seriously suggested that an appropriate form of compensation to the latter country might well be the return of her former colony subject to a reservation of rights of user by the Royal Navy much on the lines of the Simonstown Agreement of 1955. There was a strong feeling of friendship for Holland in this country based partly on tradition but also much due to the fact that Prince William (known to his friends as 'Slender Billy') had made himself well known and liked as a member of the Duke's military family and because he had shown himself to be a faithful ally at Waterloo. Had it not been for the presence of the 1820 settlers it is quite possible that a case would have been made out for the return of a body of people almost all of whom were of Dutch extraction to their natural allegiance, for the colony was far from being a valuable asset for any but strategic reasons. The presence of a substantial number of British families, however, put this beyond the bounds of possibility.

It was also the decade of the great Zulu expansion. Dingiswayo had died in 1818, having made a start towards achieving this end, and he left behind him an army which was already the most formidable that black Africa had seen. He had, for some obscure reason, left his own soldiers and was accompanied only by a bodyguard of women when he fell into an ambush laid by Zwide, chief of the Ndwande, who lost no time over putting him to death. Fired by this easy success and believing the Zulu to be masterless, Zwide moved into Zululand and attacked the army of Chaka at Qokli Hill, south of the White Umfolosi. The battle began with an exhibition of single combat between the lines of the opposing armies in which a Zulu warrior named Manyosi summarily disposed of three Ndwande champions sent to try conclusions with him. After these preliminaries, Chaka, with a much smaller force, attacked the Ndwande who were led by Zwide's son Nomahlanjani. All through an April day the fight swayed back and forth; at one moment it looked as if the disciplined impis were going to get out of hand and rush to their destruction, for Nomahlanjani staged a feigned flight as Duke William had done at Hastings. Chaka and his captains managed to rally them and at the end of the day some 7,500 of the Ndwande lay dead on the field and the remainder had fled. The Zulu had lost about 2,000 killed and badly wounded, about half Chaka's effectives, but their last powerful enemy had been overthrown and there could be no longer any question as to who would occupy Dingiswayo's throne. The remaining tribes hastened to cast their lots in with this apparently invincible clan and within the year Chaka had at his command eight highly trained regiments of 1,000 soldiers each. The era of expansion in all directions was beginning.

In July, 1819, Zwide, who had not been present at the Qokli hill battle, attempted to gain his revenge and advanced into Zululand with an army about 18,000 strong. Chaka lured him deep into the homeland and utterly destroyed him. His realm now covered about 11,500 square miles, from the Pongola in the north to the Tugela in the south and from the Buffalo River to the Indian Ocean.

The year 1820 saw a continuation of the Zulu expansion. The Zulu armies struck westwards, attacking the Tembu and the Cunu on the fords of the Buffalo River. Two pitched battles were fought by two different wings and against the Tembu the campaign was a complete success. The untrained levies were routed, their women and children massacred and their cattle, numbered in tens of thousands, were carried off. The broken Tembu poured south into Natal, heading for the Drakensbergs and the sea. The Cunu put up a better fight and drove the impis back across the Buffalo. It was the start of a kind of motorway collision in slow time, precipitated by the Xosa being compelled to stop on the Keiskamma and all the tribes of the hinterland running into the back of those ahead.

Throughout 1821 Chaka was fully taken up with domestic affairs but in the next year he struck again at the Cunu, destroying them together with what had been left of the Tembu. The multiple pile-up continued to gather way. Next year came the turn of Matiwane, chief of the emaNgwaneni, whose tribe occupied a part of the northern slopes of the Drakensbergs. Matiwane had survived an earlier attack by Dingiswayo and another by Zwide but he knew himself to be no match for Chaka. The emaNgwaneni therefore uprooted themselves and streamed over the Drakensbergs adding their contribution to the eventual smash. As they could not re-build an agricultural and pastoral society overnight, Matiwane's people took to plundering the existing tenants, the Sutu, and ranged far and wide in the process. No records exist of what happened but for years the ravaging continued and vast areas to the west of the mountain chain were turned into an abomination of desolation.

From the wreck of the tribes pillaged and driven out by Matiwane there coalesced a body of about 50,000 whose nucleus was the baTlokwa under a chieftainess named Mantatisi. As the Mantatee Horde (the name by which this great mob has gone down to history) drifted south it came upon a small tribe known as the baTlapin who had with them some missionaries from the Colony. These men were of stern stuff and had no mind to see their charges wiped out by this terrible woman. They called for help from the nearby Griqua community who had horses and guns and were part European in blood. About a hundred mounted Griquas led by their captain, Adam Kok, arrived to answer the call just as the baTlapin were about to fly. Though they had little ammunition, these hundred brave men so harassed the vast horde that they managed to turn them back to the north where eventually they split up and disappeared into

E*

the vastness of Africa. Matiwane's people came to rest in Tembu country between the southern end of the mountains and the sea. Thus, by 1825, the powerful and apparently unstoppable military empire of Chaka had emptied most of the land which we call Natal of its inhabitants and the whole of the hinterland of the colony was in a state of chaos.

In the Colony itself steady, if rather slow, progress was being made towards civilization. Lord Charles Somerset was determined to have the nebulous northern boundary properly mapped and sent out a surveying party to decide where it ought to be. The work took nearly two years but in August, 1824, it was finally completed and the first true maps appeared.

Macomo, Gaika's right-hand son, had by some mysterious means obtained leave to build himself a kraal near one of the sources of the Kat river. Although his father enjoyed a very special relationship with the government Macomo cherished a deep hatred for the white men and everything connected with them as his future life and conduct were to manifest. In January, 1822, one of the staff of the near-by mission station in the Tyumie valley had visited the young chief's kraal and had there spotted two horses which he recognized as having been stolen. Without much ceremony he took them away and returned them to their owner. Macomo, in a blind rage at such effrontery, attacked the mission and drove off all its cattle. When the news reached Fort Willshere the commandant sent a half-company under Captain Aitcheson to call on Gaika and demand redress. Gaika began by taking a high tone. Aitcheson soon deflated him and Gaika agreed to have the cattle returned; a month later the tally was still short by 73, which had probably formed a feast for Macomo and his friends. Lord Charles had gone to the limit with his favourite and sent Colonel Scott at the Fort orders to have him seized until the cattle were handed over or compensation made. Gaika gave the arresting party the slip and moved his kraal 15 miles further east. The cattle were restored but from that day onwards rustling took place on a scale that could hardly have been innocent of organization. It was followed by reprisals on the part of the farmers which the Governor could hardly prevent as he had not sufficient troops to do the business. 'In 1822 and 1823 many hundreds of oxen and cows were purchased and brought into the pastures of Albany. But often a man who in the evening looked with satisfaction upon a little herd rose the next morning to find every hoof gone, and only a spoor leading always in one direction' is how Theal describes it. Macomo was at the bottom of it all.

Clearly this could not be permitted to go on but only by the provision of troops could it be stopped and there were none save the little garrisons of Grahamstown, Fort Willshere and Fort Beaufort. The most Somerset could wring from London was permission to raise the Albany levy from amongst the settlers and to raise another two troops of Hottentots. Even when this had been done, the combined strength of the mounted and dismounted portions of the Cape Regiment totalled only a little over 500 men. Colonel Fraser of that Corps died in October, 1823, and the command of the frontier revolved on Henry Somerset, now promoted Lt-Colonel.

Henry Somerset was firmly of opinion that Macomo stood in need of a sharp lesson and he administered it. On 5 December, 1823, a mounted commando of 200 burghers and the Cape Corps squadrons made a forced march of 22 hours to Macomo's kraal on the Kat river and caught him off guard. More than 7,000 cattle were seized with hardly any resistance and taken to Fort Beaufort where those who had suffered from Macomo's depredations received back their dues. There were still nearly 5,000 left over and these were given back to Macomo. Why he was not turned out of his well-sited thieves' kitchen remains a mystery. It is probably a tribute to his glibness of tongue that Somerset accepted his customary protestations of his intention to lead a new life and let him stay.

The price for this piece of misplaced magnanimity was not to be exacted for several years but eventually it was paid in full. In the course of many petty expeditions policing the frontier, Henry Somerset acquired an encyclopaedic knowledge of every kloof and came to know the characters of every paltry chieftain better than they knew themselves. The farmers both British and Dutch liked him, for he was an engaging young man, and he commanded the eccentric loyalties of his Hottentot soldiers as few other men have done.

While Henry Somerset was acquainting himself with the practical difficulties of maintaining peace on the border, two other gentlemen were coming to Cape Town to enquire into its political theory. The House of Commons had appointed Messrs William Colebrooke and John Bigge to be 'Commissioners for enquiring into the state of the colonies of the Cape of Good Hope, Mauritius and Ceylon'. Their deliberations and the execution of their plans were to take the best part of seven years and as they had no knowledge of Dutch they fell into more than one pitfall. However, their presence was welcomed by most people for in the years immediately before the Reform Bill an autocracy such as the Colony was did not commend itself to those who either had had votes at home or who were now aspiring in that direction.

On 9 February, 1825, the first blossoms of the Commissioners' planting were put out when King George gave his consent to the creation of a Governor's Council. It was to consist of six members, three of them *ex-officio* and the others nominated by the Secretary of State, Lord Bathurst. The Governor was obliged to consult with the council over all his public acts but he was not bound to accept its advice, and its proceedings, like those of the Cabinet, were to be held behind closed doors and under oath of secrecy. Even so, it was a small step forward, though the first set of nominated members were men who already held military or civil appointments in the colony.

The commissioners sensibly recognized that the colony was now too big to be effectively administered from a place in one of its four corners and they recommended its division into an Eastern and a Western Province. This was approved and put into effect in rather an odd way, dictated no doubt by considerations of economy. The Governor was to be provided with a Lieutenant whose function it would be to administer the Eastern Province where trouble was the more likely; the Governor would remain Commander-in-Chief of all the military forces but in the ordinary way would only attend to the administration of the Western Province; however, he would keep a reserve power to take both reins in his hands and to suspend the functions of his subordinate if something of sufficient gravity to warrant such a course were to occur. The scheme was never seriously tested for after the Lieutenant-Governor had been appointed Canning succeeded Lord Liverpool as Prime Minister and formally cancelled the arrangement. It was an ill-judged decision, for the time was not far distant when the near-impossibility of one man performing the supreme military and political functions would speak for itself.

Lord Charles was already in an impossible position. He was being assailed on all sides by some very strange characters of left-wing ideas, varying from grasping parsons who were dissatisfied with their surplice fees by way of an eccentric bankrupt who had the good fortune to bear the forename of 'Bishop' to a malevolent notary and a seditious missionary. Common to them all was the factor that any stick, no matter how dirty, would serve to smite the high-born Governor. That unhappy man was being systematically calumniated by some of his own staff, Colonel Bird being the most prominent amongst them, and prosecutions for criminal libel on the Governor, though unavoidable, did not make the atmosphere of Cape Town any happier.

Lord Charles had for some time been demanding to come home and give his account of the complaints against himself which the missionaries were so recklessly making. He was given permission to return but, as he did not dash up the gangway of the first ship that passed, Bathurst found himself under the necessity of writing on 15 January, 1826, that it had 'become expedient that you should repair home immediately to furnish the necessary explanations'. Mr Brougham had sworn a great oath that when Lord Charles arrived he would personally conduct his impeachment. *The Times* for 19 January indicated that it expected Mr Brougham to make good his boast. He did not do it. Joseph Hume, the Rupert of Exeter Hall, of course made a great deal of noise.

Throughout the first half of 1827 the dismal business dragged on and Lord Charles resigned his office in disgust. Two months later the report of the Commissioners was laid before Parliament and contained two features disconcerting to the anti-Somerset faction. Mr William Edwards, the malevolent attorney, was in truth an escaped convict. The matter of Mr Bishop Burnett was decided squarely in favour of the late Governor. Mr Brougham was obliged to say that he was sorry when information reached him that the charge that Lord Charles had practically compelled a litigant to buy a horse from him at a fancy price in order to get a favourable judgment from the Governor could not be substantiated as the finding had gone against the purchaser. The only surprising thing is that Mr Brougham did not amend the charge to forcing the sale of the horse and breaking the bargain by the judgement, for he was that sort of man. Lord Charles died at Brighton in February, 1831, after a short illness.

Major-General Richard Bourke had been appointed Lieutenant-Governor during the brief existence of that office and arrived in the Colony in February, 1826, just before Lord Charles departed. He acted as Governor for two and a half years and it was under his authority that the British—one can hardly go on calling them settlers now—came face to face with the Zulu vanguard. It was not a dramatic affair. For a long time past rumours had been filtering down to Albany of terrible things going on behind the ranges. Those who had fled further and faster than most had taken service with the farmers who were glad enough of any extra labour. A small Zulu force had indeed percolated down to the Kei river where they mingled with Matiwane's folk. A patrol under Major Dundas brushed with Matiwane and reported back that the enemy were Zulus. Henry Somerset hurried to the scene with the 55th Regiment (The Border Regt.) and a mass of Tembu auxiliaries but by the time he arrived the Zulu were gone. On 28 August Somerset attacked Matiwane under the impression that his was a Zulu army and routed him. A month later Chaka was dead, murdered by his brothers. Matiwane and a few of his henchmen fled north where they encountered Chaka's successor, Dingaan, who summarily knocked them all on the head.

Somerset's allies, equally comprising Tembu and Xosa, were under the leadership of Hintza, son of Kawuta. He was the rightful paramount chief of the Xosa and resented the fact that the Government treated him as Gaika's inferior but on this occasion the interests of both colonists and Xosa marched together. It was not, however, to be an alliance of long duration. For the moment the Xosa and Tembu were content to take up the work which Somerset had left unfinished and between them they exterminated the beaten AmaNgwane. The Zulu, apparently on

the advice of Mr Henry Fynn, a resident at Chaka's kraal, withdrew shortly before the first shots were fired and contented
themselves with drawing a rake of desolation through Pondoland.

Broken tribes were reassembling on an empirical footing, small
parties joining together as best they could with those who did
not seem actively hostile. Informed opinion reckons that the
Mantatee Horde alone wiped from the face of Africa twenty-
eight identifiable and named tribes. The slain, numbered in tens
of thousands, have never ever been accurately estimated. One of
the new tribes to emerge from the debris of the old order was
the Fingoes; helpless and starving, the vestigia of half a dozen
once respected clans, they threw themselves on the mercy of
the Tembu and Xosa. These spared their lives but took them
into their own lands merely as slaves. In years to come they
would have cause to regret their inhospitality.

On the whole the Xosa and Tembu had not been badly affected
by the Zulu surges; they had had to fight for their lives against
tribes forced into their orbit by Chaka but they had been fairly
successful and their own numbers had been increased not only
by their Fingo helots but by others of their kindred who had
joined them for security. Their agriculture was not interfered
with, their herds multiplied, but the one thing they had to avoid
was a war on two fronts. For most of the 1820's their attention
was concentrated on the exits from the Drakensbergs and the
last thing in the minds of most of them was any idea of another
irruption into the old Zuurveld. Nevertheless, the pressure was
building up on both frontiers and the vacuum between black
and white was becoming more abhorrent to nature with each
year that passed. The little hunters were disappearing altogether,
for they were everybody's prey. The Griquas shot them down
mercilessly and in the face of the horrors of Matiwane's invasion
and that of the Mantatee Horde they had simply become something edible. It was during this horrible period of starvation that
cannibalism became commonplace and the Bushmen, their
women and children being eaten up in the most literal sense,
took their depleted numbers into the remotest hiding-places
they could find.

All this seemed as distant as the moon from the citizens of
Cape Town. The old settled districts went on with their farming

and wine-growing and their only troubles were political ones. The British element amongst the people on the frontier found, to their satisfaction, that the country was steadily becoming more and more akin to the home country in its institutions.* The Boers were equally conscious of the same thing but in their breasts it aroused quite different emotions.

Bourke, his period as caretaker over, went home in November, 1828, having handed over his duties to Sir Lowry Cole. He seems to have been unique amongst the early British governors in that he bequeathed his name to neither village, river nor hill. Now the Colony was coming under the administration of men who had served Wellington throughout his long campaigns; Sir Lowry had commanded the 4th Division extremely well during the war in Spain and Portugal and had also served at Waterloo. His Colonial Secretary was Colonel John Bell of the 52nd (Oxfordshire Light Infantry) who had been a regimental officer with that famous unit during the same time, and shortly to join them as Chief of Staff was the man who would be the greatest of them all, Colonel Harry Smith of the Rifles.

Smith had joined the old 95th in the year of Trafalgar and had first smelt powder at the disastrous Montevideo and Buenos Aires affairs. After that he had been with his regiment during Moore's campaign which ended at Corunna, returned after Vimeiro and been severely wounded in the foot during Craufurd's action on the Coa. As a result of this he had been translated to the staff, serving as Brigade Major in the Light Division and having been forward in every battle in which that splendid formation engaged. After Bonaparte's abdication in 1814 he had moved on to America where he had seen the burning of Washington and the bloody battle of New Orleans. He returned just in time for Waterloo where he had been the only British staff officer in the 6th Division. Since the end of the war he had been employed in Scotland, Ireland, Nova Scotia and finally Jamaica. His Spanish wife, Juana Maria de los Dolores de Leon, whom he had met and married within 48 hours just after Badajoz fell and who had accompanied him for the rest of the campaign, was almost a legend in the army. The three men and Juana were old

---

* Even rustic Grahamstown received a dash of culture when, in 1826, the courtesan Harriet Wilson paid it a prolonged visit.

1. Sir Benjamin D'Urban (1777–1849), Governor and Commander-in-Chief of the Cape of Good Hope, 1833–37.

2. Charles Grant, Lord Glenelg (1778–1866), Colonial Secretary 1835–39. "In his few years of office he did more permanent damage to the whole of South Africa than any man before or since."

friends and under such a régime the treachery and back-biting which had gone far to wreck all the work of Lord Charles Somerset would have no place.

The garrison at this time, early 1829, consisted of those veterans of Cape Colony, the 72nd Highlanders, and the 98th, a young regiment but in good shape. For the next five years they were to have little to do save ordinary garrison duties, but to break the monotony and to achieve something useful Cole put them to work making a road from the capital through the old Hottentot Holland Kloof. Sir Lowry's Pass it remains.

As the year 1829 brought new names and faces in the Colony so it took away an old one from Kaffirland. Gaika died and was buried with much circumstance in his valley; it was to be a place of significance to his descendants. His sons Macomo and Sandili (though the latter was only a boy of 8) were to give the colonial government infinitely more trouble than their former favourite had ever done.

The barometer seemed set fair. More than 12,000 Merino sheep had been introduced into Albany where the sour grass seemed to suit them well. The flood and diseases of the early '20s seemed ancient history. Everything looked as settled and as promising as it had done to the citizens of Byzantium four hundred years before.

CHAPTER 12

Irruption of the Kaffirs

LORD CHARLES, advised no doubt by Henry, had won a small victory during his period of home leave which was now beginning to produce a result. As has already been noticed, the weapons issued to the regular troops for bush-fighting were about as unsuitable for their purpose as could be designed. The Land Service musket had a barrel length of 42 inches and its bayonet added another 32. Once it had been discharged it was a considerable task to reload it in close conditions. Lord Charles and his son sketched out a design for a double-barrelled carbine with a barrel length of only 26 inches and a bore of .733 which, though still clumsy, was a far better weapon. The reduction in length naturally meant a corresponding loss of accuracy but accuracy had never been a great merit of Brown Bess. What mattered much more was handiness and stopping power and in these respects the new weapon was greatly to be preferred. The Duke, however, would have none of it. Brown Bess had served him well enough from Assaye to Waterloo and he could see no reason to lay out public money on a freak weapon for a corps of colonial gendarmerie. Lord Charles persisted, for in this instance the Duke was wrong, and during the time that Lord Hill was at the Horse Guards he managed to get his new weapon approved. About 250 were made, not nearly enough but sufficient for the mounted men of the Cape Corps, at the price of £5 1s. 2d. each. It had a formidable recoil which must almost have kicked the slightly built Hottentots from the saddle, but it gave the chance of getting in a second shot which might easily be vital. Bruised shoulders were a small price to pay for this advantage.

As the 1820's gave way to the 1830's another cloud appeared on the horizon but this time it did not blow across from Kaffirland. The abolition of slavery throughout King William's dominions suddenly became a live issue. Few people disagreed then or since that the institution was an offence to Christian people for, as Mr Lincoln (soon to be captain of a troop of volunteer cavalry fighting the Black Hawk Indians because they had moved across an agreed river boundary) had said, if slavery was not wrong then nothing was wrong. Nevertheless, it was an ancient relationship and more than one agricultural economy was utterly dependent upon it until something could be found to take its place. Cape Colony was a case in point, for it had much in common with the Deep South. The Dutch farmers were the more affected for they had run their farms by slave labour for centuries, though the rich slave-dealers and the stud-farms dedicated to the production of the necessary article in sufficient quantities had never been known in South Africa. The 1820 settlers had found slavery to be something outside their scheme of things and went in far more for hired servants as at home.

In 1833 the Act was passed and the word went forth to the King's Governors all over the world. From December, 1834, all slaves (there were about 29,000 in the Colony) were to be freed after serving an apprenticeship of 4 years to their present owners. To compensate them for the loss of the chattels for which they had paid good money, Parliament voted compensation; the amount allotted to the Cape was originally just short of £3,000,000 but second thoughts reduced this to £1,250,000. The rate was a flat one, the strong young man with years of valuable work in him ranking equally with his grandfather who did little more than sit in the shade of a maroola tree all day long. Part of the compensation was payable in cash but the bulk of it was to be handed out in bonds payable only in London. As few, if any, of the slave-owners were in a position to travel to Threadneedle Street to cash their bonds, keen financiers, which South Africa has never lacked, were willing to cash them locally at discounts of anything up to one-third of their face value. A warm, self-righteous glow expanded through Exeter Hall where well-fed citizens with substantial bank balances felt themselves to have done a very virtuous thing. In the Colony, where many farmers had borrowed necessary working capital on the security of this valuable and tangible asset, loans were speedily called in and bankruptcies with their accompanying forced sales of farms followed.

Both morally and practically the thing was right but so little thought was given to the realities of what they were doing, both by ignorant ranters and by sober politicians, that it completely alienated the Boer community. Men of the stubborn independence that was their main, and by no means ignoble, characteristic could not be expected to sit down under a direct attack on all their traditions and subject themselves for the future to the whims of a Government under the thumb of the missionaries and their mealy-mouthed friends. Some decided at once that the Colony was no longer any place for them and their wagons crashed northwards into the spaces emptied by Chaka where they would be outside the pentacle drawn on the map of Africa by Somerset's surveyors. The more patient simply adopted a policy of non-cooperation with the Government. Only a common danger which was shortly to appear kept the colony together, but when the next war came, as it soon did, the commandos of Swellendam and Graaf Reinet rode for the last time.

As for the slaves, they were for the most part like budgerigars suddenly turned out of their cages for no obvious reason. Many remained with the Baas for fear of finding something worse and of those who elected to seek their fortunes in the world outside Wonderfontein or Weltevreden many ended up in serfdom of a far worse kind under masters of another race. There was open talk of rebellion; in Stellenbosch, which was to South Africa what Virginia was to North America, there was rioting when the commissioners from London demanded to inspect the punishment-books. It was no sort of palliative to feelings so deeply outraged to be given a form of representative government in Cape Town where the next faltering step towards an elected administration was taken in the same year.

The reformers were not content with what they had done for

at the same time the old *landdrosts* and *heemraden* were swept away and replaced by English-style magistrates, strangers doing a job for pay and no more friends and neighbours. The nineteenth century had caught up with the seventeenth, but the brashness of its violent take-over came near to reducing it to the day of Charles I. The frontier had become more prosperous and softer over the years of peace but, while men argued furiously over slavery and magistrates, the simmering pot across the Keiskamma was boiling over again.

The Sixth Kaffir War broke out at a moment which gave the colonists their last chance of meeting the most serious invasion so far to take place as a united people. Macomo and the other chiefs were perfectly well aware of the dissensions between the white men, for Boers of the type of Du Buis were anything but extinct and had been carrying on a lively trade in old muskets and ammunition for some time past. Added to these were a good number of Hottentot deserters who had arrived fully armed and who were made more than welcome. Numerically the Kaffirs were stronger than they had ever been, the internecine battles of the last few years had given them valuable training in war and they had good reason to suppose that a Colony waxed fat and defenceless would be an easier prey than ever before.

Caesar Andrews, an English civilian and a fluent Dutch speaker, was living at the time in Port Elizabeth and, many years later, he wrote an account of what he had seen. 'At the close of the year 1834, the first intimation of hostilities on the part of the Kaffirs was an account of the murder by Kaffirs of Mr Mahony and his son-in-law, Mr Henderson, near what was known as the Clay Pits, where the Kaffirs were supplied with red clay, which may be termed their war paint. Two of Mr Henderson's children were in the wagon at the time of the murder, but were brought into Grahamstown by a Kaffir servant who witnessed the destruction of Mr Mahony and his master. After this event daily accounts of Kaffir aggression, burning of houses, murders and pillage continued to be received at Port Elizabeth'.

Something very much like panic set in at Grahamstown and was swiftly carried to the capital where Sir Lowry Cole had given place to another old Peninsular general, Sir Benjamin

D'Urban. Colonel Harry Smith, who was at once summoned by the Governor, describes the reports. 'The Kaffir tribes, which for many months had been greatly agitated and excited, at length burst into the Colony in what was for the moment an irresistible rush, carrying with them fire, sword, devastation and cold-blooded murder, and spoiling the fertile estates and farms like a mountain avalanche.'

D'Urban at once ordered his Chief-of-Staff to the frontier with plenary powers, civil and military, to take any action which he might deem necessary. Smith was a famous horseman and he declined the Governor's offer of a ship to take him to Algoa Bay, preferring to make the 600 mile journey overland. While the necessary relays of horses were being arranged for the journey he issued orders for the despatch of the 72nd Highlanders and some guns, half the regiment travelling by sea and the remainder following him in wagons. With only his Hottentot servant, Manie, Harry Smith rode out from Cape Town when the year 1835 was half an hour old, determined to get to Grahamstown without wasting a moment. Only the vaguest information had reached him but he knew that Henry Somerset was somewhere well forward and that the 75th Regiment (The Gordon Highlanders) was in the barracks at Grahamstown and ought to form an adequate defence for the village. After visiting his wife at their cottage in Rondebosch and snatching a couple of hours' sleep (during which Juana thoughtfully sewed his orders and warrants into the lining of his jacket) Smith rode his first stage of 90 miles 'the heat raging like a furnace'. He broke his journey twice only, first for a cup of tea at the post-house where they changed horses after the first 25 miles and again at Caledon forty miles further on where a thunderstorm of African dimensions drenched and deafened them. Next day they reached Swellendam in time for breakfast and galloped off on the next 70 mile stretch. The Buffeljagts river was in flood and forced a detour of 30 miles which they covered in 2 hours and 20 minutes, reaching the staging-post at 3 p.m. Next morning their target was the village of George, 100 miles away; Smith completed the journey to schedule but in some discomfort having unwisely accepted an invitation to stop and eat at a nameless place where a commando was mustering.

Worse was to follow, for when he got to George the authorities had laid on a civic welcome and banquet—'a ceremony I could readily have dispensed with'. He managed to excuse himself from these well-meant though ill-judged attentions and, from his bath, dictated letters to the Civil Commissioner. He and Manie were off before dawn with another 100 miles ahead of them, this time over the roadless mountains, and when about half the journey had been done they ran into a wagon train coming from the opposite direction and carrying with it the mail from Grahamstown. He opened the bag of letters from the Commandant (Henry Somerset) and the Civil Commissioner and was appalled by what he read. Somerset, for once, seemed to have lost his sense of proportion for after hair-raising tales of disaster and massacre he ended by advising the evacuation of the entire population of Grahamstown. 'I made comments on all these letters and resolved to reach Grahamstown in two days', Smith noted in his diary.

On his fifth night from Cape Town he slept at Uitenhage, almost exactly 500 miles from his point of departure. During the day's ride he had forded one river no less than 7 times because of its meandering course, knocked out a Boer who had refused to lend him a horse to replace his foundered one,* and made the impressive distance of 140 miles. Once again he was greeted by a civic banquet, the horror of which to an exhausted man was mitigated by the presence of Colonel Cuyler. He was now retired on half-pay and 'as deaf as a beetle' but Smith gratefully acknowledges the value of his wise and experienced counsel.

Early next morning the riders began the last lap to Grahamstown. Long before they reached it they encountered floods of refugees 'in the wildest state of alarm, herds, flocks, families etc, fleeing like the Israelites'. Smith had come across enough refugees in other places during his service to know that he need not take too seriously the highly coloured atrocity stories with which he was assailed. Ten miles from the village an escort of half-a-dozen Cape Mounted Rifles and 'a neat, clipping little hack of Colonel Somerset's' were awaiting them and Colonel Smith, C.B.,

* The Boer caught up with him later and apologized for failing to recognize him.

rode into Grahamstown at attention. '[I was] fresh enough to have fought a general action, after a ride of 600 miles in 6 days over mountains and execrable roads on Dutch horses living in the fields without a grain of corn. I performed each day's work at the rate of 14 miles an hour, and I had not the slightest scratch even on my skin'. As Smith was in his 48th year this was something of a feat.*

Andrews, who had found one bug-infected night in the barracks at Port Elizabeth enough to persuade him that his talents might be more usefully employed than as a private volunteer, had also set off for Grahamstown. 'A state of feverish unrest determined me to desert the following day, it being morally and physically impossible to encounter another night in the same locality. Accordingly next day I packed up a few changes of clothing, crossed the back of my beautiful little pony "Cupid", and armed with a double-barrelled flint gun and a good supply of ammunition bade good-bye to friends and rode to Uitenhage with an order in my pocket to get three horses there belonging to Lieut G, which I was requested to take to Grahamstown.

'Arrived at Uitenhage, I heard that Colonel Smith and his Hottentot servant had just arrived after three and a half days' journey on horseback from Cape Town *en route* for Grahamstown; and I learnt that the Colonel was staying at the residence of the Civil Commissioner (Mr Van der Riet), who I knew personally very well. My object being to proceed to Grahamstown and the seat of war, I asked the Civil Commissioner to introduce me to Colonel Smith, and was told he was taking a bath, but would soon make his appearance, which he shortly did. I was duly introduced, and observed that I understood the Colonel was on his way to Grahamstown, and that I should be happy to form one of his escort. Rather to my surprise, the Colonel said "Escort be damned. I have ridden from Cape Town with my man Manie, and I shall ride into Grahamstown with him tomorrow." Seeing that I looked somewhat blank at this reply to

* Sir John Fortescue, in a rare error, insists that he was ten years younger. If the parish register of Whittlesey is not to be relied on (his date of birth is given there as 28 June, 1787) he would have been Adjutant of a detachment of the 95th at Buenos Aires at the age of 9.

my well-meant offer, the Colonel smiled and said "Mr Andrews, although I do not want an escort I shall be glad of your company, but I start at four o'clock a.m., and if you wish to go with me you must be punctual as to time." '

Andrews was punctual. He describes the day as 'one of the hottest I have experienced in South Africa'. During the ride he found himself greatly taken by the Colonel who 'at the Sundays River Hotel, at that time kept by Mr Webber', appointed him his A.D.C. and Secretary.

Smith had a strongly developed sense of the ridiculous and the scene at Grahamstown made it difficult for him to keep a straight face. 'On reaching the barricaded streets, I had the greatest difficulty to ride in. I found Colonel Somerset parading the night duties. Consternation was depicted on every countenance I met, on some despair, every man carrying a gun, some pistols and swords too. It would have been ludicrous in any situation other than mine, but people desponding would not have been prepossessed in my favour by my laughing at them, so I refrained, although much disposed to do so. I just took a look at the mode adopted to defend Grahamstown. There were all sorts of works, barricades etc, some three deep, and such was the consternation, an alarm, in the dark especially, would have set one half of the people shooting the other. I at once observed that this defensive system would never restore the lost confidence, and I resolved after I had received reports and assumed the command, to proclaim martial law, and act on the initiative in every respect.' To the seasoned soldier it was plain that the only thing Grahamstown needed was a leader and the right man for that office was now present.

The Colonel's secretary, who had found himself quarters in a store kept by another of his numerous friends, puts it mildly enough. 'We found the streets in Church Square strongly barricaded and most of the women and children collected inside the church, and all the stores inside the barricade were full of people, many from the country, and there were fears (perhaps groundless) of an attack on the Town. A good deal of panic and want of order prevailed until the arrival of Colonel Smith was announced, when some measure of confidence was restored.'

Smith, after a meeting with Somerset and Captain Campbell,

the Civil Commissioner, was left in no doubt as to what needed to be done. 'Despondency did exist to a fearful extent, originating from the sight of the horrors perpetrated by the remorseless enemy, but any vigorous steps and arbitrary authority boldly exerted would still ensure a rallying-point for all. I said, "Very well, I clearly see my way. At as early an hour as possible tomorrow morning I shall declare martial law, and woe betide the man who is not as obedient as a soldier. Be so good as to prepare the necessary documents and copies to be printed for my signature. I will be with you soon after daylight in your office where I shall take up my abode." . . . I learnt the number of regular troops to be a little above 700, the civil force under arms 850, then occupying Grahamstown, Fort Beaufort, and the connecting post of Hermanus Kraal (the civil force being at the Kat River Settlement, a location of Hottentots, where Captain Armstrong with a troop of Cape Mounted Rifles acted in a civil and military capacity). Fort Willshere had been most shamefully abandoned. I received a report that a body of 200 Burghers of the Graaf Reinet district under their Civil Commissioner Ryneveld was approaching. I knew the front of the 72nd Regt in wagons would reach me in a day or two. I resolved, therefore, as soon as possible to make an inroad into the heart of the enemy's country in one direction, re-occupy Fort Willshere, and thence march to rescue the missionaries who were assembled in one house, 'Lonsdale', in Kaffirland, and whose safety could not be calculated on for one moment. I then directed the population of Grahamstown, so soon as martial law was proclaimed, to be formed into a Corps of Volunteers, and I would issue them with arms. The church in the square of Grahamstown being occupied as a military post and a council chamber, I desired the principal gentlemen to assemble, to name their own officers, etc, and to submit them for my approval, and told them that they and the organization of the corps should be instantly gazetted.'

The strong hand was not immediately appreciated by some of the self-selected civilian leaders and it was not long before Smith had a visit from Campbell, suggesting that he ought to attend himself at the inaugural meeting of the Grahamstown Volunteers if he wanted that incipient Corps ever to come into existence. This was a business for which Harry Smith was admirably suited;

like many small-statured men, he had a loud voice, enjoyed authority and had a strong streak of the actor in his composition. Let him tell for himself what happened. 'When I went in, there was a considerable assembly of very respectable looking men. I asked what was the cause of the delay in executing my demands? One gentleman, a leader in what was called the Committee of Safety, which I very soon complimentarily dissolved, stood up and began to enter into argument and discussion. I exclaimed in a voice of thunder, "I am not sent here to argue, but to command. You are now under martial law, and the first gentleman, I care not who he may be, who does not promptly and implicitly obey my command, he shall not even dare to give an opinion; I will try him by a court-martial and punish him in five minutes." '

The volunteers paraded in varying degrees of enthusiasm later in the day outside the church and their command was given to a regular officer, Captain Sparks of the 49th, who happened to be visiting his family in Grahamstown at the time. The military career of Caesar Andrews was nearly cut short in the mustering process. His friend the store-keeper kept a good stock of guns and old muskets; as Andrews was sitting on his bed above the store he heard a great clicking of locks going on, followed by an explosion and a bullet whizzed past within a foot of him before going through the slate roof. 'I followed a practice I had already acquired from my Chief and gave those below my blessing.'

Smith inspected his command; as he walked down the ranks one man touched his hat to the passing Chief-of-Staff. 'None of your damned politeness in the ranks' growled Smith. Andrews was sworn in by Colonel England of the 75th as Secretary to the burgher forces when they should arrive, for his ability to speak Dutch was not to be wasted and in any event Smith's usual A.D.C., Paddy Balfour of the 72nd, was on his way.

England, too, had started off on the wrong foot with Smith. Having left Fort Willshere (possibly a wise decision for reasons already seen) he had occupied himself with making a fortress of his barracks which would have withstood any attack. He had not, however, thought it necessary to detach a solitary section for the defence of the village. It is not clear whether he had done this under orders from Henry Somerset or whether England had displayed initiative. Smith did not approve and said so; he was never really appreciative of Somerset even when that officer's performances improved as greatly as they were to do in the future. Probably he made his military capacity permanently suspect by his actions at this time. The amateur fortifications were pulled down, proper alarm posts fixed and, as Smith says, 'the aspect of affairs had changed. Men moved like men, and felt that their safety consisted in energetic obedience'. Within a couple of days the Graaf Reinet commando, 200 strong, rode in and shortly afterwards the first wagons hove in sight bearing the advance guard of the 72nd, 'conspicuous in their splendid Highland uniform and black, ostrich-plumed bonnets' as Andrews enviously calls them. Grahamstown was not now open to attack.

That seems to be a convenient moment at which to consider affairs from the other point of view. Comparative prosperity had forced the Kaffirs for some years to give thought to what was once called 'lebensraum'. As their numbers increased, and with them their flocks and herds, so did their problems. The ante-diluvian methods of agriculture which they practised brought a law of diminishing returns, for land will not continue for ever to give bounteous crops if the heart is taken out of it and never replaced. Manuring was entirely a fortuitous business and the arable land was becoming exhausted. The cattle also demanded more and more grazing, different places being required for winter and summer. Before very long they were going to have to expand or starve and the decision had to be taken in which direction the expansion should be. On either side were people stronger than themselves and they knew that when the time came for them to fight they must inevitably lose. To fight Dingaan and to be exterminated by the only trained, professional army in black Africa would be a counsel of utter desperation; there would be no mercy found for the vanquished in that quarter. On the other hand, a war against the white people, while it hardly carried with it better hopes of a victory in the long run, was a more promising prospect. If the Kaffirs could score some swift initial successes, which was well within their power since the border was so slightly defended, they might be in a fairly strong bargaining position when the peace talks came. They knew that the Europeans were no more enthusiastic than themselves for a long campaign and would probably be willing to buy them off rather than face a protracted guerrilla war. The prize was the empty quarter between the rivers, a kind of Polish Corridor which could not exist for ever, and it was on the cards that the colonists might resign it to them as the lesser evil. To take Grahamstown would be a pointless proceeding; once it had been sacked it would be untenable and valueless. Worse still, it would act on the minds of the government as the burning of Washington had done on the Americans in the War of 1812. (The analogy probably did not strike them, but the sense of it certainly did.) A war that was short and not too bloody was the best prospect.

There was only one way in which the white men could be soundly defeated and that would be by persuading the Hottentots to change sides. The possibility was not too far-fetched, for many of these volatile people could probably be persuaded to defect by a judicious mixture of superstition and promises. Indeed many did, but the loyalty of the Cape Regiment and of the new levies shortly to be raised stood the strain. The fact that they remained true when they had nothing to gain beyond the usual soldiers' pay is a tribute to the quality of their British officers, for nothing would have been easier than to murder them and decamp across the river. It is at moments like this that the qualities of the officers and their capacity for making themselves respected and liked by their firmness and fairness alone stand between a civil population and massacre.

Unable to count on the Hottentots, the Kaffir chiefs found themselves rather in the position of trade union bosses demanding a pay rise; demand the impossible but be ready to settle for what you can get, or, in terms more suited to the occasion, overrun all the land you can, carrying off all the cattle you can, do as much damage as you can and then be ready to say, magnanimously, that you will accept the empty quarter and be satisfied. By the time Harry Smith reached Grahamstown they had made a promising start.

Smith's plans were those which his old master, the Duke, would have made in his place. Never show fear or irresolution in the face of a primitive enemy nor wait for him to attack you.

The base of Grahamstown being now secured, the next step must be to seek out the enemy wherever he may be found and harry the life out of him. This demands troops in large numbers and such did not then exist, even on paper.

He was fortunate in one respect. The only source of assegai-fodder was amongst the Hottentots but many of these were lounging about with their occupation gone since their masters, mainly the farmers of Bathurst and Albany, men to whom the traditional art of laagering up was unknown, had decamped into Grahamstown. 'I organized two corps of Hottentots, consisting of every loose vagabond I could lay my hands on, called the 1st and 2nd Battalion Hottentot Infantry. It is scarcely to be credited how rapidly these men trained as soldiers.' Indeed Smith thought so highly of his raw material that he asserted that 'no nation in the world, with the exception of the inhabitants of the South of France, have such a natural turn to become soldiers as the Hottentots'. He refers to the Basques, of whom he had seen much during the battles of the Nivelle and Nive; few people would have regarded the Provençals, of whom Smith had seen nothing, as a race marked out by martial ardour.

Andrews had something to do with the 'Q' side of the new force and his observations have a pleasing cynicism about them. 'The two battalions mustered about 2,000 men. A contract for clothing was called for. Kaffir truck was down in the market; brown Kaffir cloth was cheap, and a contract was taken to clothe the Totties in brown Kaffir cloth. It looked very well when new, but a march into the Fish River bush which soon followed made the bush brown and the Totties scarecrows. A fresh contract to clothe the naked being inevitable, a little foresight dictated to the previous contractor that something more substantial than Kaffir cloth would be required. All the obtainable moleskin was therefore purchased. When the second contract was called for, the first contractor got it, but with the understanding that he must abandon the military rank of Major in the Hottentot battalion which he held; of course, the military rank was readily parted with and the contract retained.'

Sir Benjamin D'Urban, pounding along in the wake of his Chief-of-Staff, arrived in Grahamstown. The first detachment of the 72nd was sent to re-occupy Fort Willshere; they found that the barrack buildings had been put to the torch, the thatched roofs had disappeared and the walls were cracked with the heat. Patiently they set to work to rebuild the place. Somerset was sent off with the commandos to clear communications with Algoa Bay, the maintenance of which was critical to the situation, for only by this route could men and supplies be brought in by sea, and a force of the new Hottentot levies, about 300, was scraped up to raid behind the Kaffir leading elements. Its commander was Major Cox, a brother rifleman of Harry Smith in Peninsular days who was now serving with the 75th, and whom the latter describes as 'the most useful and active officer under my command'.

His objective was the kraal of a chief who bore the memorable name of Eno. Eno was an old man, artful in war but not particularly aggressive, who had been chosen by the paramount chief, Hintza, to play the part of Uriah the Hittite. Hintza was a highly intelligent man. He had fought alongside Henry Somerset in 1828 and was under no illusion about the possibility that a day might come when he would be seeking help from Somerset again. Eno's clan happened to be the nearest to the border and it seemed politic to Hintza to put him into the forefront of the battle. If Eno's affairs prospered, Hintza could draw every advantage from them when the day arrived for a parley. If they did not, then a dead Eno could give no cause for embarrassment and a living one could be easily disavowed. Eno was on quite good terms with Somerset and they had already postponed the opening of the war by a month when some stolen cattle were traced to Eno's kraal and a young British officer wounded whilst retaking them. Tact and forbearance on the part of both men had damped down an explosive situation but by February Eno was no longer his own master. Hintza was calling the tune, invisible in the minstrel's gallery.

Cox, his little force accompanied by some mounted settlers and ninety burghers of Uitenhage, carried out his raid in the best style of Jeb Stuart. Before they realized what was happening, Eno's warriors were scattered and the smoke was rising from the roofs of his burning kraal. Eno himself was not in residence; a cordon of Cape Mounted Rifles and other riders had been laid to catch him on his return from a foray but he slipped between them and was no more to be seen. Eno was, indeed, expendable.

Nonetheless, the flood-tide was rising. Macomo's men had passed beyond the Kat River just below Fort Beaufort; further inland, Tyalie's people were flowing on and, nearest to the sea, the clans of Umhala, Botumane, Siyolo and the Gunukwebe and Galekas had crossed the Fish River by every possible ford or drift. From the ocean to Somerset East and from there nearly as far west at Uitenhage, no living white man remained except in hiding. Twenty-two farmers had been killed, though the Kaffirs had been most scrupulous about allowing women and children to go free and unharmed; four hundred and fifty-six houses had been burned to the ground and, so far as could be reckoned, about 115,000 cattle had been carried off, together with nearly 6,000 horses and 162,000 sheep and goats. All the hard work, the heart-breaks of the early years and the fruits of courage and hardihood by the 1820 Settlers had gone whistling down the west wind. The physical damage was estimated at about a third of a million pounds, but that was only a paper figure. It took no account of the time and difficulty that would be needed to make good the losses when the time came. Many of the older hands were bitter against the government. It would not have been necessary for the settlers to fly like chaff before a storm if there had existed machinery to mobilize them for war as in former days; the *landdrosts* and field-cornets would have had the men mustered and ready and the non-combatants sent to sanctuary long before this; but all their authority had been taken away and only the far-away Civil Commissioner was now permitted to give orders. Their grievance was not ill-founded. The farmers, Boer and Briton alike, were brave and hardy men and all of them could ride and shoot. As the almost comical events in Grahamstown had shown, all they lacked was leadership.

They were to lack it no longer. At least 15,000 Kaffir warriors were now in colonial territory but men who had fought at Vittoria and Waterloo were in the saddle on the European side of the border. Cox was sent off almost as soon as he returned to perform another cutting-out expedition. With a small body of mounted men he led a dash into Kaffirland and released the missionaries who, according to Harry Smith, were expecting to

3. Colonel Henry Somerset, son of Lord Charles Somerset.

4. Lieutenant-General Sir Harry Smith (1787–1860); from a picture painted in Paris after Waterloo.

5. The meeting of Sandili and Colonel John Hare at Block Drift,
30 January, 1846.

6. The Battle of the Gwanga, 8 June, 1846.

have their throats cut at any moment. They were probably in no real danger; Hintza was perfectly capable of distinguishing his friends from his enemies and knew quite well that the Rev. John Philip was numbered amongst the former. This man of God had a voice that rivalled that of Harry Smith and it was raised loudly on the side of the Kaffirs from the security of Cape Town. When the *Commercial Advertiser* arrived from the capital containing an apologia for the Kaffirs it took all Somerset's efforts to avoid a riot. Whatever emotions the released missionaries may have manifested, gratitude was not one of them. For the rest of the war and, indeed, for long after, they never flagged in their efforts to vilify their liberators.

By mid-February D'Urban and Smith were ready. Mr (ex-Major) George Wood had clothed the two Hottentot battalions in their moleskins, drawing from the missionaries the charge that he had personally prolonged the war, with the aid of a few friends, in the expectation of handsome profits. Lieut-Colonel John Peddie, who had lost an arm at Salamanca, was at the head of his Highlanders and thirsting for a fight. Cox's timely beating-up of Eno's kraal had decided the wavering Hottentots of the Kat River settlement that their interests would be best served by an European victory. They repaired to Fort Adelaide, a more resounding name than the nearest post really deserved, and put themselves at the commandant's disposal. That sensible man, Captain Armstrong, accepted their services on the condition that their pastor, the Rev. Mr Read, was not permitted to come near them again until the war was over.

The first thrust was made by Somerset with several companies from the 72nd and 75th as a hard core and with a troop of the C.M.R. and all the burgher forces from Uitenhage, George and Graaf Reinet. With these experienced practitioners there rode for the first time the Englishmen of the Albany Sharpshooters, and the Port Elizabeth Yeomanry. Both the new Hottentot battalions marched with them.

Somerset, with the commandos, cleared the difficult country of the Zuurberg and Oliphant's Nek without much trouble and the clans of Eno, Siyolo and Botumane fell back across the Fish River determined to fight the quarrel out in the kloofs. Smith divided his army into three divisions, Somerset with the burghers

F

and local English levies taking post nearest to the sea with the Chief of Staff himself commanding the centre division and Colonel England being the furthest north.

On 11 February, Smith crossed the river at Trompetter's Drift while more or less simultaneously England went over Committee Drift and Somerset made his passage by Kaffir's Drift only a few miles from the sea. The work of clearing out the dark and sinister kloofs was harder than it had been in 1819 but the weather was far better. Andrews was thoroughly enjoying it. 'Could not help thinking if this is campaigning it is very jolly, but who shall say how long this state of things shall last?', he confided to his diary. The troops had worked out a battle drill for kloof-clearing of a kind that their descendants were to know in Burma more than a century later. The kloofs were, so far as as was possible, ringed by a screen of riflemen except in one place where an exit offered itself. The musketry from the men perched above and firing down drove the occupants out into a killing-ground where the heavy, leaden balls tore into them. This done, the troops reformed and worked their way down the length of the ravine to flush out any who might have escaped. They then moved on to the next one where the process was repeated and so, as it seemed to weary men, *ad infinitum*.

Though the drill worked, it was by no means the bloodless and, to the Kaffirs, disheartening business it had been on the previous occasion. Against 73 Kaffirs killed, Smith lost 4 Highlanders, a soldier of the 75th, a Tottie and 7 burghers together with another dozen wounded. The Kaffirs fled back to the Keiskamma, abandoning some 4,000 cattle and the usual proportion of sheep and goats, but they were anything but beaten. Tyalie attacked the Kat River settlement at Fort Adelaide, but the blue-cranes' feathers were not used to best advantage by being thrown against concealed riflemen. Under the brave leadership of Field Cornet Groepe, a veteran of more than one of the earlier wars, the Hottentots, together with a sprinkling of Griquas who made up Mr Read's congregation, threw them back with quite heavy losses.

To balance this, a raid on the post at Trompetter's Drift, where a party of settlers was building a raft for the use of Smith's commissariat, caught the little garrison completely by surprise. The post was promptly abandoned with the loss of 4 Englishmen and 4 Hottentots. Commandant Rademeyer, with the men of George and Uitenhage, came to the rescue but 40 of them, including Rademeyer, were surrounded in one of the thickest of many thick woods. They fought their way out with *herneuker* and butt, though 5 were killed and another 8 wounded. Rademeyer realized that a substantial number of Kaffirs must have trickled back into the deserted kloofs and the whole scouring operation had to be gone through again. It cost the lives of another four burghers and caused hurt to five more. The Kaffirs, pretty well unscathed, made for the even more forbidding kloofs of the Amatola mountains, from which they would take a lot of dislodging. Neither side had gained any real advantage over the other.

D'Urban decided to have one last try at coming to terms with Hintza. On his orders, Commandant van Wyk went twice under a flag of truce to talk. Hintza was giving nothing away. It was useless for the Governor to address him as paramount chief of the Xosa and to claim that he was, or ought to be, answerable for all the things done in the course of the invasion by his lesser chiefs. Hintza had the complete answer to this and one cannot deny that, from the legalistic point of view which the Kaffirs loved, he had the right to it. It was perfectly correct to describe him as paramount chief of the Xosa. He knew the title to be rightfully his and so did all his people. Nevertheless, it did not lie in the mouth of a government which had publicly acknowledged his supplanter Gaika to be the incumbent of that office to shift its ground when it suited it and to round on the inoffensive Hintza. There was no evidence that he had waged war against the colony, nor was he found in a place where he had no business to be. Van Wyk had to concede that there was no case against Hintza and so the war must go on.

Smith, on the Governor's orders, prepared his force for a full-dress invasion of Kaffirland. His command was much the same as before, six field guns with 25 gunners, 371 officers and men of the 72nd, 358 C.M.R., about 1,500 mounted burghers, 62 English volunteers, 40 of the corps of guides (mostly settlers) and 760 Hottentot infantry, a total of just over 2,000 mounted men and just under 1,000 on foot. D'Urban, in personal command with Smith as 2 i/c, divided it into four approximately equal columns under Peddie, Somerset, Cox and Van Wyk. Colonel England with the 75th, 461 strong, about 1,000 burghers and half a battalion of Hottentots was left to guard the length of the Fish River.

The planning of operations fell entirely on Colonel Smith, for D'Urban, in spite of his excellent qualities, had never been a field commander. In the Peninsula he had been Quartermaster-General of the Portuguese army under Beresford and, although he had laid manfully about him at Salamanca at the head of that country's only brigade of cavalry, his duties had mainly been in the field of training and supply. He had no false pride and very willingly allowed the more experienced man to have his head. Smith began by clearing his feet. He personally led a force of mounted burghers, mainly the men of Swellendam, from his camp at Trompetter's Drift north westwards by way of Fort Brown into the Umdizini bush and the mission station of Lovedale. His striking force comprised the 72nd, whose ostrich plumes must by now have begun to droop a little, and the 2nd Hottentot battalion. Lovedale had been burnt to the ground and only a few Kaffirs were encountered but the many little smoke pillars rising from the peaks of the Amatolas proclaimed that the strongholds were occupied.

Andrews, irrepressible as ever, had some comments on the burgher cavalry. 'They looked well in line, but though the men were willing enough to ride by threes their horses did not understand it. I had, on behalf of the Colonel, to do a little swearing in Dutch. One of the burghers, willing enough to obey the Colonel's orders, after many fruitless efforts addressed his neighbour, saying "Neef Jacob, slaat toch mijn paard als het u belief, de Colonel is te danig kwaai", which means in English "Cousin Jacob, whip my horse if you please, the Colonel is very angry". The best spirit, however, prevails among the Dutch Burghers, and all learnt before the war was over to like the Colonel, who did his best to look after their comfort in the field'.

In clear weather Smith's men patrolled far afield for a week. Andrews' diary for 1 April gives a glimpse of what it was like. 'Marched through a beautiful country and came to a hill affording a fine view of T'Slambe's Kop, Gaika's Kop, and the wooded kloofs of the Amatola Mountains; observed the smoke of Kaffir fires under T'Slambie's Kop; encamped for the night on the Debe Flats, near beautiful water; had a delightful bathe, but while enjoying it, it was reported that a large body of Kaffirs was approaching; dressed rather hastily, and found it was a false alarm, and that it was Colonel Somerset's second division, which encamped two miles distant from ours. The night passed quietly.' The following day Major Cox made another raid, this time taking the light company of the 72nd and the Hottentots from Kat River (now known officially as the Kat River Legion) into the foothills of the Amatolas where they killed a few Kaffirs and recaptured 800 cattle and many horses and goats.

There were casualties of a kind inevitable amongst troops experiencing for the first time the frightening conditions of the African bush, where everything seems hostile. On one night, a Highlander let off his musket by accident; before the officers could get their sub-units in hand they had opened a brisk fire on each other under the impression that the Kaffirs were upon them and 4 men were killed before order was restored. One should not be too swift to condemn them for only a day or two before Sergeant Burt had 'unaccountably fallen a few paces in rear of his company and was immediately overpowered'. In their own element the enemy were not to be despised.

On 3 April the army left the Debe Flats. The 3rd division marched north to Keiskammahoek without opposition; the 1st moved eastwards to the left bank of the Buffalo river while the 2nd encamped about three miles lower down the same water. The 4th was about 25 miles away to the north-west where it had been engaged in cleaning out Gaika's old home in the Tyumie Valley. On 7 April came the first serious engagement. Captain Murray of the 72nd was sent with 100 Hottentots into the mountains to catch any Kaffirs who might be withdrawing in the face of the advances of the 3rd and 4th divisions. They marched off during the hours of darkness and at first light found themselves facing a high and rugged cliff held by some 600 of the best Kaffir warriors under the chief Tyalie. The position appeared impregnable and Tyalie certainly considered it to be such. Harry Smith described it as 'a sort of castle of rocks, steep and scarped by nature'. Murray went straight for it, bravely followed by his

Hottentots and, as they scaled it hand over hand showers of assegais and great boulders descended on them. An assegai carried away Murray's cap, another took him in the side and four of his Hottentots fell. The first frontal attack failed but Murray's Highland blood was up and he was not to be deterred from taking his objective.

Smith was watching the battle through a glass and his quick eye saw that a means existed of turning the position. When Murray received his message, he attacked again, coming in on the flank of the Kaffirs, and he drove them before him, taking in the process another 4,000 of the ubiquitous cattle. Only then would be allow his wounds to be dressed. Smith calls it 'the prettiest affair by far of any during the war, and the most like a fight'. Andrews adds his comments on the cattle and other things. 'No one who has not heard it can conceive the bellowing of such an excited herd. The rebel Hottentot, Stoffel Arnoldus, was captured in the castle by some of Major Bagot's battalion, the stock of his gun, carrying half-pound balls, had been smashed by a shot . . . forty of the enemy were killed and many wounded.' For years afterwards the place was known as Murray's Kranz. The only fatal casualty was a sergeant of the Hottentot battalion who was shot by a deserter from his own corps. To add to the embarrassment caused by the cattle, many Kaffir women came into the camp and gave themselves up. Smith is guilty of no over-statement when he says that 'the care of these cattle and the sending them to the rear were a very laborious and arduous duty'. The women were fed and sent away. The evacuation of wounded through possibly hostile country was also an arduous duty; Richard Southey, an 1820 Settler who was captain of Smith's corps of guides, tells that on one occasion when a burgher had his leg pinned to the saddle by an assegai it took a wagon, a span of oxen and 20 men as escort to get him to safety. Some of the intelligence that came in was not to be trusted too far. In a letter to Somerset dated 15 March, D'Urban wrote that 'The report of Kaffirs between Hermanus Kraal and Bothas Hill was altogether groundless, the fumes of a drunken fit of Mr Piet Lowe'.

On 8 April the army moved again, this time to comb out the mountains where the Keiskamma, the Buffalo and the Kabousie

Rivers all have their sources. This very steep and rugged country, then known as the Poorts of the Buffalo, leads into the more open land which undulates to the banks of the Kei and beyond that lay Hintza's territory. This was *terra incognita* to all save a few of Southey's guides, some of whom (including his brother George) had been traders in Kaffirland. These were the fortunate ones, for the Xosa, whilst sparing the missionaries, had made a point of murdering every trader who had not been able to make his escape in time. No enemy were encountered and the army continued its march in four columns to concentrate at the old mission station of Butterworth. Emissaries were sent to Hintza, giving out that the troops were there to recover stolen cattle and inviting him to come in and talk. After 'constantly receiving shuffling messages from Hintza' for some days, and an accretion of strength from many Fingoes who had thrown themselves on Smith's protection, Hintza's ambassador came into the camp. 'His Prime Minister, Kuba, is a sharp, wolf-like looking fellow with the cunning of Satan. I would back him at eating beef-stakes against any devil.' Kuba argued as persuasively as a Kaffir is able, but it was soon quite clear that any question of restoring stolen cattle or any other form of reparation was not in his brief. D'Urban heard him out and then declared war in regular form.

Smith was given permission by the Governor to set off with 300 mounted men to try and capture the paramount chief. This was the sort of task he loved for it gave an opportunity of burning up some of his fearsome energy and appealed to the strong romantic streak in his nature. Led by some Fingo guides, who were equally delighted by the prospect of avenging themselves on their oppressors (the customary address from a Xosa to a Fingo was 'Dog'), he rode swiftly to the kraal of Hintza's great wife, Nomsa, in the Tsomo mountains. The 72nd and one of the Hottentot battalions followed at a foot-pace. 'I reached it', says Smith, 'just before dark and had a smart brush with the enemy and took a lot of cattle. The next morning at daylight I pushed forward to the bed of the Upper Kei where information led me to believe a considerable quantity of colonial cattle were secreted. I had a tremendous march this day and the heat on the banks of the river was excessive. At dark this night I had captured

THE KAFFIR WARS

14,000 head of cattle, mostly colonial. I ascertained some months afterwards that these were Macomo's booty. The next day I joined the headquarters column to get rid of my cattle and to get some fresh troops. At daylight on the following day I crossed the rocky bed of the Tsomo, very deep and rapid, and made a most precipitate march on Hintza's kraal. He was not there but many of his followers were; his cattle were all driven off. I immediately burnt his kraal—in Kaffirland regarded as the possession of his territory—the only kraal I burnt in his country.'

Hintza thought very little of this; his plans had been based on the well-known habits of the white men which should have meant merely that they would repulse attacks so far as they were able but do nothing more drastic than that. Invasion of his own dominions with intentions at which he could only guess had never been considered a serious possibility. If war paid no dividends, then diplomacy must do what it could to retrieve the situation and abate the indignity. 'He therefore rode into our camp in an undaunted manner.' Kuba did not accompany him. He was more usefully employed in driving the remainder of the stolen cattle to places that ought to be beyond the Governor's reach. Sir Benjamin read out the indictment, to every count of which Hintza blandly pleaded guilty. When the demand for the return of the cattle was made, however, he announced that he must have time to consider this high matter.

Not every effort to impress the Xosa with the irresistible power of Britain was a success. The story belongs to Andrews. 'A high medical officer conceived the idea of astonishing the natives. Lucifer matches were in those days a new idea, drawn through a piece of sandpaper to ignite them. Seeing a few Kaffirs in the neighbourhood, he motioned them to approach, which they did. Taking out a box of lucifers from his pocket he said "Kom hier zo", and sitting on the grass placed the open match-box between his legs, when on the part of the Kaffirs all was attention. The medico pulled the match through the sandpaper, it exploded, but unfortunately a spark fell into the matchbox which also exploded, singeing the whiskers and eyebrows and half suffocating the exploder, who looking up saw an expression of wonder and surprise in the faces of those he had intended to astonish, and he heard something that sounded like "maa wough".'

That night Hintza and his son Kreili dined with the Chief-of-Staff. 'He showed (much to the disgust of our A.D.C.) a particular partiality for the potatoes out of an Irish stew and for coffee'. Present at the table was 'Mr Shepstone, a very clever youth of 19, the son of a missionary. He had been born among the Kaffirs and the language was as familiar to him as that of his father.' Hintza argued his case with skill. He had accepted the responsibility because it would have been unbecoming in a paramount chief to do otherwise. Nevertheless, the real trouble lay in the fact that many of his subordinate chiefs were contumacious. Tomorrow he would agree to all the Governor's demands. 'He then left me having eaten enough for seven men. I walked with him to his people where the protruding omentum [caul] of the slaughtered bullock was prepared for him. Curiosity induced me to remain. He ate every bit of this fat fried lightly; there could not have been less than four pounds'. Admiringly, Smith bade his guest 'Good night'. He always had a softer spot for Hintza than the ruffian monarch deserved. His appearance may have had something to do with it, for in a letter to his wife Smith calls him 'a very good looking fellow, and his face, although black, the very image of poor dear George IV'. Even when Hintza sent one of his men to gain audience with Smith and to knife him during the course of it Smith forgave him. Hintza, when told how his plan had miscarried, made no bones about it but laughed uproariously.

Next morning a durbar was held and Hintza went through a solemn charade of consenting to the Governor's demand for the return of the stolen cattle and despatched messengers in all directions. Sir Benjamin, well satisfied, declared peace. The message to Hintza's underlings contained no mention of cattle; they were only orders to massacre every Fingo as a warning against treachery to him. Richard Southey, who understood Hintza better than any other European, took the unmilitary step of getting all his corps of guides to put their names to a round robin addressed to the Governor deprecating the weakness he appeared to be showing and giving a truer picture of the paramount chief's character than the one which he had himself impressed on Sir Benjamin. It was a waste of paper.

As the April days moved on, Hintza regaled his hosts with

tales of his prowess with his 15 wives, but no cattle came in nor news of any on the move. Instead, there arrived disquieting reports of the slaughter of the wretched Fingoes. Sir Benjamin D'Urban, enraged out his usual placidity, sent for Hintza and told him firmly that if any more were killed he would hang two Kaffirs for every Fingo. He named the first two candidates as Hintza and Kreili. Hintza adopted the attitude that it was a great deal of fuss about nothing but word went out that the killings must stop. It became clear that Hintza had no intention of keeping his bargain and that the longer matters were allowed to drag on the less would be the chances of any cattle ever being restored to their owners.

Harry Smith, never the most patient of men, suggested going across the Kei with the chief to ascertain the reason. Hintza asserted that for him to be taken amongst his own people in the guise of a prisoner would be an insult of massive proportions. He proposed instead that he should be permitted to return alone but not surprisingly this arrangement found no support. In the end it was arranged that he should travel with Smith as a guest and that his brother Boku and his son Kreili should remain as hostages. They set off on 9 May with a strong escort comprising 50 C.M.R., 2 companies of the 72nd under Murray, who had recovered from his wound, 3 companies of Hottentots and 15 of Southey's guides under his brother George. Hintza demanded that his position be clearly explained and Shepstone interpreted. 'You have lived with me now for 9 days; you call yourself my son and say you are sensible of my kindness. Now I am responsible to my King and to my Governor for your safe custody. Clearly understand that you have requested that the troops under my command should accompany you to enable you to fulfil the treaty of peace you have entered into. You have voluntarily placed yourself in our hands as a hostage; you are, however, to look upon me as having full power over you, and if you attempt to escape you will assuredly be shot. I consider my nation at peace with yours and I shall not molest your subjects provided they are peaceable. When they bring the cattle according to your command, I shall select the bullocks and return the cows and calves to them.' It could hardly have been more plainly spelt out. Hintza replied that no intention of escaping was in his mind. 'Very well, Hintza; act up to this and I am your friend. Again I tell you, if you attempt to escape, you will be shot.'

Soon after the party had marched out odd things began to happen. First, a couple of Kaffirs driving a few cattle approached; Hintza, without a word to Smith, sent one of his men to them and then explained that it was only with a message for them to come in. Instead of that, the whole party, messenger and all, rode swiftly off. Southey was worried by this and said so. Hintza only commented that they were going in the right direction. Next afternoon, they crossed the Gwanga and bivouacked, Smith keeping 'a very Light Division watch' on the hostages. In the morning he demanded to be told exactly where they were going. Hintza gave a glib reply but was obviously excited about something. At the usual halt for breakfast he became peevish, saying to Smith, 'What have the cattle done that you want them, or why should my subjects be deprived of them?'. Smith gave him a short answer. After marching for another hour, Hintza suddenly became facetious. 'See how my subjects treat me; they drive the cattle away in spite of me'. He asked leave to send his councillor Umtini on ahead to announce his imminent arrival and to this Smith agreed. As they neared the river Xabecca, the spoor which they had been following bifurcated. Hintza, now hilarious about something, said that they must follow the fork to the right, up a very steep and heavily wooded bank. Smith had noticed that for some while Hintza had been manifesting an unusual solicitude for his horse, walking him up every hill in order to spare him. Half way up the river bank, Hintza and his followers suddenly swept past Smith on either side of him. He shouted to the chief to stop; as Hintza had chanced to become entangled in the bush, he did as he was bid with a disarming smile. Smith returned his half-drawn pistol to its holster, feeling ashamed of his suspicions. At the top of the bank, a tongue of land a couple of miles long ran to a bend in the river where a Kaffir village stood. As Smith waited for the sweating troops to make their way up, Hintza was off at full speed. Southey and another guide named Shaw called out and in a split second Smith was in pursuit. Hintza had a good furlong start but the distance gradually closed, for Smith was a superb horseman and well

171

mounted. At about 40 paces distance, Smith pressed the trigger of his pistol. It misfired. He drew the other and tried for a second shot. That misfired also. Having no sword, he struck at Hintza with the butt of the pistol while the chief stabbed fiercely at him with the assegai which he always carried. By consummate horsemanship, Smith managed to get himself on to the right-hand side of the fugitive, so close that the assegai could do no harm, and grabbed him by the collar of his leopard-skin kaross. He wrenched Hintza from his horse, but in the process his own had got out of control and was bolting towards the village to which Hintza had been trying to lure him. Luckily for Smith, all the Kaffirs had gone down to the river and the village was empty, but while he was mastering his horse Hintza leapt to his feet and ran fast towards the river. Southey, in response to Smith's yelled order, fired a snap shot at Hintza and hit him in the leg. Still he picked himself up and vanished down the river bank. Southey, joined by Balfour, pursued him. As Southey was looking around him in the thick bush, an assegai clattered down from a stone beside him. With the speed of a veteran, he whipped round and saw a Kaffir almost near enough to be touched, with his assegai drawn back for a stab. Southey fired and his bullet took Hintza between the eyes. Smith had the body taken with decent respect to be placed in the village.

Such was the manner in which Hintza, paramount chief of the Xosa, died. It is extraordinary how the legend has persisted that he was in some fashion murdered. Nobody need be surprised that Exeter Hall took it up and branded Smith as an assassin, but in the last few years and with at least half a dozen accurate and reliable accounts to choose from, it still crops up. Even Mr Donald Morris in his admirable book *The Washing of the Spears* asserts that Hintza was 'shot under a flag of truce'. The truth was not like that.

Smith was now in a position of great difficulty. With a small force in an unknown country, far from his base and surrounded by thousands of maddened savages, the prospect was not cheerful. He despatched Hintza's remaining henchmen back to their people in the hope that they would give a true account of their chief's end but without much confidence that they would do so. He knew the Bashee river to be choked with stolen cattle and he was not going to return without them if it could be helped. After a march of 14 hours they came upon the Bashee and there indeed the cattle were waiting, about 3,000 of them. His force crossed the river just before darkness fell and they bivouacked on the far bank without much expectation of a peaceful night. The men had been on the march for 3 days since leaving the Kei and had made good some 84 miles. As the moon rose, he set off with the least exhausted men in chase of more cattle which he had noticed at dusk to be moving towards the Umtata. Captain Ross of the C.M.R. was left in command of the camp with the cattle, the 'jaded horses, weakly men and as large a guard as I could afford', with the heartening information that he was certain to be attacked. Ross was another Peninsular veteran and Smith was not unduly worried.

He himself set off with no guide through country of which he had a very defective map. His vigorous action went un-rewarded, for the Kaffirs' first thought had been to drive the cattle well away and all he had to show for the night's exertion was one prisoner. On his return to the bivouac he was greeted with long faces. Major White, a settler who held rank in the Grahamstown Volunteers, had gone out with a small escort to do some mapping. Smith had extracted firm undertakings from him that he would not stray far from the bivouac and that he would keep a very sharp look-out. Apparently White had allowed his enthusiasm for sketching to out-run his prudence, for Ross heard a shot and when he reached the place from which it had come all that he found were the corpses of White and his 7 men. They had been stripped of everything and not a Kaffir was to be seen. It was a salutary reminder that the enemy could not be treated with contempt.

Smith was now worried about the safety of a body of 60 men under Captain Baillie which he had detached during his night march to carry out a separate cattle-raid. At about midnight they came in, having been on the march since three o'clock that morning. Baillie's men snatched their first meal that day and all save the sentries got such sleep as they could with Kaffirs beyond number drumming and screaming all around them. The Hottentots were uneasy for they could understand the cries coming from the bush which forecast the fate which awaited them if things were to go wrong. Smith assembled as many as he could and impressed upon them that safety depended upon silence, obedience and never firing a shot without orders. An elderly man spoke for them all; 'We will do all our father desires, if he will stay near us, and not go galloping about to get his throat cut; for if we lose him, we are all lost.' Hottentots were sound judges of character.

Smith posted parties in the river above and below the ford to cover the crossing of the cattle. Expert stockmen such as the Kaffirs were might easily have started a stampede and that would have been the end of Harry Smith's expedition. The Hottentots, no less skilful, saved the situation by driving the bellowing beasts safely over in a way that no European troops could have done. Many attacks were made during the crossing, including some clever feints to distract attention, but the carbines and muskets of Highlanders and Hottentots kept their assailants at a respectful distance. Once the open country had been reached, the column's troubles were over though, as Smith puts it 'with the thousands of brawny savages all round us, screeching their war-cry, calling to their cattle and indicating by gesticulations the pleasure they would have in cutting our throats, the scene was animating to a degree'.

They re-crossed the Kei and joined up again with D'Urban on 17 May, having 'completed a march of 218 miles in seven and a half days over a rugged and mountainous country, intersected by deep rivers at the bottom of precipitous ravines and rivulets difficult to cross, having had to search for hours without any road at all, bringing with me 3,000 captured cattle and 1,000 Fingoes who had flocked to me with their families for protection, and added considerably to my difficulties.' The Governor, knowing more about politicians than did his Chief-of-Staff, was much disturbed to learn of the end of Hintza. A subsequent Court of Enquiry completely exonerated both Southey and Smith but was only petrol on the flames to the zealots of Exeter Hall.

D'Urban had never been taken in by Hintza. In a letter to Colonel England dated 14 May he wrote of the chief being 'a cunning old savage as slippery as an eel and as wily as a fox', which was not an inaccurate description. His unease at the shooting is shown, however, by a letter which he sent to John Bell, carrying on the Government at Cape Town during Sir Benjamin's absence; 'The death of Hintza . . . I am sorry for, inasmuch as it may serve as a handle of mischief to a certain party at home. It was, however, nobody's fault but his own. He was a most irreclaimable and treacherous villain.' D'Urban had had much to do with the corrupt Regency in Portugal and had no high opinion of politicians afterwards. The uproar which followed did nothing to alter his view. Bell told him that already there had been an outcry in Cape Town where the word 'murder' was being freely bandied about. The Rev. Dr Philip, to whom the death of a Kaffir in almost any circumstance merited that name, raised his voice loudly and wrote prolix accounts of the matter to his friends in London. The fact that he knew nothing whatever about the manner in which Hintza came to his death inhibited him not at all. He had been shot by Southey and that was all he needed to know. The newspapers with which he had influence took their cue from the missionary and soon Harry Smith was publicly held up to execration as a bloody-handed butcher who loved his work.

Sir Benjamin broke the news to Kreili and Boku, both of whom remained unmoved. It was right and wise to acknowledge Kreili as the paramount chief for his title was beyond question. NSutu, the widow of Gaika, had been doing what she could for the government in the Tyumie valley where the lives of several traders had been spared on her insistence. It may have been done entirely out of goodness of heart, but NSutu was plainly anxious that her son Sandili, a boy who was handicapped by lameness, should step into his father's sandals. As time went on Sandili proved himself to be a relentless enemy of the government and it is highly probable that the earlier mistake in promoting Gaika to an office that was not his provoked his hatred of the English.

On 24 May, the Governor entered into an agreement with Kreili which was duly recorded in writing and translated to the new chief by Shepstone. His uncle Boku and a councillor by the exotic name of Kinki were also present. The treaty was simply an announcement that the government had chosen to exercise rights of conquest and Kreili was in no position to argue. It is safe to assume that he preferred the Rev. Philip's

175

version of his father's death to that given by Harry Smith but Kreili could do no other than bide his time. He was a patient young man and had another fifty years left to him for revenge.

Though the campaign in the east was to all intents and purposes over, the clans of Macomo and Tyalie in the Amatolas were not completely subdued. D'Urban had written to Smith on 27 April that 'Cox and Van Wyk have given the people who remained in these hills a very decent stirring-up, sending into the Colony some 5,000 head of cattle' but they were not privy to the treaty, if such it can be called, with Kreili.

Sir Benjamin determined to act upon his own initiative and to remove the emptiness which had so invited trouble. On 24 May, he issued from his camp on the Kei a Proclamation. It began with the bald assertion that 'The King of England's Colonial Dominions now extend to the line running along the right bank of the River Kye . . . which boundary is hereby acknowledged by Kreili'. It was annexation of the simplest kind but the reason for it was by no means discreditable. Sir Benjamin was determined to see a frontier which could both be defended and administered without too much effort and expense. For a long time past he had been urging upon the Government at home the absurdity of one man in Cape Town attempting to control so large an area with such primitive communications. He had advised the appointment of a Lieutenant-Governor with his seat at Uitenhage but the proposal, while approved in principle, had been firmly turned down for the customary reason that it would cost a little money. This time Sir Benjamin was going to act first and then report what he had done. He proclaimed the existence of a new Province between the old frontier and the Kei which he named the Province of Adelaide and ordered the building of a capital on the left bank of the Buffalo River which would be called King William's Town. Its administration was to be the charge of his Chief-of-Staff; 'Colonel Smith, C.B., is appointed to the command of the District of the Province of Queen Adelaide and all the troops therein until His Majesty's pleasure be known'.

With the energy which everybody expected of him, Harry Smith addressed himself to his new task. 'My first object was to provide for the security of the various posts established by His

Excellency; to facilitate communications by improving roads, fords etc; then to endeavour to compel the Kaffirs in conformity with my instructions to withdraw beyond the Kei and sue for peace. I endeavoured by every means in my power to assure them that peace was within their reach and that, if hostilities were continued it would be due to them alone.' There was no easing of the 'stirring-up' of the unreconciled for patrols were still sent out in all directions. This was quite deliberate, for, as Smith wrote to D'Urban on 3 June, 'I cannot conclude the detail of these operations without observing to Your Excellency that such is the terror of the enemy at the sight of a British soldier that he flies with the utmost rapidity. If, because small patrols are kept constantly moving through his holds and fastnesses in every direction, his cattle captured and his corn destroyed, he must abandon the country which his treachery and defeat have cost him.' Pato, whose people lived between King William's Town and the sea, was the first to come in, putting 1,000 of his best warriors at Smith's disposal.

One patrol, however, was not so successful. Two officers of the Hottentot battalion, Lieutenants Baillie and Biddulph, were sent with 60 men to comb out a section of the Amatolas near the abandoned mission station of Pirie. Smith himself accompanied it for a short distance and ordered Baillie (whose father was the officer who had commanded the detachment on the return from the Bashee) that on no account must he allow the party to be split up. For some reason which will never now be known, Baillie disobeyed his orders and divided the patrol into two parts, giving Biddulph a rendezvous at which to join him. Baillie and his men were never again seen alive. Biddulph waited as long as he dared at the appointed place but, having no idea of where Baillie had gone, he eventually returned to camp alone. No sound of firing had been heard and Biddulph took it that Baillie had changed his mind once more and was making his way home independently. Some weeks later, when the war was over, the bodies of Charles Baillie and all his men were found in a kloof which they had entered in search of cattle. The evidence showed plainly that they had fought hard for their lives and that, when their ammunition was exhausted, they had disputed it with butt and bayonet until the last man fell fighting. Andrews, writing of it in 1877, says that the spot was then still known by the name of Baillie's Grave but. like Murray's Kranz, it has now disappeared from the map. Harry Smith was struck by the fact that the bush had completely swallowed up all the firing and noise of battle for, although the place was not far distant, nobody heard anything at all of the worst calamity of the war.

Cox and Van Wyk were given every man Smith could spare in order to make one last push into the Amatolas; this time it was enough and Macomo sent in his emissaries to treat for peace. Cox rather unwisely sent back the extra troops and Macomo had second thoughts. Smith, who had expected something of this sort to happen, summoned Macomo to attend upon him at the newly-created Fort Cox, just by the former mission station of Burnshill at the foot of the mountains. Macomo was truculent until Smith showed him that the troops had been disposed in a manner to make any retreat by him impossible. This was followed by a threat to 'sweep him and all his host off the face of the earth', whereupon Macomo suddenly became a very humble man. He explained, probably with truth, that his men had been decimated, his corn-pits were empty and his women had left him because they were starving. Smith reminded them that their father Gaika had conjured them never to make war on the British and 'in their own mode of incantation, invited Gaika to our council'. Smith treated the chiefs as he had done the Grahamstown Committee of Safety, 'not allowing them to have an opinion, much less to give one'. He weighed into them for some time, ending with a threat of utter destruction if they did not instantly surrender. This they did. Smith then admitted them to the Fort and feasted them, assuring them that so long as they behaved themselves they would find him a friend.

A durbar extending over six days was held at Fort Willshere attended by the Governor and all the chiefs who were still in arms, including one surprisingly called Yo Yo. Both sides exchanged protestations of future good-will and a formal treaty was concluded. Kreili was sent home to his mother Nomsa; Macomo and Tyalie went back to their disarmed people. The settlers returned to their farms and began laboriously to clear the wild mimosa from the fields, to re-build their houses and to re-stock their flocks and herds from the small resources available. The Sixth Kaffir War had ended in complete military victory for the Government but its loose ends remained.

CHAPTER 13

Lord Glenelg and the Trek

THE fruits of victory had not been so much as peeled when the order came from London that they were instantly to be thrown away. The Rev. Doctor Philip had hastened thither as soon as he could, taking with him two companions named Tshatsu and Andries Stoffels. The first was a mission-educated Kaffir and the latter a Kat River denizen, half Hottentot and half Xosa, who had been strongly suspected of treasonable intentions during the war. While D'Urban, Smith and half a hundred others were trying to rebuild the shattered community, these travellers were busy spreading a word of their own composition. The moment was a perfect one for them; the abolition of slavery was still a fashionable subject and anything which tended to show that Japheth was being horrid to Ham was welcome in liberal circles. Their tour was 'a triumphal procession', said one enthusiast, 'in which such incidents were not omitted as Tshatsu and Stoffels taking ladies of rank to the dinner tables of houses where they were guests'. At public assemblies of a certain kind they were received with enthusiastic cheers.

The government of Lord Melbourne had not been long in office and the post of Colonial Secretary, never much sought after by professional politicians, had been conferred on Charles Grant, soon to be the first Lord Glenelg. His intentions were good and his ignorance of his subject majestic. It is doing him no injustice to say that Charles Grant in his few years of office did more permanent damage to the whole of South Africa than any man before or since, though several seem to have tried hard enough to snatch the palm from him. He had been born in India and at the time of his supreme achievement was 48 years old. Within 2 years his Cabinet colleagues Lord John Russell and Lord Howick were to inform the Prime Minister that Glenelg's incompetence was of so shattering an order that either he must go or they would. He went, but by then it was too late.

Mr Fowell Buxton was at that moment chairman of a House of Commons committee enquiring into the conditions of the aboriginal inhabitants of various British colonies and to his room Philip and his crew eagerly repaired. He introduced his companions; Tshatsu was a powerful chief who could bring 2,000 warriors into the field. The fact that his father was a minor dignitary in a clan of less than 1,000 all told was not publicized. If he appeared to be slightly drunk most of the time, the committee must understand that this is how great potentates appear in dark Africa. The committee, quite out of their depth, swallowed the whole rigmarole. Philip did not linger long enough for anyone to be found who might be able to catch him out, but he had done his sowing and the harvest would follow. Stoffels did not live to see it, for he died of tuberculosis, caught in London, soon after reaching Cape Town. Tshatsu did better. 'He had become so conceited and so fond of wine that he was utterly ruined'.

Unfortunately, a witness much more formidable than these comedians was also on his way to the committee room. Andries Stockenstroom, son of the murdered *landdrost*, had become a changed man. He had done much good service, some of which we have seen, but for all his ability he was described as being self-willed and crotchety to such an extent that his equals found it a burden to work with him. His judgment was distorted by his jealousy of Henry Somerset and he had a calculated hatred of all that family. It looks as if Lord Charles had been in the habit of issuing orders to Henry on the frontier without going through the proper channel of Stockenstroom, who, when speaking of the Somersets, expressed his feelings in the colourful phrase that 'his blood had been distilled into bile'. None the worse for this experience, he went to London. His evidence was, succinctly put, that all colonists were evil men and all the woes of Africa derived from their bad conduct to the Bantu. He held the Kaffir tribes out as being well governed communities of honest and harmless pastoralists, getting in a dig at Henry Somerset whenever opportunity presented itself. Some of his wild statements were downright lies, but when the former *landdrost* of Graaf Reinet whose father had been killed by them spoke of the Kaffirs in such enthusiastic terms it is no wonder that he was believed. He gave his evidence to the committee in August, 1835. Not until March of the following year did the news of it reach an incredulous colony when Colonel Wade at once left for London to rebut practically everything Stockenstroom had said. But by then it was too late, for the committee had made up its mind what its recommendations were going to be.

Glenelg wrote to D'Urban. He complained that he had not been furnished with 'a clear and comprehensive explanation of the causes which provoked the irruption of the Kaffirs into the Colony'. He had 'read with pain that it would be difficult to describe' Sir Benjamin's description of the Kaffirs as 'irreclaimable savages'. The despatch was a long one and it contains such extracts as 'In the conduct which was pursued towards the Kaffir nation by the colonists and the public authorities of the colony through a long series of years, the Kaffirs had an ample justification of the war into which they rushed with such fatal imprudence at the close of the last year . . . urged to revenge and desperation by the systematic injustice of which they had been the victims, I am compelled to embrace, however reluctantly, the conclusion that they had a perfect right to hazard the experiment, however hopeless, of extorting by force that redress that they could not expect otherwise to obtain . . . the claim of sovereignty over the new province bounded by the Keiskamma and the Kei must be renounced. It rests upon a conquest resulting from a war in which, as far as I am at present able to judge, the original justice is on the side of the conquered, not of the victorious party'. The despatch went on to announce the appointment of a Lieutenant-Governor for the eastern district and enjoined the Governor to enter into treaties with the Kaffir chiefs as if they were heads of the most ancient and cultured

states of Christendom. No European except approved missionaries was to cross the Fish River on any pretext. An Act of
Parliament would be introduced to provide for the punishment
of any of the King's subjects who might injure the person or
property of a Kaffir even outside the colony.

When this news reached the Cape, utter consternation resulted.
The chiefs could now raid and steal with impunity and Dr Philip
was in fact if not in theory the new Governor. It was soon
followed by an announcement of the name of the Lieutenant-
Governor for the eastern province. It was to be Captain Andries
Stockenstroom of the Cape Mounted Rifles.

Glenelg was aware that the frontier was still under martial
law and that Harry Smith considerably outranked Stockenstroom
in the Army. In order to make quite sure that the wind of
change should not be obstructed by a technicality of this kind,
peremptory orders were given to the Governor that there should
be an immediate return to normal civil law no matter what the
conditions prevailing there might be.

Smith, entirely unaware of what was happening in London,
was putting all his abundant energy into the task of civilizing
the new Province. In this he was greatly helped by an old councillor named Ganya who had once been Gaika's principal adviser.
'With this old fellow I spent six hours a day for several successive days until I made myself thoroughly acquainted with their
laws and rights of person. Although these closely resembled the
law of Moses given in Leviticus, and, if correctly administered
were excellent, I soon discovered that might was right, that the
damnable forgery of sorcery and witchcraft was the *primum
mobile* of oppression and extortion and that, under the cloak of
punishment for this offence, there was committed oppression of
so barbarous and tyrannical a kind as it was hardly to be conceived that beings endowed with reason could perpetrate on each
other.' He learnt at first hand of the smelling-out of suspected
witches and the hideous tortures, which included death by roast-
ing or pegging-out on ant-hills, that the chiefs employed on any
man unlucky enough to win their displeasure. 'I found I had
upward of 100,000 barbarians to reclaim who had no knowledge
of right or wrong beyond arbitrary power, desire and self-will.'
These bloodthirsty despots were the sovereign princes with whom

Lord Melbourne desired to enter into relations regulated by treaty as if he were dealing with Louis Philippe or President Van Buren.

Smith appointed magistrates among the tribes and gave them means of enforcing their decisions by setting up a regular Kaffir police force. He himself assumed office as a final court of appeal. The chiefs, hardly surprisingly, did not like it but they respected Smith for his complete and inflexible uprightness and attempts to slide back into the old ways were few. When they did occur, punishment was condign and swift. The ordinary tribesmen became secure and happy as never before. Macomo came within an ace of being broken and only saved himself by an abject and public apology for his contempt of Smith's authority. The building of King William's Town progressed satisfactorily, the Fingoes were settled in various empty tracts of land and all seemed set for a bright future.

Then the blow fell; Smith wrote his account of it in Simla some years later but even after so long a period for reflection his feelings remained as bitter as ever. 'In the midst of all I had effected, and all my visions of what I could effect, the most crooked policy ever invented by the most wicked Machiavellians blasted all my hopes for the benefit of the 100,000 barbarians committed to my rule, and the bright prospects of peace and tranquillity for the Colony (for the frontier inhabitants began to be in a state of security which was security indeed) . . . I was removed from my command and replaced by a man violently obnoxious to Kaffirs and colonists. Owing to the view Lord Glenelg had taken and the *"ton"* given, I was upbraided with every act of violence and oppression the curse of war can impose, and branded as the murderer of Hintza throughout the newspapers of the world . . . while our country's treasury and private contributions were open to the sufferers of the world from the temperate regions of Portugal to the snows of Poland, the ears of the public were deaf to the cries of the widows and orphans in the once happy and rapidly thriving province of Albany, although its settlers had been induced to come from England and there lay out their capital, were good subjects, loyal and true, and regularly paid their taxes, and therefore had a right to expect protection from the government. All rule and just and

good government was banished under the influence of the philan-
thropic party, who, by perversion of facts evidently desire to lead
others (this Colony certainly) to the devil for God's sake.'
Nobody can say that British governments are inconsistent.

Stockenstroom disembarked at Cape Town on 4 July, 1836.
D'Urban received him cordially and was rewarded by a
lecture on Lord Glenelg's principles of governorship. Stockenstroom did not dally in the capital and was soon on his way to
his headquarters at Grahamstown where he was to enjoy a
salary of £1,000 a year and a free residence. Ganya told Smith
that he would not long survive his departure and died within a
month.*

The Lieutenant-Governor reached Grahamstown on 3 September. An address was presented to him by 412 British settlers in
which they expressed their loyalty to the Crown but called in
question the evidence he had given to the committee. Stockenstroom refused to accept it. This incident set the tone for the
whole of his period of office. The next the colonists heard from
London was that the statute tactfully called The Cape of Good
Hope Punishment Act had been passed into law. Its preamble
read: 'The inhabitants of the territories adjacent to the Colony
of the Cape of Good Hope, to the southward of the 25th degree
of south latitude, being in an uncivilized state, offences against
the persons and property of such inhabitants and others are
frequently committed by His Majesty's subjects within such
territories with impunity.'

For one section of His Majesty's subjects, this insult was going
to be the last. The descendants of Joseph had come face to face
with their Pharaoh and they had their Moses ready to hand.
Piet Retief was a man as well liked and respected by the British
as by the Boers. He had shown himself to be a fine leader during
the wars and was by no means a wild man out of the Bezuidenhout and Prinsloo stable. On 22 January he issued his manifesto

---

* At about this time (1837) there was published in London a book by
the appealing title of *The Wrongs of the Caffre Nation*, the writer
employing the pseudonym of 'Justus'. One reviewer says of it 'The
statements in this book are not only untrustworthy but absurd. The
author of such a production could not be expected to put him name to
it'. The author had another reason for his anonymity, for Justus was
Charles Grant, First Earl Glenelg.

from Grahamstown and few will quarrel with the natural justice of it. There were 10 counts to his indictment of which these are the first and the last:

'We despair of saving the colony from those evils which threaten it by the turbulent and dishonest conduct of vagrants, who are allowed to infest the country in every part; nor do we see any prospect of peace or happiness for our children in a country thus distracted by internal commotions.'
'We are now leaving the fruitful land of our birth, in which we have suffered enormous losses and continued vexation, and are about to enter a strange and dangerous territory; but we go with a firm reliance on an all-seeing, just, and merciful God, whom we shall always fear and humbly endeavour to obey.'

The quiet dignity of these words bears comparison with those of Thomas Jefferson and his friends.

Including those who had gone already, some 2,000 of the Colony's best men and women took to their wagons having either sold their farms at knock-down prices or simply abandoned them. Outraged in all their finer feelings, but with the stoutest of hearts and fortified by a simple faith, they took the way to the north, into the land devastated by Chaka and now held down by his successor Dingaan and also the fierce Matabele. As their struggles and adventures do not form a part of this story, we can only watch and listen as the dust of their passage slowly dispels and the cries of 'Wey, Wey' from the Hottentot drivers grow fainter in the distance. Their victories over the Matabele at Vechtkop and over the Zulu at Blood River, the murder of Retief and his companions and the catastrophe of Weenen are more than adequately told elsewhere; for the purposes of this book it remains only to take stock of what they left behind and to measure the depleted garrison left to defend the Colony during the trials which lay ahead.

The Boers were not the only people who set out to expand the frontiers of Europe in Southern Africa. Quite a number of adventurous Englishmen had taken up residence in the lands of Dingaan with the object of making money by trade and hunting. By and large, they were not molested and their firearms had made them useful auxiliaries to that chief during his native wars. When Sir Lowry Cole had been Governor he had received orders from London to appoint an officer in Natal to exercise authority over the white men there but as the government was not prepared to lay out more than £100 a year in salary it is not remarkable that no candidate put himself forward for the post. At the end of December, 1835, these people petitioned D'Urban to have the district made into a British possession and D'Urban, at the height of his Empire-building activities, advised compliance. Needless to say, Lord Glenelg would not hear of it.

There had been some friction with Dingaan because the settlers refused to hand over fugitives from the chief's wrath to be executed but a *modus vivendi* was reached at about the same time under which Dingaan agreed to cede the land around Port Natal to Captain Gardiner, the acknowledged leader, on the understanding that no more refugees should be allowed sanctuary there. Gardiner was on good terms with Dingaan and eventually the latter agreed that he should have authority over all white men in Natal and that he be at liberty to set up mission stations there. Gardiner went home to England to recruit people to man them and within a couple of years several stations were opened. In fact, Dingaan exercised little authority over the land south of the Tugela which remained largely depopulated and the Cape of Good Hope Punishments Act applied with full rigour to the white community.

In December, 1838 a company of the 72nd had arrived at the Port, sent by the Governor without instructions from home. The cause of it had nothing to do with the action of the Boers. A lot of talk had been going on among the Europeans in Natal about forming another independent republic and such a phenomenon on a coast with excellent port facilities and free access to the interior was not tolerable to the Cape government. The harbour was declared closed and it was made plain to all that this was purely a military operation of limited time. Major Charters, in command, marked out a line two miles from high-water mark around the inlet and declared the strip to be under martial law. He collected up all the arms and ammunition from the settlers, to their fury, and placed it in store. The Boers, under the leadership of Mr Pretorius, had no more enthusiasm for the sight of the

187

Union flag flying over land which his people regarded as having been purchased with their blood. They need not have felt any apprehension for as soon as the news reached Lord Glenelg he and his cabinet colleagues denounced the Governor's action and at the end of December, 1839, the long-suffering Highlanders embarked again. There were about 640 men, mostly English, capable of bearing arms and about 3,200 women and children left behind.

D'Urban's reward for all he had achieved was an intimation dated 1 May, 1837, to the effect that the King had decided to dispense with his services as Governor and that he was to consider himself as holding office only until his successor should arrive. It was a shameful insult to a fine officer and great gentleman. Smith, shortly to leave on appointment as A.G. in India, wrote of 'my everlasting feelings of respect and veneration' for him and the colonists spoke of him for many years after as 'Sir Benjamin the Good'. It is some satisfaction to record that his public services were not ended, for after the fall of Glenelg Sir Robert Peel advised the young Queen to confer upon him the G.C.B. and he ended his long life as C.-in-C., British North America. He is buried in Montreal.

The supply of the Duke's old Peninsular officers was by no means exhausted, for the next Governor was Major-General George Thomas Napier. Captain Napier of the 52nd had been amongst the bravest of the brave in the golden days of the Light Division. With his brothers Charles (later to be Governor General of India and one of Britain's finest Generals between Wellington and Roberts) and William the historian, he was descended from Charles II and his mistress Louise de Kerouaille. George had lost an arm when he plunged into the heart of the fire in the lesser breach at Ciudad Rodrigo, an event which had not prevented him from coming back after his recovery and seeing much more service. He had been carefully indoctrinated by Lord Glenelg and arrived with the belief that the Kaffirs were a deserving people ruthlessly exploited by flagitious settlers. He was far too honest a man not to acknowledge before very long that the truth was other than that. Affairs on the eastern border were chaotic and, to add to his troubles, he was deprived almost at once of the 98th who were sent home. To all those with eyes to see, it was plain that the future of the Colony depended entirely on the temper of the Hottentots. There were still plenty of Boers who had not trekked but the commandos were terribly weakened, not only in numbers but by the loss of the best of the young men who did the actual fighting. Quite apart from that, it was idle to expect those who remained to saddle up again in aid of the British unless it should chance that their own interests marched with them. They could not be expected to feel loyalty to a government which had so mistreated them and the news from Natal seemed to indicate that the same government was quite capable when it thought fit of pursuing their kinsmen who had escaped from it and making them again into a subject people.

There was an ugly mutiny amongst the Hottentots, now 6 mounted companies strong, on 19 February, 1838, at Fraser's Camp, one of the new works between Grahamstown and Trompetter's Drift. While the officers were dining in their mess, 16 Hottentots broke in and fired on them, killing a young Ensign named Crowe. Murray of the 72nd was called in with a detachment of Highlanders and swiftly put it down. There was, naturally, a strong fear that worse was to come but a subsequent Court of Enquiry came to the conclusion that it was an isolated act by a few malcontents.

The root of the trouble lay with the missionaries. The Hottentot population found itself faced with a bewildering choice of various brands of Christianity which appeared to have little love for each other but one tenet they all had in common. The Hottentots were an oppressed race, in every way the equal of the white men, and they had been wrongfully deprived of their own land. Memories of the old name of 'Khoikhoi' began to stir in their unpredictable breasts and at Kat River, Theopolis and other places a steady stream of doctrine which some might call evangelization but others deemed sedition was pumped over them. Nobody realized this more clearly than Napier. He wrote to Glenelg on 12 July, 1838, asking for 3 regiments of the line and some more artillery 'to prevent the ruinous stock stealing and provide against a sudden rush of Kaffirs into the Colony', while at the same time proposing that the Hottentot establishment be reduced. He received the kind of answer one would expect. In reliance on Stockenstroom's advice, he entered into a treaty with the Gunukwebe under whose terms they were to be allowed to seek shelter west of the Fish River should they be attacked, on the understanding that they would assist the government in the event of another war. Macomo wanted the Hottentots turned out of their Kat River settlement but this Napier would not accept. These were the people who must be kept sweet at all costs.

Somerset continued at his Sisyphus task of keeping cattle raiding down to reasonable proportions though he now had less than 500 C.M.R. with which to do it. The only bright spot was the downfall of Stockenstroom, though even this was achieved by unworthy methods. An old charge was dug up that 25 years ago he had shot a Kaffir boy during his pro-settler days. The Court found it to have been a lawful act of war but such was the outcry that Stockenstroom had to go. His most implacable enemy could not deny that the administration he left was far more efficient than he had found it. Colonel John Hare of the 27th (The Royal Inniskilling Fusiliers) took over as acting Lieutenant-Governor. Stockenstroom went home to see Lord Glenelg. That nobleman was suitably impressed by the mistreatment of his protégé and was in the process of arranging for his reinstatement when the ground was cut from under his feet. Lord John Russell and Lord Howick had had enough and it was Lord Glenelg who bowed out. Stockenstroom's disappointment was assuaged by a baronetcy and a pension of £700 a year.

Raids and reprisals went on for several years. In 1840 the 72nd were at last sent home. They had something to show for all they had done; the citizens of Cape Town presented them with a fulsome address and in 1836 they were granted the rare battle honour of 'Cape of Good Hope'. This had nothing to do with their behaviour during the late war but was a belated recognition of the part they had played in the taking of Cape Town in 1806. There were left on the frontier the 27th, 75th, a wing of the 91st and a few gunners and sappers. The only reserve was the 25th finding guards at the capital.

The farmers glumly planted their corn in the faint hope that they might be permitted to harvest it and tended their flocks and herds in the knowledge that any night they might disappear. All the same, the colony continued in a state of reasonable prosperity behind the line of new defences named Forts Cox, White, Montgomery, Williams and Peddie. Fort Willshere was abandoned to the bush, which also took back to itself the neat little village that had been called King William's Town. It is hardly remarkable that when the next draft of settlers left England in 1840 they preferred to sail on past Table Mountain and make for New Zealand.

CHAPTER 14

'Harry Smith's Back'

N APIER saw out his time without a major conflict and in his place came yet another Peninsular soldier, Lieutenant General Sir Peregrine Maitland, the same officer who had received at Waterloo the imperishable order of 'Now, Maitland, now's your time'. Hare had been confirmed in his office as Lieutenant-Governor and remained at Grahamstown. Maitland had been brain-washed in the now customary manner before sailing but it did not take him long to find out that the authorities in London were utterly out of touch with reality. The absurd treaties were being broken every day by the Kaffirs. When he wrote to Lord Stanley, the new Secretary of State, asking what he should do, there arrived eventually the helpful reply that everything must be left to Sir Peregrine's judgment with a reminder that there 'were limits beyond which the military force of Great Britain could not be employed'. Maitland, for all his 67 years, went to see things for himself. His findings appalled him. 'The Xosa were sinking deeper in barbarism, owing to the policy pursued towards them, and the Scotch and Wesleyan missionaries gave some information which shocked him. They stated that an ancient custom which permitted the chiefs to ravish any girls they took a fancy to had recently been revived though Lord Charles Somerset in 1819 had induced Gaika to abolish it. But that was not the only evil result of the Stockenstroom treaties that they had to tell of.'

He saw at once the military absurdity of the Fish River as a frontier and set up another fortress, defended by earthworks, on the watershed between it and the Keiskamma and about 15 miles north-west of Fort Willshere which he named Post Victoria. It did something to keep the adjacent clans of Sandili in order but little else. He also distributed a couple of hundred old muskets amongst the Fingoes, for they, owing even their existence to the Government, could be relied upon to aim them in the proper direction.

More and more fatuous treaties were drawn up, recognizing the colony's frontier as being the old line agreed with Gaika in 1819. Even so, there was very nearly a war in January, 1846, when Sandili attacked and beat an English trader at Tyumie Mission and sacked his store. Hare, with a hundred men of the 91st at his back, marched to Block Drift, in the Tyumie valley near Post Victoria, and demanded redress. Sandili returned a fighting answer; let the governor come for payment of the trader's goods, his warriors were ready. He came to meet Hare with an escort of 3,000 men but so firm was that officer's demeanour that Sandili faltered and made restitution. Probably the main reason for his climb-down was the knowledge that he could not count on the support of Macomo. That chief had discovered a taste for brandy and passed much of his time in the canteen of Fort Beaufort in a state of advanced insobriety. 'When in this condition,' says George Theal, 'he was a source of terror to his wives and attendants, whom he assaulted at will, as it would have been deemed a dreadful crime to resist a chief of his rank.' The state of affairs on the frontier was an impossible one. Since the signing of the treaties 106 people had been murdered by the Xosa and everybody knew that war could not be long delayed.

It started on 16 March, 1846, almost by accident. This time there was neither irruption nor punitive expedition, but the rescue of a prisoner from his escort in the old Van Jaarsveld tradition. The prisoner was a Kaffir known as Kleintje, who had been caught at Fort Beaufort stealing an axe. He was arrested and sent for trial to Grahamstown. The chief Tola demanded his release in insolent terms and was given the answer he deserved by the agent-general. Aggrieved by this, he sent 40 of his warriors to overpower the escort of two Hottentots. One of them was killed and his hand cut off in order to release Kleintje from his handcuffs; the other escaped with the tidings to Fort Beaufort. Hare demanded of Tola that he hand over the murderer and the fugitive but Tola refused. Sandili, who was known to be harbouring them, also sent back a defiant answer. In this way began the Seventh Kaffir War, usually spoken of as 'The War of the Axe'.*

Colonel Hare acted promptly. He sent out warning to the farmers to be alert and distributed muskets to those who might need them. The garrisons of Fort Beaufort and Fort Peddie were reinforced and prepared to move against Sandili's kraal. The traders in the land across the river took fright and fled westwards; most of the missionaries remained, Mr Brownlee at the kraal of the inebriate Tshatsu even being sufficiently infatuated to suggest that his host be served out with weapons. Hare, instead, called out the settlers to establish a line of posts to prevent another invasion while he dealt with Sandili. Maitland sent, by the war-steamer *Thunderbolt*, every man he could raise. They numbered exactly 80 soldiers of the 27th and a couple of small field-guns. Hare had at his disposal just under 1,000 infantry drawn from the 27th and 91st, 337 mounted men of the 7th Dragoon Guards and about 400 C.M.R. He raised another 1,500 by sending for the Hottentots of Kat River (for the last two years infelicitously re-named Stockenstroom) who responded readily.

Hare was neither a Harry Smith nor a Willshere and he had the misfortune to be in ill-health. His previous encounter with Sandili had led him to believe that he had only to show his teeth and Sandili would abase himself. In this grievous error, he began his operations too soon and without sufficient preparation. From Post Victoria to Sandili's kraal was only a short ride; there could be no need of wagons for a laager nor were great quantities of stores essential. Nevertheless, Hare deliberately encumbered himself with 125 wagons which, allowing for a full span of oxen each, straggled in single file for more than 3 miles. Henry Somerset came to take over command on 11 April and 4 days later the force, which had started from 3 different places, coalesced at Burnshill. Sandili's kraal, which might have been

* Sir John Fortescue says that it was not an axe but an ox.

taken by a swift dash, was found to be empty and the Kaffirs had once again taken themselves into the fastnesses of the Amatolas. Somerset moved out to attack them with his infantry and C.M.R. leaving the cavalry in camp. That night they were attacked but beat off their assailants without much difficulty.

In the morning came the order for the wagon train to move out under escort of the 7th D.G. to join Somerset in the hills. The consequences should have been predictable. As the column struggled through a narrow defile, one of the wagons in the middle stuck fast. A horde of Sandili's Gaikas, who had been waiting in the bush for this to happen, poured down and cut loose the oxen. The dragoons, who were, for some reason, concentrated at the rear of the column, could not even get near them and half the wagon train fell into Kaffir hands without a fight. Luckily the ammunition wagons were in the rear and escaped. Major Gibsone of the dragoons extricated these and took them back to Burnshill and those which had passed the obstruction safely joined up with Somerset. He, believing that the boost to Kaffir morale would precipitate a flood over the river into the colony, drew all his force back to Burnshill. The reverse had cost the lives of a dragoon officer, a colonist, 10 men of the 91st and 5 Hottentots apart from the loss of the wagons and teams. Somerset brought 1,800 cattle back with him but it was an unprofitable exchange.*

His fears had been well grounded. Thousands of exultant Kaffirs spread into the colony raiding far and wide. Thanks to Hare's warning, the farmers had had time to band together and the loss of life amongst them was inconsiderable but the burning of crops and buildings and the driving off of flocks and herds could not be checked. So much were the Kaffirs in command of the situation that there were many instances of them driving their loot merrily past the posts and taunting the few soldiers in them to come out. The line of fortlets along the Great

* Bissett tells us that 'The baggage wagons of the 7th D.G. contained all the valuable mess plate etc belonging to the officers . . . some had 2 or 3 guns in their wagons by the best makers, Purdey, Rigby, Wilkinson, Moore, Westley-Richards etc. These superior arms, unfortunately, fell into the hands of the enemy'. It is, perhaps worth mentioning that an N.C.O. who particularly distinguished himself during this melancholy episode bore the honourable if antique name of Telemachus.

Fish River eloquently proclaimed their utter uselessness. Despite the conventional protestations to the contrary, every Kaffir tribe was soon in arms against the colonists. Only the Fingoes remained. Kreili's people drove a great herd under the walls of Fort Peddie, the strongest post of all, commanded by Lt-Colonel Martin Lindsay of the 91st, who 'was not held in much esteem either in military circles or by the colonists, and he certainly did nothing that would entitle him to regard'. Lindsay was perhaps the least attractive figure amongst the British officers who served in the colony. The Boers hated him because he had had one of their people flogged without trial as a result of some supposed misdemeanour and, for obvious reasons, this was at a time when relations between Boer and Briton were in a very delicate state. His next feat surpassed even this. At about 4 miles from Fort Peddie lay a mission station named Beka inhabited by a clan of Fingoes. On 30 April a message arrived at the Fort that these people, tested allies of the colonists, were being attacked by about 1,000 Kaffirs; the news reached Lindsay at about noon on 30 April and, two hours later, he sent out a squadron of Dragoons, a half-company of the 91st and two guns to relieve them. The officer in command, 'observing that the Fingoes were holding their own', fired off a few shells and returned to the Fort, explaining that it was late in the afternoon, his horses were tired and, anyway, it was only a ruse to draw the Kaffirs after him. With this lame excuse Lindsay professed himself satisfied. The result was that the mission was burnt down and the Fingoes abandoned to their fate under the eyes of 200 British soldiers. This heartened the Kaffirs even more than their success against the convoy had done and many who had been wavering joined in the war.

Sir Peregrine Maitland, 'the dear old General' as a subaltern on his staff, later to be General Sir William Bissett, called him, had already reached Post Victoria. The news of the disgrace at Fort Peddie decided him that the only possible course was for him to supersede his indifferent commanders and personally take over the conduct of operations. Help was at hand, for he had taken the precaution before leaving Cape Town of ordering that any troops which might arrive there from any quarter should be commandeered and sent to the frontier with all speed. This had netted 9 officers and 283 men of the 90th who had put in for refreshment. Almost more important was the return of Stockenstroom. Sir Andries, as he now was, had altered course again and, while remaining as cantankerous as ever, had decided that the Kaffirs had only themselves to blame for this war and he would do everything in his power to encompass their defeat. Maitland gladly appointed him a Colonel on the Staff and entrusted to him command of all the burgher forces. The Boers, as soon as they realized that sanity had returned to him, were delighted. Stockenstroom's re-conversion was explained by the analogy that one does not seek the cause of its collapse when one's house is tumbling about one's ears. He gave it out uncompromisingly that in his opinion the Kaffirs should be driven from the strongholds of the Amatolas and never permitted to return. To this most people echoed 'Amen'. With the arrival of Stockenstroom in the field, the tide, even if it did not begin to turn, at least reached slack water at its height.

Stockenstroom's bailiwick was north of the Winterberg, from which place he could move to block the exits from the Amatolas which led back into Kaffirland. While he was organizing and victualling his men there, Somerset began to purge the districts of Albany and Uitenhage with his C.M.R. Little parties embattled in lonely farm-houses were relieved and so were the Hottentots of Theopolis. The emboldened Kaffirs came out to meet him in formed bodies of unusual size and were shot down by the carbines of the Hottentot horsemen. First they cleared the valley of the Kowie, then the land around Olifant's Hoek and by the end of May the colony had been almost completely evacuated by the invaders.

Outside the border, things did not look so promising. Not a mission nor a trading post remained in Kaffirland and it had become necessary to abandon Post Victoria because of its unreliable water supply. The time was one of great drought and the problem of forage dominated almost everything. The Lovedale mission at Block Drift (later to become Fort Hare) was the only exception and here a substantial tented camp had grown up around the original buildings.

By the middle of May it had become necessary to revictual Fort Peddie and a convoy of wagons was assembled for the purpose at Grahamstown, 43 of them, each with a full span of 16 oxen. It is only a matter of about 20 miles from Grahamstown to Trompetter's Drift, where a fairly strong post existed, and only a small escort could be spared. It was therefore arranged that a party should come from Fort Peddie and collect its wagons at the Drift, providing protection during the rest of the journey from its own resources. All went well as far as the river but, when the post lay about 3 miles behind the convoy, the Kaffirs burst out of the thick bush. Their first priority was to shoot sufficient of the draught animals to bring the column to a halt and this they promptly did. The escort, 80 soldiers of the 91st and about 40 burghers, made their escape back to Trompetter's leaving 4 men dead on the ground; the Kaffirs plundered the stores, which were as welcome to them as they would have been to the garrison of Peddie, burnt the wagons and drove off the oxen.

This second success against the colonists so persuaded them of their superior prowess that they decided on attacking Fort Peddie itself. Slight though their chances may have seemed against trained soldiers firing from behind loop-holed walls, the enterprise came within sight of victory; for once in their history, the Kaffirs tried out a stratagem. The 'feigned flight' ploy is as old as war; it was a standard practice of the Vikings, had won the day at Hastings, had been employed on occasions by Chaka, and used at Amalinde. On the morning of 27 May several thousand warriors appeared before the Fort and some rather aimless skirmishing took place. Lindsay was on the point of making a sortie when one of the Fingoes happened to overhear a Kaffir chief announcing his plan in an excessively loud voice. The Fingo, heaping coals of fire, reported this to an officer and soon afterwards a second horde was observed, obviously the one which would storm the fort in the absence of the greater part of its garrison. In the event, the Kaffirs stayed just outside cannon shot and had to content themselves with looting and burning a trader's store and lifting the cattle belonging to the luckless Fingoes. Officers in the look-out tower observed the figure of Tshatsu unsteadily directing operations.

Though the assault had luckily turned into a fiasco, the supply situation was becoming serious. Maitland prepared a second convoy, twice the size of the first, with an escort this time of 1,200 men under the personal command of Henry Somerset. It was to travel by way of Committee Drift and Breakfast Vlei, as the Kaffir scouts behind every thicket realized from an early stage. In the densest bush between these two places the attack came in. This time the troops were ready for it and a hard fight took place. Bissett was particularly impressed by the conduct of a sapper officer named Captain Walpole. Walpole was extremely short-sighted and no Victorian officer could be expected to wear glasses to correct such an infirmity. With a double-barrelled percussion pistol in his hand, Walpole went from bush to bush, pulling aside the foliage and blinking myopically at whatever was revealed. Whenever it chanced to be a Kaffir, Walpole shot him, reloaded and went on to the next bush. Somehow he remained unscathed and seems to have accounted for quite a number of the enemy. The convoy crashed its way through by brute force and reached Fort Peddie on the following day at a trifling cost.

On 7 June a diversion was staged to occupy the Kaffirs while the empty wagons made their way back to Grahamstown. Somerset was in command and a raiding party of 300 Hottentots and 200 Fingoes under British officers were marched out of the fort to go and beat up Stokwe's kraal. A troop of Dragoons, a squadron of C.M.R., a troop of volunteer cavalry, a hundred George burghers, four guns and a rocket tube followed as the sun rose next morning. They met up at about 7.30 and, after a smart little fight, the kraal was over-run and put to the torch. It was then noon, no time for marching tired horses, and Somerset resolved to make for the nearby Gwanga streamlet to water them and to rest.

There was only a small rise to be crossed before the stream was reached. As the cavalry rode slowly up it, Bissett's horse, which had been restive all the morning, suddenly got out of control and carried him at speed to the top from which there was a long view over the river to the hills beyond. To his amazement he saw, just over the ridge and on an open slope, a body of some 600 Kaffirs marching at their leisure across Somerset's front. These were the men of Siyolo and Umhalla, waxed over-confident by their successes. Siyolo, as he later said, had pointed out the unwisdom of this, reminding Umhalla that Siyolo meant wild-cat, an animal that prowls and strikes by night. Umhalla had taunted him with cowardice and Siyolo, stung, had agreed on a movement by day although this was contrary to everything in the Kaffir habit.

Somerset deployed his guns, two 6 pdrs and two 12 lb howitzers, along the top of the slope, the rocket tube with them. When they opened fire the result was not what he expected. The ammunition had been in store since the 1835 war and the fuses of the shrapnel shells were all set wrongly. Most shells exploded as soon as they had left the barrels, and the rocket exploded in its tube. The Kaffirs opened fire with musketry, some of their projectiles being 'long junks of lead and legs of iron pots', but did no more damage. The country was ideal for a cavalry charge and an opportunity like this would probably never come again. Somerset launched his horsemen in the only attack of its kind during these wars. The Dragoons led, for they were the only men to carry sabres, and the C.M.R. followed in line. The Kaffirs broke, though their casualties were not heavy at that stage, for to slash at one of these athletes with a long, straight sword is like trying to decapitate an eel. Many were bowled over, but they rolled away and usually picked themselves up unscathed. When the carbine-armed C.M.R. arrived it was different. 'The charge was the prettiest thing I have ever seen in real fighting. You might have placed a long tablecloth over each troop, they kept in such compact order and the C.M.R. went through the Kaffirs in one long line'. That was how Bissett saw it. He himself returned his sword to its scabbard as soon as he could and took from its bucket his double-barrelled gun. With this, he fired more than 30 rounds never at more than 20 paces and at the end of the day he disfigured the butt by cutting 7 notches in it. The C.M.R., firing from the saddle, did most of the killing and it was reckoned that about 400 were slain or died of wounds. It was a little victory which came at a very timely moment. Bissett with his own hand brought down one of Kreili's chief counsellors from whom much interesting information was obtained, including the fact that Siyolo had been badly wounded. Bissett, incidentally, mentions that everybody, officers and men alike, carried double-barrelled guns in those days and from his frequent references to caps it must be that most of them were percussion weapons. The battle had also ended the plan of Umhalla and Siyolo to place their men in the jungle around Trompetter's Drift to block communication between Grahamstown and Fort Peddie. While the fight was in progress the empty wagons had safely passed over the Drift and were well on their way to Grahamstown. After the battle, Bissett walked over the ground. He noticed that 'One Kaffir was shot with a quantity of blister ointment in and about his mouth, their notion being that English medicine makes you strong.'

The battle of the Gwanga, as it came to be called, did not end the war at a stroke but it marked the moment at which the tide began perceptibly to ebb. Within a few days of it, the Kaffirs lost a powerful ally. The Rev. Dr Philip had suffered a personal tragedy in the death of his son and grandson in a boating accident and he had begun to realize that perhaps his protégés were not, after all, the down-trodden heroes of a golden age. During his last days he was told of the mass murders of helpless Fingo women and children and of the hideous tortures to which British prisoners had been subjected at Kaffir hands. The unfortunate man's spirit was completely broken and he died in July a model of Christian meekness.

By late June the government had in the field forces far exceeding anything that had been seen before. Something like 3,200 regular troops were on the border drawn from the 7th Dragoon Guards (325), two battalions of the 91st amounting to nearly 1,000 effectives, the 27th (416), 151 officers and men of the 45th (The Sherwood Foresters), the 90th (The Cameronians) (439), 624 of the C.M.R. and about 300 British artillery and engineers. The burgher forces facing the enemy numbered over 5,500 and Cuyler, dragged out of retirement at a great age and promoted Major-General, was in charge of a further 3,000 forming a kind of Home Guard in Uitenhage and Lower Albany. On top of these, Commandant Groepe disposed of about 800 Griquas and Hottentots, serving without pay, and a labour corps of all races under British officers totalled yet another 4,000. Though this constituted a formidable fighting force, it also created the problem of how to feed 14,000 mouths, to say nothing of numbers of unenlisted wagon drivers, and forage for their animals all at

G*

a time of severe drought. This factor alone inhibited any large-scale campaign.

The Royal Navy eased the situation considerably by making a landing place on the coast about a mile east of the mouth of the Fish River from which point the journey overland to Fort Peddie was reduced to a mere 22 miles. The sailors also made a raft crossing over the river about a mile upstream of Waterloo Bay, as the new landing place was called, which opened a short route to Grahamstown. A small fort, named for Admiral Dacres, was built to cover the landing. It was garrisoned by seamen and Royal Marines.

The Governor, deeming it the best communications centre available, moved his Headquarters to the Fort. From there he organized his army into two divisions, the left under Hare around Block Drift and the right under Somerset nearer to the sea. Somerset was the first to strike. In the early days of July, he moved out with 880 cavalry and 750 infantry in pursuit of Pato who inhabited the land between the site of King William's Town and the sea. Pato had never been among the most rancorous of the Kaffir chiefs and he was regarded as the weakest link in their chain. Spies had already informed Somerset that he had moved eastwards carrying with him great numbers of stolen cattle. Somerset's force, as usual, was made up entirely of burghers and Hottentots and their march was not opposed. Pato, however, had added to the difficulties created by the drought and had burnt all the grass in their path. The result was that, by the time they had reached the Kei, the burgher forces had been compelled to shoot many of their foundered horses and those left were in no state to continue campaigning.. Only the Hottentot infantry went over the river on 21 July and within 48 hours they were back, driving about 5,000 cattle triumphantly before them. Somerset, to save his horses, fell back again to the Gwanga leaving a strong force of Hottentots near the former town.

Maitland, reasonably satisfied with the result of the first stroke, decided that the time had come when he was strong enough to raid the Amatolas. His plan was for the last-mentioned force to spread out in a half-moon to block all the eastern exists while the division under Hare and the burghers of Stockenstroom should drive the garrison into their arms from west and north.

On 29 July, the drive began. Stockenstroom, with the burghers of Graaf Reinet (sadly reduced in numbers but still to be reckoned with), Colesberg and Beaufort, plus the Kat River Totties, started from the Upper Tyumie valley. With that in his hands, he sent a large part of his burghers up to the Bontebok flats where they were to spread out to the east and seal off any exit. The infantry struggled up the steep ridge of the Hogsback (where the Hydro Hotel now stands) and plunged into the ravines and forests beyond. Stockenstroom, who permitted himself no luxuries that his humblest follower could not share, went with them on foot, gun in hand. Hare's task was to move from Block Drift with most of the regulars along the foothills scouring and clearing all the bush that lay in his path. The Amatolas appeared to be effectively sealed off and certainly no army organized in European fashion could have had any chance of escape. For the Kaffirs, however, the task was by no means an impossible one. Having no impedimenta beyond their weapons and a skin bag apiece and knowing intimately every inequality in the ground, they oozed themselves between the two forces, many escaping through a gap unaccountably left between Somerset's left and Hare's right, and vanished. The army had sustained casualties of 10 killed and 7 wounded, all by the fire of muskets of which the Kaffirs had too many for comfort, and had nothing at all to show for their great efforts. The Amatolas were, for the moment, empty of enemy but they could not be occupied and the Kaffirs could return whenever they pleased.

However, for the moment Pato, Sandili and Macomo had had their teeth drawn. There remained Kreili. Maitland resolved that he too must receive a lesson and he allocated a force, mostly of burghers, to do the business. In all there were about 2,500 of them in two wings under command of Stockenstroom and Lt-Colonel Johnstone of the 90th. Hare remained at Fort Cox, whose re-occupation was the only tangible evidence of the last sweep, and Somerset went back to his old camp on the Gwanga. The two columns rode out on 14 August to be greeted early in their march by a messenger from Kreili. Why were they attacking him? He was at peace with the colony and there were no stolen cattle in his land. Stockenstroom returned the answer that he would speak with Kreili at his kraal and nowhere else.

The expedition moved on without opposition but at the cost of a number of foundered horses.

A conference took place at the kraal on 21 August; Stockenstroom demanded redress for all Kreili's misdeeds and was met with a flat denial that the chief had anything with which to reproach himself. He had made war on none, had not stolen a single beast and had indeed punished one of his captains whom he had learnt was taking a part in the hostilities. After much argument, Stockenstroom agreed to withdraw if Kreili would make certain promises. Would he agree to be responsible for the acts of the Gaikas and their vassals if the Government would accord him his title of paramount chief? Would he compensate the traders and missionaries who had been plundered, return any cattle he might happen to find and acknowledge British sovereignty over all land west of the Kei? Kreili unhesitatingly said that he would. All those present knew perfectly well that Kreili was lying and that Hintza's old corral on the Bashee river was full to overflowing with stolen colonial cattle. The passage of herds of sheep was eloquently proclaimed by the amount of wool sticking to the mimosa. Nevertheless, Stockenstroom affected to believe him and went back by the way he had come. A small independent raid carried out at the same time by Captain Hogg of the 7th D.G., operating from Fort Cox with a body of Hottentots against Mapasa, a minor Tembu captain, recovered 4,000 cattle with colonial markings but Stockenstroom thought it better not to make an issue of this.

The governor was displeased with Stockenstroom, for he had expected the expedition to bring back something more valuable than empty promises. Stockenstroom's nature did not allow him to accept criticism from any quarter and a noble quarrel followed. It ended only on 27 November when he was relieved of his duties. This happened at a most unfortunate moment for, unlike previous wars, the War of the Axe had brought about much ill-feeling between Boer and Briton. In addition to the reasons already mentioned, the burghers were feeling, as irregular troops often do, that they were being exploited. All the hard work and all the danger were their portion while the regulars were carefully shielded from either. There had probably always been a germ of truth in the argument for experienced frontier Boers were more serviceable in some operations than green British regiments. No doubt pleasantries had passed on earlier occasions about this but now for the first time there was real venom in it. The root of the trouble was that it had been exceedingly difficult to ration so large a force and the commissariat officers had been perhaps too strictly guided by regulations, in ensuring that the British troops were served first. The dismissal of Stockenstroom and the contemptuous demeanour of the occasional bad officer like Lindsay did nothing to remedy this unhappy situation.

Maitland informed Kreili that he would not ratify the arrangement and again demanded the return of cattle known to be in his territory. There was, however, nothing he could do to impose his will and, as his horses were dying of hunger, he was forced to fall back to Waterloo Bay. The burghers were sent home with the thanks of the Government as want of provisions made it impossible to keep them in the field. Many a farmer walked back bitterly, his saddlery over his shoulder, and with empty pockets. Hare's precarious health broke down completely and he was sent home. The fact that he was no malingerer was made plain, for he died at sea four days out of Cape Town and was buried at St Helena.

Drought paralysed the army until the young grass appeared in October. As soon as the countryside began to turn green, wagons were once more hired and the atmosphere became more animated. Another 1,100 regulars arrived to be fed, the 2/45th and the 73rd (The Black Watch) from Montevideo and about a hundred details from Cork. Earl Grey, Secretary for the Colonies in the new administration of Lord John Russell, not to be outdone by the War Office, sent out six middle-aged half-pay Lieutenant-Colonels and Majors for whom jobs had to be found or created. At the end of October there arrived 9 officers and 285 men of the Rifle Brigade from Gibraltar and on the next day another 13 officers and 400 men of the 6th. Soon after came the other half of the Rifles, 10 officers and 328 men. From such a force great things were expected.

There had been some insincere overtures from various chiefs. Macomo, suffering from dysentery, had met a deputation on the slopes of the hill near the present village of Alice still known as Sandili's Kop to enquire what terms were to be had. He was told that nothing short of the surrender of all their guns and booty, the acceptance of locations of the Governor's choosing and the acknowledgment of British sovereignty up to the banks of the Kei would suffice. He went home in disgust. Those present could not fail to notice that out of an escort of several thousands about half had muskets, supplied, no doubt, by European traders. The killings went intermittently on. In August a patrol of 19 Stellenbosch burghers were trapped in a kloof in Albany from which 5 never emerged; between then and October, 13 farmers and many of their servants were murdered in the same district. The Tembu chief Umtirara sent in protestations of friendship but nothing else. Talks dragged on everywhere as the grass and corn grew and ripened. No Kaffir chief had the smallest intention of making peace but the time gained was of inestimable value. The crops were reaped, the corn-pits filled and with the reinforcements that had come in from tribes not in immediate contact with the colony, they would soon be ready for the next round. Maitland was beginning to feel the strain of campaigning in Africa at an age when most of his contemporaries were enjoying a quiet retirement and had become almost senile. He did, however, decide that Pato, the chief nearest to the sea, should be the first to be eliminated. The long-suffering burghers were called out once more and in the closing days of 1846 another expedition set out. Maitland went with it, for the old Guardsman of Waterloo was not the man to sit in his office while others did the fighting.

The real commander, however, was Henry Somerset and the object of the operation was to surround and crush Pato after which a demand would be made of Kreili for the return of 15,000 cattle believed to have been secreted by him. If he refused, he would be attacked and the force would then go on to liberate the 3,000 Fingoes at Butterworth. The first stage was neatly carried out. The 73rd were marched to the nearest ford on the Kei as a feint; as the Kaffirs were moving to dispute their passage, a force of C.M.R. 600 strong crossed by a ford several miles nearer to the sea while Somerset swept round from the other side to complete the encirclement. They came back 3 days later with droves of cattle but Pato had evaded them. This time, however, Somerset returned at once and the whole force made straight for Butterworth which it reached without difficulty. Kreili had refused the demands made on him and Somerset therefore tried to bring him to battle. The result was the usual one. There was no battle but in the forest of Manubi, about 18 miles east of the Kei, Somerset found great quantities of stolen cattle and came back to King William's Town with about 10,000 head. The liberated Fingoes were settled in the neighbourhood of the old Post Victoria and given arms for their own protection. The losses during the sweep were negligible but again the lesson of eternal vigilance was taught. Three officers who had galloped off on their own were found in a thicket later on, their bodies horribly mutilated.

On 6 January, Maitland was superseded as Governor. His successor was Sir Henry Pottinger, an experienced colonial administrator but not a military man. A separate Commander-in-Chief also arrived, Sir George Berkeley. Pottinger's service had been in India and China and he was accustomed to dealing with organized native states; his brief was to 'make some arrangement with the hostile tribes that would bring the war to a close and tend thereafter to preserve peace'. He found Maitland to be in a state of surprising euphoria and under the impression that he had already achieved something of that sort. In the belief that the war was all but over, he had raised martial law and was on the point of sending the 90th home. Many of the burghers had already adopted the same course on their own initiative. Pottinger at once countermanded the orders and appealed to the colonists to provide him with seven or eight hundred volunteers to meet him at Fort Peddie on 18 March under promise that they would not be required for more than a month. He also attempted to stop the illicit trade in arms to the Kaffirs by proclaiming that any person caught in trade of any kind would be treated as a traitor and would, after conviction by court-martial, be shot.

The response to his appeal for volunteers was poor. They carried out a sweep into Pato's country with scant success and, at the end of the month, disbanded themselves. Some progress, however, was made. The 73rd, after their diversion on the last occasion, had moved on to the Buffalo River where they had built a fort named, strangely for a Scotch regiment, Glamorgan.

From this nucleus, more posts were set up, a small one six miles further in being called Need's Camp after the Rifle Brigade officer who built it. Fort Murray was re-built and a large post established in the scrub-covered skeleton of King William's Town. The colonel of the Rifle Brigade who commanded it bore a name later to become well-known, if not always distinguished, in the army's record of its campaigns in Africa. He was Lt-Colonel Buller. Another makeshift port was established to supply the new fortresses, this time at the mouth of the Buffalo. In time it was to become East London.

The war now moved into that depressing condition which was to mark the last stage of the greater struggle of half a century later. Large British forces were kept in being to do little more useful than guard places that were not threatened and consume vast quantities of rations. The enemy carefully avoided any concentration of his forces and took the offensive only to the extent of raiding isolated farms and butchering the unwary. The only difference, in this case, was that the forces of the government were gradually establishing themelves in the old disputed lands and, with their supplies secured by sea, they could not easily be dislodged.

It was not until June, 1847, that another action deserving of mention took place. Sandili decided that the time had come for him to trail his coat. A handful of stolen goats were traced to his kraal; he restored all save a couple of them on demand, but the gesture of defiance could not be allowed to pass unmarked. A company of the 45th with a half-squadron of Dragoons and some C.M.R. were sent to arrest him. Sandili called out his warriors and nearly a thousand of them were observed drawn upon a hill near by, Sandili conspicuous at their head. As the officer in command of the patrol took stock of the situation, more and more Kaffirs appeared until every hill was covered with knots of them. They were clearly too many for the patrol to tackle on its own, so Captain Moultrie decided to fall back on his main body at Block Drift. The Kaffirs dogged their steps, hooting and yelling and keeping up a sporadic musketry in which two men were wounded.

For once there were troops enough and to spare and the opportunity of chastening the most forward of the chiefs (with the possible exception of Macomo) was not to be lost. The decencies were observed by sending a pacific mission to demand the handing over of the thieves and 200 muskets into the bargain. Sandili returned a rough answer. Pottinger, working on the Napoleonic principle that war should be made to pay for itself, called on the burghers for help with a promise that they should keep any cattle they might manage to seize. Very few were tempted, for they knew perfectly well that at the first hint of an attack all the cattle would be driven away into the hinterland where friends would look after them until things had blown over.

Sir George Berkeley himself assumed command of the troops taking part. He began, with commendable foresight, by establishing 3 forward depots in the Amatolas, one on the eastern bank of the Tyumie which was christened Fort Hare, another at Fort White and the third at King William's Town. A substantial blocking force of Hottentots was established at Shiloh on the Klipplaats River to prevent any break-out over the Bontebok flats. The Tyumie basin was temporarily cleared of its inhabitants. Three patrols, totalling about 2,000 men, moved out in light marching order on 19 September under Somerset, Buller and Colonel Campbell of the 91st. Once again it was swatting at a mosquito, for Sandili had gone and the Amatolas were empty. All the frustrated soldiers could achieve was the burning of a few huts and the destruction of some corn-pits, mostly empty.

The time, however, was not wasted, for by a relentless pressure of continual patrolling Sandili was brought near to starvation and on 19 October he sent in his chiefs to surrender to Colonel Buller. Either Sandili was of a more forbearing nature than his conduct suggests or he was short of powder or, more probably, a great liar, for he insisted that he had been hiding amongst the crags of the Wolf River. He claimed that on one occasion a rifleman had been on the point of opening up the thicket in which he lay but inexplicably turned aside and that on another an officer had passed so close to him that he could recognize him again. He and his sub-chiefs were sent off under strong escort to Grahamstown. The original cause of it all, the axe-stealing Kleintje, was also picked up. It is good to know what became of him for otherwise he might have passed into unremarked oblivion in common with those other individuals who, since Helen of Troy, had set men at war with each other. Kleintje can join Jenkins the Ear, M. Jecker of Mexico and M. Dupont of Tonkin in this distinguished number.

Next, Sir George turned his attention to Pato. An offer similar to that made to Sandili was sent to him with the same result. Somerset, from his camp on the Komgha, made a lunge into his country and harried him for three weeks. At the end of that time Pato, too, had had enough and, having first ascertained that his life would be spared, he submitted on 19 December. No chief now remained in arms west of the Kei.

It was not, however, an unblemished success. Once again a small party of officers, refusing to learn from past experience, allowed themselves to become separated from their troops and were cut off by a party of Galeka's under Hintza's brother Boku. Their mangled remains were found some days later.

At this time there came also a change at the head of affairs. Pottinger had made a mark on the colony only by his unbridled licentiousness; Theal says that 'His *amours* would have been inexcusable in a young man, in one approaching his 60th year they were scandalous. In other respects a cold, calculating, sneering, unsympathetic demeanour prevented men of virtue being attracted to him' and ends, rather unkindly, with 'He was much better adapted for office in India than in South Africa'. Be that as it may, to India he went, regretted by none, and at Cape Town the cry soon went up 'Harry Smith's back'.

He was Sir Harry now, victor over the Sikhs at the brilliant little battle of Aliwal and commander of a division at Mudki, Ferozeshah and Sobraon. Most important, he was a man who needed no education in the ways of Africa. Sir George Berkeley accompanied Sir Henry Pottinger to Madras and Harry Smith once more set off for Grahamstown. Within hours of his arrival he had proclaimed a new frontier for the colony, broadly speaking along the line of the Keiskamma. At his former provincial capital of King William's Town on 23 December, 1847, Harry Smith gave it out that the land between the new frontier and the Kei (it was a little more precise than that, but the description will serve) would henceforth be British Kaffraria, a dependency of the Crown quite distinct from the colony, to be kept for the

Kaffir people over whom would be placed a High Commissioner. The War of the Axe had ended with the lack of precision which had marked its beginning.

It could not be claimed that the Kaffirs had been decisively defeated in the field but the largest military force ever seen was encamped in various places throughout British Kaffraria. It was clearly within the power of the Governor to wreak a severe vengeance on the invading tribes if he had a mind to do it. The Governor would have been within his rights on any view of the matter for massive and flagrant treaty-breaking was easily provable against practically every chief. Harry Smith, however, was no eye-for-an-eye man. He distrusted the whole idea of treaties and held firmly to the belief that only by putting it beyond doubt that early, easy successes inevitably meant eventual massive retribution could the Kaffirs be kept within their boundaries. Quite apart from humanitarian reasons, it was in the interests of the colony that Kaffraria should be so governed that its people did not need to seek adventure abroad. Harry Smith had a taste for the theatrical gesture. At Port Elizabeth he saw Macomo in a crowd and summoned him to step forward. After Macomo had obeyed the order to kneel, Smith placed his foot firmly on the chief's neck and said loudly enough for all to hear, 'This is to teach you that I am come hither to teach Kaffirland that I am chief and master here and this is the way I shall treat the enemies of the Queen of England'. It was not the way to win friends amongst the tribesmen; Macomo may have been a drunken brute but he was chief by divine right and so public and grave an insult gave as much offence to his people, even to those who hated him, as if, for example, William of Orange had meted out the same treatment to the fallen James II.

At King William's Town on 23 December, 1847, a great indaba took place. It was the sort of thing at which Smith excelled and he believed in the necessity of creating an event which would live in the common memory of his audience. First there was a military parade by the 7th D.G. and the Rifle Brigade which was watched by about 2,000 Kaffirs squatting in a hollow circle. When the soldiers had finished Smith rode into the middle of the circle and read out his proclamation. Between the Keiskamma and the Kei, north to the junction of the Klipplaats and Zwart Kei Rivers, he, Harry Smith, would henceforth be Inkosi Inkulu, the Great Chief. Colonel Mackinnon would be his vice-gerent and would live at King William's Town which he was to lay out in squares and streets on each bank of the Buffalo. A chain of four forts, named Juanasburg, Woburn, Auckland and Ely, would surround it. The chiefs were then presented with two staffs, one an ordinary sergeant's baton and the other an affair with a large brass knob, denominated respectively 'the staff of war' and 'the staff of peace'. Each chief was put to his election between them. The result could hardly have been in doubt. Next, from the saddle, Smith demanded that each chief in turn should kiss his boot. 'This they did also without hesitation'. As their humiliation before their people had now gone far enough, Smith then wrung each chief by the hand and presented him with a generous number of cattle for a feast.

Superior people in England sneered at a way of conducting public affairs in a manner which appeared to them childish and Smith was accused of having allowed the applause for Aliwal to run to his head. In fact he was right; a people in many ways child-like and whose records are passed down by word of mouth are not likely to forget that a war which had started with so much promise ended in such abasement. There could be no argument about what had happened so publicly no matter what some future witchdoctor might protest to the contrary.

Smith had not yet finished his lesson. On 7 January, 1848, he summoned a second meeting. First he exacted an oath of allegiance and reform, coupled with an undertaking to pay an annual quit-rent of one fat ox to be delivered at King William's Town on every anniversary of that day. Then he pointed out the sanctions for those who might disobey. 'Look at that wagon', said he pointing to one, 'and hear me give the word "Fire"'. The train was lit and the wagon exploded in a thousand pieces. 'That is what I will do to you if you do not behave yourselves'. Then he took a sheet of paper in his hands, tore it to shreds and threw the pieces to the winds. 'There go the treaties,' he exclaimed, 'Do you hear, no more treaties?' Nobody can say that this was not open diplomacy. British residents were appointed to each tribe, the Kaffir police under a British officer were strengthened and a strong military force was left in Kaffraria. The Rifle Brigade, 45th, 73rd, 2 squadrons of C.M.R. and a hundred gunners occupied 7 positions apart from the provincial capital itself, Forts Murray and Glamorgan on the Buffalo, with an outpost called Fort Grey on the road to King William's Town, Fort Hare on the Upper Tyumie, Fort Cox on the Upper Keiskamma, Fort White at the source of the Debe and Forts Wellington and Waterloo near the Gonubie.

Two men who had turned out on the side of the colonists, Kama and Hermanus Matroos, received grants of land for which they were not in the least grateful. The chiefs appeared to accept the new order but none intended to do so for one moment longer than he could possibly avoid.

The re-building of King William's Town was carried out almost entirely by the Rifle Brigade. Colonel Evelyn, then one of its young officers, wrote in the *R.U.S.I. Journal* (vol. xiv, p. 103) that 'They built a town, they built barracks, they built houses for their officers, some of "wattle and daub", some of bricks, and roofed with various materials. They also made an aqueduct some 3 or 4 miles long to supply the camp with water and for the purpose of irrigation. When we left, they had more than half built permanent barracks of stone. That was all done by one battalion, without neglecting any of its military duties . . . we had a daily parade, inspected arms &c, and saw that the men were in proper order and then dismissed them to their working parties.'

There were lessons from the war which had to be digested. Nobody suffered from the illusion that the War of the Axe would end the conflict. The only question was when would the next round begin and who would be found in which corner. Plainly the commandos were nearly a spent force. It was sure that they, or what was left of them, would fight in defence of their own farms but that was as far as they would go. At a period when the colony was approaching the moment of its greatest peril, relations between Boer and Briton were far worse than they had ever been and were still deteriorating. It was futile to rely on the British government maintaining an adequate force of regulars; indeed, the colonial government could count itself lucky if it were not deprived before long of those already there.

The great imponderable was the attitude of the Hottentots. From the earliest days, all experience had shown that these people, neither European nor Kaffir, were essential allies. Without their active help the wagons would not roll, the intelligence of Kaffir movements would not come in and the operation known as beating about the bush could only be carried on in a very limited way. Men would not dare to leave their farms if they could not rely on the Hottentot servants' loyalty during their absence. What would happen if the Totties were to be subverted and turned into active enemies simply did not bear thinking about. Nevertheless, the problem of how to keep them contented was not easily solved. If a Hottentot soldier was not permitted a little plunder, he would regard his joining the Army as equivalent to going to sea just to be sick. If he were permitted some, the settlers would be almost literally up in arms. Unless he were generously treated he would not remain a trustworthy soldier; if he appeared to be pampered, the others would be jealous. Add to this that the missionaries were unflagging in their efforts to persuade the men of Kat River and Theopolis that they were under-privileged, exploited and the true heirs of Southern Africa and it is not difficult to conclude that it was a question to which no answer could be the right one. Desertion continued, on much the same scale as in the past and merchants traded muskets and powder for ivory and cattle.

The Axe War had not ended in peace but with a conclusion on the Kaffir side that the best policy was to rest a little and recoup the losses. The border farmers knew this, but away to the west the colony was absorbed with other kinds of trouble inseparable from the growth of a new state.

CHAPTER 15

Colony in Danger

IT is necessary for continuity to leave the Colony for a while in order to see what had been happening beyond the borders. It will be remembered that the British garrison had left Natal at the end of 1839. It was not long before they returned. The Trekkers had established their long-desired Republic by 1840 with its seat of government at Pietermaritzburg, if government be the word for democracy carried to the point of anarchy. The republicans, wishing to enter into diplomatic relations with the Queen they had rejected as their sovereign, entered into correspondence with the Governor at Cape Town, then Sir George Napier. Napier was firmly of the opinion that Natal, properly so-called and not including much of the new settled land, should become a British possession. His motives were by no means ignoble; a poverty-stricken Republic which could not even pay its chief servants and which was constantly at war with the Zulu was not a comfortable neighbour; the farmers themselves would be better off with the might of nineteenth-century Britain behind them. Lord John Russell was in two minds about it. He did, however, go so far as to instruct the Governor to send a detachment of troops to Port Natal in June, 1840.

Quite a number of ships were now making their way round the Bluff into the harbour that would be Durban and from there it was not too difficult for goods to be transported into the interior. In particular, cargoes of muskets, powder and lead were believed to be reaching the Kaffirs through the tradesmen's entrance and the colonial government could hardly watch this unmoved.

Another factor was the need for protecting the friendly Kaffirs. The Pondo, the people lying beyond Xosa and Tembu and nearest to Natal, had had little or nothing to do with the colonists' wars with the Kaffirs. About the only contact with them had been a meeting between Major Dundas and the paramount chief Faku at the time of the rumour of Chaka's invasion in 1828. A Republican burgher force under Commandant-General Pretorius had recently attacked the Baca clan in reprisal for some cattle-stealing and practically wiped them out. Faku, though the Baca were his enemies, could easily see the same thing happening to him and appealed to the missionaries who wrote to the Governor. Napier was quite as disturbed by what had happened as was Faku. The Zulu pressure from the north had long been relaxed; if the burghers of Natal were to take the place of Chaka and drive the Pondo south, then inevitably the build-up of pressure on the Tembu and the Xosa would push them over the frontier once more.

Napier saw only one course open to him and on 28 January, 1841, Captain Thomas Smith of the 27th marched out of Fort Peddie with 2 companies of his own regiment, 50 C.M.R. under Captain H. D. Warden and 8 gunners under a subaltern. They were going overland to Port Natal by way of Pondoland. Correspondence between Cape Town and Maritzburg became bogged down over the usual question of whether or not the trekkers remained British subjects. After a long and hard march, broken by periods of waiting for orders, Smith, his force augmented to 263 all ranks and 3 small guns, arrived at 'the few scattered buildings that then constituted the town of Durban'. They made camp at the base of the Berea. Much to-ing and fro-ing went on between Smith and the Volksraad, ending in a demand that he should go.

A fight was provoked on 23 May when a number of cattle were seized by Boers from a transport in the harbour. That night Smith marched out with about a third of his command to attack the farmers by moonlight; he underrated his enemy, was soundly beaten with 16 killed and 31 wounded, and chased back to camp. His two field-guns fell into Boer hands. Smith's camp was prepared to resist immediate attack and it was in order to get the news to Grahamstown that Dick King made his famous ride. When he reached there after a nightmare journey of about 600 miles—almost exactly the same as Harry Smith had covered from the opposite direction—he saw Colonel Hare who, of his own initiative, sent another company of the 27th by sea from Port Elizabeth in a coaster which he chartered himself. The frigate *Southampton* brought more troops from Cape Town, collared on their way to India, and rounded the Bluff on 25 June. One broadside was enough to disperse the farmers who were lying in wait for her at the entrance to the inner harbour, and Smith was relieved.

The burgher forces lost heart at the reminder of the enormous resources still possessed by Queen Victoria and went back to their homes. Colonel Cloete, who had taken over from Smith, went by invitation to the Volksraad at Maritzburg to discuss matters but the uproar there made such a course impossible. In the end a kind of temporary *modus vivendi* was agreed for want of anything better. Smith, promoted Major, remained with a small garrison.

As the subsequent political events in Natal are not of imme-diate relevance to this narrative, it is enough to say that a British colony of Natal, bounded to the north by the Tugela and the Buffalo (not to be confused with the Buffalo river in British Kaffraria) came into existence in the autumn of 1845. It was probably inevitable, for the Republic had only kept in existence because of a vague idea that the King of Holland was going to make a take-over bid, but it was hardly calculated to inspire the Boers who had stayed behind with enthusiasm for the British cause. There had also been a treaty with Faku acknowledging him as paramount over the land between the Umtata and Umzimkulu rivers and from the Drakensbergs to the sea. Any Boers wishing to escape from the unsought status of British subjects must trek on.

Pretorius, erstwhile Commandant-General, and many of the original trekkers did exactly that. Harry Smith, having been on tour to arrange the affairs of the colony *vis-à-vis* Moshesh, chief of the Basuto, and Adam Kok, the Griqua leader, met them at the foot of the Drakensbergs in February, 1848. 'These families were exposed to a state of misery which I never before saw equalled except in Massena's invasion of Portugal . . . the scene here was truly heartrending.'

Smith and Pretorius had much in common and got on well together. The Boers agreed to remain where they were for the time being and Smith undertook to do his level best to meet their grievances, some of which he regarded as entirely legitimate. Pretorius had no personal feelings of kindness for the British as he had been rudely treated by Pottinger. Harry Smith, however, was a very different kind of man, with whom business might be done. It was from the Boer camp on 3 February that Smith proclaimed the existence of the Orange River Sovereignty; all the land between that river and the Vaal (which means 'yellow' in Afrikaans) would henceforth be subject to the Queen and organized into magistracies in the traditional fashion. Pretorius, who clearly understood the proclamation to cover only those settlers then north of the Vaal which excluded the country his people were occupying, raised no objection and set off to sound out opinion beyond the mountains. Smith was full of confidence that a happy issue would result for he had an unfeigned affection for the rugged Dutchmen and believed that they returned it. Unfortunately, personal feelings play only a limited role in public affairs; Smith installed Captain Warden as Resident in the Sovereignty and ordered him to send practically all his troops back to the colony. He would, he said, have none other than Boers there as soldiers.

His confidence was of short duration and Smith found none to approve his work. The home government very reluctantly accepted the accretion of 50,000 square miles of territory, (had they known what underlay it the answer would hardly have been the same) and issued a stern prohibition against any more feats of this kind. Pretorius found the farmers to share the feelings of the Privy Council but for different reasons. Only in Cape Town, where Smith was threatened with the erection of an equestrian statue, was enthusiasm demonstrated. The farmers of Winburg announced that they would never recognize British sovereignty over them and invited Pretorius to place himself at their head. Smith issued a manifesto suggesting that the disaffected should count their blessings, which he enumerated, and stating flatly that if they forced him to fight them, the crime would be theirs. Pretorius replied by expelling the British magistrate from Bloemfontein; Warden, with no troops, surrendered and was courteously escorted to Colesberg with all who wished to accompany him. The commandos of the Orange mustered at a camp on the banks of their river near Colesberg.

Smith, with a heavy heart, accepted the fact that his duty could only be done by undertaking a civil war. Never a man to shirk responsibility, he took personal command of the troops which gathered at Colesberg early in August. The Boers faced him from the bank opposite. On the 26th he crossed the river using a newly invented rubber pontoon, and began his march on Winburg. With him were about 1,200 men mainly drawn from the Rifle Brigade, the 45th and the 91st with 3 guns and a handful of C.M.R. for use as orderlies. If there had to be a battle between white men, Smith was not going to be open to the accusation of bringing in non-European troops to shoot or ride down his temporary enemies.

The battle was fought on 29 August near a farm called Boomplaats on the banks of the Krom Ellen Bok stream. It lasted no more than an hour. It is described by the then Lt Edward Holdich, Smith's A.D.C.: 'The White Company (or Europeans) of the C.M.R. under Lt Salis were ordered to cover the front of the column in skirmishing order, and to feel round the hills, but not to fire a shot unless fired upon. General and staff rode to the front with tried troops . . . the column had not advanced many paces when someone from the front cried out "There they are", and on looking in the direction intimated the hills were suddenly observed to be lined with Boers in their duffle jackets and white hats, who soon opened a brisk and regular fire, which at first did not cause much more harm than to throw the leading party rather into confusion. The order was given for the troops to go "threes about" and make way for the guns . . . the guns being brought to bear upon the enemy, the infantry were deployed into line (and the wagons laagered). The order of attack was Rifle Brigade to skirmish over the hills to the right; 45th to bear on the centre and follow up any opening made by the artillery; 91st to escort the guns and the C.M.R. to sweep round to the left, where the Boers were advancing from their right in good skirmishing order into the plains, with the evident intention of getting round our rear and in at the wagons. The 45th suffered a good deal in the centre, and the Rifle Brigade on the right being too eager and not taking sufficient advantage of cover lost a good many, Captain Murray being mortally wounded at the head of his company. The 91st were ordered in support of the 45th and the General's escort (a party of the Rifle Brigade) to form the escort for the guns.

'In about 20 minutes the first range of hills was cleared, and, pushing on with all arms, we observed the Boers re-formed at a farm house below, where they made a good defence from behind walls, and especially from an old kraal and the bed of the river. From the kraal Colonel Buller was shot, a bullet taking a piece out of his thigh and killing his horse. The guns were advanced over a stony hill, which in ordinary times would have been deemed impracticable, and by their steady fire . . . soon drove the rebels out of their defence works and they spread across an open plain that intervened in great disorder. (No cavalry available to pursue).'

For all practical purposes, the battle of Boomplaats was over. As was said of the battle of Pinkie, 'None took more joy of it than did the tooth which bit the tongue'. The army moved on to Bloemfontein, picking up a few prisoners—some of whom were allowed to go after a lecture by the General—and caring for the wounded who fell into their hands. Smith was smarting at having been deliberately potted by a Boer marksman, though his wound was very slight.*

Two prisoners in particular were singled out for attention. One was a deserter from the 45th, named Michael Quigley, taken in arms against his former comrades, who could expect nothing other than the firing squad. The other was a Boer named Dreyer; he appears to have been the only Boer actually made prisoner

---

* The history of the 45th (First Battalion The Sherwood Foresters) gives up a picture of Harry Smith at this time. 'Sir Harry was wherever the firing seemed to tell most and when he saw a few falling and their comrades stopping to look at them, he would ride up and shout "Forward, boys, forward". Ensign Fleming who had thoroughly enjoyed his first battle wrote home to his mother that he would rather go through Boomplaats again than face another parade.

with arms in his hands. The others had either disposed of their
roers or asserted that they were loyal men and their presence
near the battlefield was fortuitous. Colonel Buller, whose wound
cannot have been all that serious, was president of the court
martial which found both men guilty and pronounced sentence.
Both were shot in the presence of the assembled army in Bloemfontein on 4 September. Dreyer promptly joined the Boer
martyrology with the rebels of Slachter's Nek; nobody bothered
about the renegade soldier.

There followed a flag-showing march through a large part of
the Sovereignty, the building of yet another fort at Winburg
and a return to the colony at the end of the month. Whatever
the juridical rights and wrongs of the business, Boomplaats left
a bitter taste in every Boer mouth. The British were, as always,
magnanimous to a defeated enemy but it did no good. Every
Dutchman made a mental resolution never again to lift a finger
to help the government no matter in what straits the colony
might find itself. Looked at critically, one can say that their
attitude was unreasonable but in South African affairs reason
always seems to occupy a lowly place. Emotion is all that
matters and that commodity was not in short supply. None of
this was lost upon Sandili, Macomo, Kreili, the Hottentot
captains or the missionaries.

The year 1849 was one of preparation for the next round in
the struggle and it provided the Kaffirs with a useful bonus. The
Governor had been ordered by Lord Grey to prepare the colony
for the next stage of a genuine representative constitution. This
was well received at Cape Town for the settlers had been demanding something of the kind for several years past. All the good-
will towards Downing Street, however, was instantly dissipated
by one act of supreme folly emanating from that address. Lord
Grey suddenly decided that he had found a way of strengthen-
ing the numbers of able-bodied white men there and of saving
the tax-payer a good deal of money at one stroke. For a long
time now, people sentenced to transportation had been con-
signed to Botany Bay. Why should they not instead be sent to
the Cape? This would mean that the productivity of each ship
would be doubled and a substantial body of extra manpower
would be created at minimal cost. After all, argued the Cabinet,

the convicts were for the most part people who had committed only quite minor offences and, indeed, many of their crimes were only of a political nature. Irish peasants who had been forced into crime by the starvation of the Hungry Forties far outnumbered the thieves and murderers and surely men of the kind which filled the ranks of regiments like the 27th and 88th could only be an asset to a country desperately short of fighting men?

Neither the inhabitants nor the Queen's representative saw it in that light. The word 'convict' was one charged with emotion and it was insulting to the people who had made a country out of a wilderness to expect them to mingle on terms of equality with those from whom they would have drawn in their skirts at home. Smith forwarded on the petitions and begged Grey to alter his decision. The colonists formed an 'Anti-Convict Association' and besought the Governor not to allow the ship to land her reluctant freight. It made not the slightest difference. The transport *Neptune* was known to be on her way and all but one of the unofficial members of the Legislative Council resigned. The dilemma was, for Harry Smith, a cruel one. He was heart and soul with the colonists in their objection to what was being foisted on them but his public duty to obey orders was inescapable. The most he could achieve was to order that the convicts remain on board until the Queen's pleasure be known, which meant that he assured Grey that if he persisted on going through with his mad plan he must first find a new Governor.

The ship remained in Table Bay from September, 1849, to the end of January, 1850, during which time some fairly decorous rioting took place in the capital. As usually happens on such occasions, the troops were insulted and stoned as if the whole miserable business were of their contriving. Officials resigned in shoals and only a series of rather desperate expedients kept the government functioning at all. Grey gave way in the end and the unfortunate Irishmen continued their voyage to Van Dieman's Land. Not only the Boers but the British also were in a violent anti-government frame of mind when the next blow fell. Stockenstroom went back to London to agitate against what he said were the Governor's high-handed methods of carrying on his administration.

The missionaries, or many of them, continued to behave as the Jesuits were doing in Paraguay. To them, the souls and bodies of the non-white people were their private and exclusive preserve. It was for them to elevate these down-trodden and oppressed people and to restore to them the rights that had been so brutally wrested from them over the centuries. To assist in the consummation of this pious wish, a steady trade in fire-arms, many of them the latest type of percussion weapons, was carried on mainly by way of Natal. The merchants were Europeans almost to a man.

The 400 armed Kaffir police, under a British officer named Davies, had been doing good work in the tracing and recovery of stolen cattle. Davies, like many more senior officers in India a few years thence, was wholly unaware that they had been skilfully indoctrinated in their off-duty time and were as rotten as tinder. Very few, however, discerned the cloud on the horizon. Harry Smith, once the convict business was over, persuaded himself that prospects were fair and, in order to mute the strident demands for economy which came from London in every ship, he sent the 1st Battalion, The Rifle Brigade home in May, 1850.

No sooner had they gone than a great drought struck the colony; its worst effects were felt amongst the Gaikas, whose chiefs Sandili and Macomo were highly inflammable material. Colonel Mackinnon, the British Resident in Kaffraria and a man who could read the signs, became suddenly uneasy. Servants were leaving their masters, sometimes without even collecting their pay, and there were rumours of a new witch doctor of the Makana school plying his trade under the umbrella of Sandili. The rumour was true; Sandili was a feeble, malevolent creature of whom it could be said that his opinions were those of the last person with whom he had conversed. His only inflexible tenet was a bitter hatred of white men which the moderate feelings of his mother NSutu had only exacerbated. His principal councillor now was the seer Umlanjeni who explained with an unanswerable lucidity that the drought and its accompanying distress had been created by the wicked British in the exercise of their well-known talent for such things. He also asserted that by the infiltration of their residents they had darkened the faces of the chiefs by stripping them of traditional authority and that as soon as it suited them they would arrest all the Kaffir grandees and put them to death. The seed fell on fertile ground.

Harry Smith, as soon as he learnt of Mackinnon's misgivings, travelled to King William's Town to see things for himself. He summoned a meeting of all the chiefs on 26 October; all attended except Sandili. He was given three days in which to present himself, coupled with a threat that if he did not put in an appearance the Governor would 'throw him away'. Still Sandili did not come. The other chiefs went through the motions of approval and Smith wrote to Lord Grey that 'The crisis has passed, and, I believe, most happily'.

The crisis, in fact was still to come. Within a fortnight the usual symptoms appeared. Farms were raided by large bands of Kaffirs, crops were destroyed or carried off and cattle mysteriously disappeared in large numbers. Bitterly chagrined, Smith wrote to Grey on 5 December that, 'The quiet I had reported in Kaffirland, which I had so much and so just ground to anticipate, is not realized, and I start this evening'. He sailed in the transport *Hermes* with the 73rd and was not to leave the frontier for 16 months.

The scene at King William's Town reminded him forcibly of a similar one at Grahamstown 16 years earlier. Panic was striding across the eastern frontier on winged feet with families in flight to the west, anywhere where they could get out of the reach of bands of well-armed Kaffir warriors. The customary invitation was sent to the chiefs, desiring them to come to King William's Town on 26 October to discuss the menacing situation; not a solitary leader of the tribes of Gaika attended. This was regarded by the Governor as tantamount to a declaration of war, as no doubt was intended. Smith still cherished the delusion that the power of his name was all that would be needed to bring the recalcitrants to heel and he solemly purported to depose Sandili, appointing in his stead the popular Civil Commissioner, Charles Brownlee. The Kaffirs were totally unmoved by such at attempt to interfere with their well established hereditary principle and, while treating Brownlee with courtesy, quietly disdained to acknowledge his new status. Sandili for his part took himself off into the wilderness around

7. The Action at the Boomah Pass.

8. Sir Harry Smith's escape from Fort Cox.

9. & 10. Colonel Mackinnon's patrols destroying Kaffir kraals.

the headwaters of the Keiskamma and waited to see what would happen.

Sir Harry went back to Cape Town confident that he had arranged everything; he greatly deceived himself, for Sandili and his brother Anta soon made their position clear. They were the lawful chiefs and would assert their authority over their people no matter what any white man might say. They refused flatly to attend another meeting and were promptly declared outlaws, the government of both their clans being entrusted to their mother NSutu. Mackinnon set off at the head of such troops as he could muster to arrest them and Smith had to come back to King William's Town with every reinforcement on which he could lay hands following behind. Mackinnon's column was led by the Kaffir police of Davies who were to a man behind Sandili and who made it their business to ensure that he knew exactly what Mackinnon was going to do. Next behind them was a contingent of Hottentots from the C.M.R. and finally came the infantry, comprising parts of the 6th, 45th and 73rd.

The whole force numbered about 700 and Mackinnon was so certain that it would be a peace-time excursion that he had ordered all troops to march with unloaded weapons for fear of some accident which might provoke trouble. They were, of course, watched every step of the way by unseen eyes and when the column reached the Boomah Pass, a rugged defile between thickly wooded ridges which enforced movement in single file, Sandili decided that the moment had come. The Kaffir police and C.M.R. were suffered to pass without molestation. As soon as the first of the infantry appeared, thousands of Kaffirs debouched from their hiding-places and threw themselves on the British who were unable to fire a shot. However, the red-coats were no feeble antagonists and instantly charged into the bush and, after a hard battle in which steel played the dominant part, they put the Gaikas to flight. They lost in the process 23 killed and the same number wounded, but their fate was kinder than that of an outlying picket of the 45th. These men, 15 in number, had been waylaid and slaughtered in a fight against impossible odds and those who did not die instantly were tortured and decapitated. Mackinnon's men found them on the next day, on their way to Fort White by the track through

H

225

Keiskamma Hoek. Thus began the Eighth and greatest Kaffir War, on Christmas Eve, 1850.

On Christmas Day parties of Kaffirs appeared in the military villages of Woburn, Auckland and Juanasburg; they seemed peaceable enough and many joined the local people at their Christmas dinner. To the Kaffirs, however, it was not Christmas but St Brice's Day. At a signal, they turned on their hosts and stabbed them to death. The Gaika tribes sprang to arms and all but a handful of Davies' police went over, with their weapons, to their kinsmen. Only Pato did not join in, a fortunate circumstance since his people dominated all the country between King William's Town and the sea at East London.

It was not the result of any loyalty on Pato's part for, as most people believed, he was merely waiting for the most propitious moment to carry out his promise, made during the previous war, to 'convert Major-General Somerset's skin into a tobacco-pouch if he could only catch him, dead or alive'. The moment never came and he remained sufficiently active and friendly for Smith to pay a public tribute to him in the despatches which he wrote when the war was over. Until then, however, he was kept under strict surveillance. William King-Hall, the Captain of H.M.S. *Styx*, found him living in a back room at Fort Murray with a sentry over him, 'which is managed extremely well, the sentinel over his body supposed by the Kaffirs as a species of Guard of Honour'. King-Hall found little to admire in this essential ally, describing him as a 'drunken dog' who, when the Commissioner's back was turned, 'managed to beg a few shillings from the visitors with which he will probably buy liquor at King William's Town'.

It did not alter the fact that his adherence was essential, for Harry Smith was in serious trouble. On the day of the massacre he was in Fort Cox which, together with Fort White, came under immediate attack. The latter place was garrisoned only by 120 men from the 6th together with a number of wounded from the Boomah Pass battle. It was not a fort in the generally understood sense of the word but a wounded officer, Captain Mansergh of the 6th, assumed the command and 'every available man was set to work to build an earthen parapet, breast high, between each hut and to construct a couple of flanking bastions

at corresponding angles of the square'. Bissett wrote of Mansergh that 'he was one of the best war officers I have ever
known'. The defence of Fort White needed just such a man
and his small force, fired by such an example, fought off Sandili's
men in an earlier Rorke's Drift kind of battle which went on
for two days. Sandili, because of his lameness, took no part in
the assault but Bissett saw him plainly 'on Colonel Mackinnon's
cream-coloured charger', captured a few days before, directing
operations. Steady volley-firing on the word of command, in
the Duke's old style of Busaco and Waterloo, broke the attacks
and it was Mansergh's 'soldier-like qualities that saved the Fort
from being taken by the enemy'. Bissett himself, disabled from
taking any part in the fight, was cared for by Dr Fraser of the
C.M.R. with the assistance of a Mrs James who had arrived
fortuitously just in time and with a turkey as her companion.
Turning this over to the cook, she made herself generally useful.
Early in the siege, two European ladies whose farms had been
raided and their menfolk slaughtered, appeared before the Fort.
Sandili had permitted them to pass unharmed but, to amuse his
chiefs, had stripped them both naked before exhibiting them to
the garrison. Mrs James courageously went out with clothing
and brought them in.

Whittlesea also held out with its small and very scratch
garrison but it was on Harry Smith that the responsibility fell
and he was completely immured; from Fort Cox, all that could
be seen was that the entire bush seemed alive with excited
Kaffirs, confident in the knowledge that Umlanjeni had, by his
magic, rendered them invulnerable to the soldiers' bullets.
Somerset, going to the wars again at 57, tried twice to cut his
way through from Fort Hare but was forced back by sheer
weight of numbers. During the second engagement, in which he
lost a gun and 24 soldiers of the 91st, he managed to get a man
into Fort Cox with a message. On no account must Smith try
to sally out with his infantry alone for they would certainly be
cut to pieces. His only chance was to make a dash for King
William's Town with the 250 mounted men of the C.M.R. who
were with him.*

'This Sir Harry, in the daring, dashing way so characteristic

* 'Memoir of J. Montagu', W. A. Newman, London, 1855.

of him, gallantly did, wearing the forage cap and uniform of one of the Cape Rifles, and by this timely incognito he rode 12 hazardous miles through the desultory fire of the Kaffirs on the way to King William's Town. At the Debe Nek, about half way there, a strong attempt was made to intercept the Corps, but Sir Harry Smith and his escort vigorously spurred through their opponents and, after a smart ride reached the town having eluded six bodies of Kaffirs who little suspected how great a prize was then in their power'.

In all his long years of campaigning Smith had never been in greater danger than this. In the breach at Badajoz, before the long wall at New Orleans and at Waterloo he had risked a clean death by bullet or shell. If he had fallen into the hands of Sandili an unspeakable end by torture would almost certainly have been his fate. A few weeks later all the men who had formed his escort on this occasion deserted and went over to the rebels. It can only have been the affection in which the Hottentots held him and which his past behaviour and example had so well merited, that had inhibited them from selling him to the Kaffirs.

On the last day of 1850, Smith issued an uncompromising proclamation from King William's Town. 'He hopes that colonists will rise *en masse* to destroy and exterminate these most barbarous and treacherous savages, who for the moment are formidable. Every post in British Kaffraria is necessarily maintained.'

Formidable they were, but a sufficient military force would not take too long to put down the rebellion. There was, however, none to hand. The Boers adopted an attitude of dogged impassivity and the commandos would not ride. The British army was in its customary inter-war condition of having been pared to the bone by Parliament. Sir John Fortescue did not over-state the case when he said to his audience at Trinity in 1913 that 'It is actually a fact that at this time the military power of England was strained almost to breaking point by 3,000 naked savages'. In February, 1851, came bitter news; the Hottentots of Kat River, who had rendered such good service before, had to a man revolted and gone over to their hereditary enemies the Kaffirs. Smith, in the position of a climber on a high mountain who cannot go back but finds each hand or foot-hold crumbling to the touch, issued another call to arms. 'I regard this almost general disaffection of the coloured classes within the colony as of far greater moment than the outbreak of the Kaffirs.' His resources were pitifully small; four weak regiments (6th, 73rd, 45th and 91st) mustered only about 1,700 effectives and of these 900 made up the garrisons of a dozen posts. As he wrote to Grey, he had only 800 'available to control 4,000 Hottentot auxiliaries of doubtful loyalty and to meet the hordes of well-armed, athletic and intrepid barbarians in the field'.

These auxiliaries, for what they were worth, had been raised by Montagu, the Colonial Secretary. Normally an impeccable civil servant, when the rebellion came Montagu remembered that he had carried a colour long ago at Waterloo and the old soldier in him rushed to the surface. Without waiting for orders, he raised a levy of Hottentots on a six-month engagement and drafted them to the frontier. 'Your exertions are incredible, and they will enable me to take the field,' wrote his grateful Chief. With their aid he was able to re-victual the essential posts of Fort White and Fort Cox, but for the moment he could do little more.

He was forced to act on two lines, one based on King William's Town and maintained from East London and a more westerly one from Forts Hare and Beaufort to Grahamstown and Port Elizabeth. Forts Cox and White connected the two lines between Fort Hare and King William's Town. The first line was under command of Mackinnon while Somerset was responsible for the second, his headquarters being at Fort Hare.

It was Somerset, appropriately enough, who scored the first success. He had in all about 2,900 men of whom 900 were needed as the permanent garrisons of his forts. With a striking force drawn from the remainder and consisting almost entirely of loyal Boer farmers and C.M.R., he made a furious attack on the Kat River renegades within a matter of days after receiving the news of their defection. The rebels shut themselves up in Fort Armstrong but Somerset was not to be denied. His men stormed the fort on 23 February and brought back those who had survived the battle in chains to Fort Hare.

A fortnight later, 335 of the C.M.R. deserted from King

William's Town in a body; they included the men who had formed Sir Harry's escort. The reason appears to have been that these were Kat River men and they had been persuaded that all their friends and relations captured at Fort Armstrong were going to be summarily executed. Smith, terribly grieved at the mutiny in a Corps which he loved second only to his own Rifle Brigade, took the decision that the remainder, probably tainted, must go also before they did worse damage. All, save a handful of men whose loyalty was beyond doubt, were disarmed and sent home.

Smith had now no mounted troops at all in a country where they are of the essence. However, all experience of warfare of this kind had taught that the only successful strategy is to 'Go straight at 'em' and this was by no means uncongenial to the Commander-in-Chief for all his 63 years. Leaving his posts garrisoned, though they could no more halt the tide than do the piers of a bridge, he moved out to break up the force which was said to be collecting for the rescue of the prisoners at Fort Hare. With a force of which the 73rd was the core, he cut off the rebels on the Keiskamma and beat them soundly, spent the night of the 20th at Fort Hare with Somerset and, on the following day, defeated another band on the Tab'Indoda range. He rode back to King William's Town by way of Fort White, bringing with him 1,000 head of cattle and leaving many discomfited rebels of both kinds to realize that war against Harry Smith was not to be taken lightly.

Another small but useful success came his way. Hermanus Matroos was a man of mixed blood who had been a particular pet of successive governors. He had been useful to the Government in the war of 1835 and, in consideration of his services then, had been given a grant of some beautiful land on the Blinkwater stream a few miles north-west of Fort Beaufort. The settlers complained that, unlike them, Hermanus was not exacted of any quit-rent, so, in order to keep them happy and to perfect the grantee's title, Smith had required him to pay 'a mere trifle'. This seems to have exacerbated Hermanus, for his land soon became an African Alsatia to which every vagabond could safely resort. On the outbreak of the war, Hermanus threw in his lot with the rebels and, in a moment of supreme confidence, attacked Fort Beaufort with a horde of masterless men. His assault was beaten off and a nameless marksman on the walls brought down Hermanus with a musket-ball in the brain. So perished one of the most dangerous of the rebel leaders.

Though operations on the grand scale were out of the question, Smith was not inactive. Mackinnon scoured the Poorts of the Buffalo in mid-April and even penetrated some way into the Amatolas. Captain Tylden, R.E., in command of a garrison of 60 volunteers and 300 Fingoes, his Kat River men of the C.M.R. having gone over to the enemy, defended Whittlesea (founded by Smith and named after his home town in Cambridgeshire), fought off a dozen attacks and probably saved the colony from invasion. Sandili, however, was unaffected. 'Had the Kat River Rebellion and the defection of the Cape Corps not presented themselves', wrote Smith to his sister Alice (for whom the village of that name was christened), 'Sandili's reign would have been a transient one. I have been obliged to steer a most cautious course, one contrary to my natural desire in predatory warfare, but imperatively imposed on me by the dictates of prudence and discretion, my force being composed generally of a race excitable in the extreme . . . a few spirited farmers have performed good service, but where are the men who so gallantly fought with me in 1835—Van Wyks, Greylings, Nels, Rademeyers, Rynevelts etc? Once more, my advice to the frontier inhabitants is to rush to the front'.

They showed little enough enthusiasm for taking it. The heart of the war was plainly in the Amatolas. Pato was steadfast and Kreili was, on the face of things, lying low. It was the children of the favoured Gaika and their Hottentot allies who had brought the colony to this pass. As soon as troops became available, it was to the mountains that they must go.

There was a school of thought in the Colony during the earlier stages of the war that held Smith to be ill-served by his senior commanders. Mackinnon in particular was taken to task for his slowness which seemed to verge on lethargy. An article in the *R.U.S.I. Journal* for 1851 (vol. 3, p. 28) asserted that this shortcoming won for him the nickname of 'Regulate the Pace' while Captain William Hall R.N., confided to his diary that 'Not a word is said about Mackinnon's patrol who it is generally supposed will do nothing to speak of. I have never heard anyone mention him except to accuse him of very great incompetency and only fit for an office'. Much odder things, it seems, were being attributed to Henry Somerset. Hall again is the source of information. 'The general expression is "That fellow Somerset made his fortune by waggon hire last war and is trying to do it this." He wishes to prolong the war from getting so much more pay and allowances. The Cape Corps is a species of family monopoly, to him, having his relatives in it as officers, and they also say as men, bastard children in the ranks . . . from two sources I was informed that although he had many empty waggons on his return from the Vlei, he hired 3 at £1 a day each from a Trader named Crouch to whom he is said to owe money . . . they also publicly report that he had 3 or 4 prostitutes—Hottentots—with him, and from the care he takes of himself, travelling with every luxury and convenience, keeping well in a General's place; these patrols which are killing work to all under his command are a species of pleasure picnic to him with the knowledge of his getting out of debt by the prolongation of the war. It is an indisputable fact that during the previous wars many waggons hired by him were his own under the name of others.'

Captain Hall was an honourable man so it must be assumed that these stories were indeed current, probably to a large extent due to the fact that the General bore a famous name. Much the same things had been said about the financial transactions of Marlborough and with probably the same degree of veracity. One can be quite certain that if there had been any truth in them, Henry Somerset would not have remained long under the command of Harry Smith but would have been brought sharply to a court-martial. In particular the introduction of the name of Mr Crouch ought to settle the matter. This gentleman enjoyed much notoriety as the principal supplier of firearms and ammunition to the Kaffirs, from which occupation he amassed a substantial fortune. The only intercourse with him which Somerset would have welcomed would have been the command of a firing squad. The charge of being father of his regiment can hardly be taken seriously. His eldest son, a legitimate sprig of the great house of Beaufort, certainly served under his command.

232

It is not easy to believe that he would have been willing to command a troop of his father's colourful bastards. Liaisons with Hottentot women were, of course, not unknown but they were usually confined to the back-veld Boers who had the choice between taking one of them or having no woman at all. Henry Somerset, it is true, enjoyed a full share of Plantagenet lustiness for at the age of 54 he married as his second wife a lady of 17 years. The fact that his Hottentots and his alone remained true to their salt could have a more charitable and creditable explanation than the one apparently bruited about.

Luckily quite a lot of information survives about the equipment and training of the British troops already in the colony when the war started. Captain Gawler of the 73rd came out of retirement in 1874 long enough to deliver a lecture on it at the R.U.S.I. for the edification of officers about to embark for Ashanti. The standard infantry weapon was still a smooth-bore musket though flint had at last given way to percussion. This meant that rain no longer rendered shooting impossible but it was a fiddling business taking the small copper caps from their box and putting them firmly on the nipples with wet fingers. Gawler advocates the ideal weapon as being a double-barrelled gun, something after the fashion of the modern Paradox, with one barrel rifled for the last few inches and loaded with ball while the other threw an ounce and a quarter of buckshot. Undoubtedly many weapons of this kind were in use by those who could or had to provide their own arms. A carbine to much the same specification was ordered from Enfield Lock for the 12th Lancers (who did not arrive until October) but it was not delivered in time to be put into service. Gawler did not find much use for artillery in bush warfare because it held up movement and hardly ever had a worthwhile target; rockets, in Gawler's opinion, could 'do all the frightening that was necessary' and the 24 lb. Hale rocket and tube were certainly used to good effect.

On minor tactics, the 73rd (and doubtless other regiments also) were soundly taught; the first two essentials were silence and quickness of thought. Men were taught to forget the upright military carriage and to stroll along bush paths at a comfortable slouch, never raising their voices above a whisper. When in

H*

single file, as they usually had to be, at every halt men moved a few paces into the bush, turning outwards; the leading man faced to the right, the next to the left and so on. If the thickness of the bush was not too great, flankers moved on either side of the path, looking up into the trees and down into the thickets. The drill for an ambush on a path was simple and effective; a bend was the best place, where a few men could fire one volley as soon as the enemy were at point-blank range. This done, the remainder of the party who had been disposed on one side of the track and parallel to it, hurled themselves on to the shocked Kaffirs with whatever weapon each man fancied, bayonet, axe, knife or musket-butt. If ambushed themselves, they were instructed not to stand up and shoot but to rush straight at the Kaffirs who seldom, if ever, waited to fight it out. On one thing Gawler insisted; bush is not as impenetrable as it looks. As he explained, 'you may leave bits of your uniform on it but the Kaffir will leave bits of his skin.' It was a little overstated but the regiments found out the truth of it and became skilful at their work.

Uniforms were a problem, for the Army at home was still tied to the fashions of that great military haberdasher, King George IV. Nearly all this had to go. The ridiculous coatee was discarded for a simple and practical blouse made locally from grey canvas. Next to follow was the shako, in place of which the forage cap with an improvised leather peak made a hat which kept the sun out of the eyes and did not catch in every branch. Boots disintegrated as time went on and were replaced by anything their owner could find; beards were in fashion and as these were mature men, long-service soldiers on 21-year engagements, they soon looked as tough as they were.

The prisoners from Kat River, under strong guard at Fort Hare, were tried by court-martial and 47 of the ring-leaders were sentenced to death. It fell to the lot of Harry Smith to make the agonizing decision as to whether or not they should receive clemency and he wrestled with the problem for a long time before taking a final determination. As a young company officer he had been shocked when, after the assault on Ciudad Rodrigo, he had been compelled to witness the execution of a number of British deserters who had been taken in the act of firing on their own comrades and bringing down many of them. His view of retributive justice was as inflexible as that of any other man of his day, as the executions of Dreyer and Quigley had shown, but he had to balance the deterrent value of putting these men before a firing squad for the same reason that Admiral Byng had been so treated against the chance that such action might cause the Hottentots who still remained loyal to go over to the enemy. In the end he came to the conclusion that the public service would be better carried out if they were spared and he commuted the death sentences to transportation for life. This action was ill-received by many a colonist; Somerset in particular was furious and felt, with some reason, that he had been badly let down. The Boers were swift to contrast the treatment meted out to Dreyer who, like many of the Slachter's Nek men, had not been proved to have shed the blood of any man, with that of the Hottentots who had almost certainly been guilty either as principals or accessories in atrocious murders. The only people to be pleased were the Exeter Hall fanatics at Cape Town and even these regarded the act of mercy as having been inspired by no more Christian virtue than naked fear. It is hard to disagree with the conclusion of Sir John Fortescue who observed that 'there can be no doubt that some of the ring-leaders deserved to be shot and it would not have been amiss if certain of the missionaries had shared their fate'.

By the end of February things were beginning to look up a little. Thanks largely to Mr Montagu, Smith now mustered about 9,000 men of one kind and another, of whom about a third could be called regulars. The number included the loyal C.M.R. and a small but extremely useful body of blue-jackets and Royal Marines from the ship's company of H.M.S. *Castor* who could turn their hands to almost anything. On the 25th he sent out a strong patrol of about 400 of his precious regulars and 1,600 Fingoes to scour the country between King William's Town and the Keiskamma. They found it almost empty. Hardly a Kaffir or a cow was to be seen and only a little musket fire from extreme ranges interfered with their progress. He despatched another on 5 March under Mackinnon, this time in greater strength and with the addition of a couple of field guns, to re-victual Fort White and Fort Cox. This time, the Kaffirs stuck

235

closer to the column and made some determined attacks on it in the course of the return march. Mackinnon, however, knew his business and was entirely at home in the country. He led a skilful counter-attack in which his foot-soldiers drove the Kaffirs under the waiting guns which came suddenly to life and blasted them to pieces. More than a hundred corpses were counted and the loss to the column was trifling. A few days later a third sweep into the upper reaches of the Buffalo found nothing but emptiness. The work was necessary but it exhausted the soldiers and did little to encourage them in the belief that victory was just around the corner.

Another serious blow fell on 13 March; at King William's Town itself, 43 men of the C.M.R. deserted in a body, taking their arms and equipment with them. Smith acted with the speed of desperation. At first light the Regiment was paraded, dismounted, the 6th being posted on one flank and the 73rd on the other. In rear were the guns, loaded with grape and the port-fires burning brightly in the gloaming. Harry Smith himself gave the order to ground arms. After an instant of hesitation, the C.M.R. obeyed; all except the European element were dismissed from the army on the spot and so 300 invaluable mounted infantry were lost. It was a scene to become painfully familiar in India a few years thence and the best that can be said of it is that Smith, devoted to the Corps though he was, did not allow himself to be deluded into believing that rottenness could not exist amongst tried men. The consequences of such misplaced loyalty by officers to their coloured troops was to be extremely costly in 1857 and there can be no doubt that Smith's promptitude and realistic hardening of his heart saved the colony from a great catastrophe. The same thing, on a smaller scale, happened at East London and it seems a moral certainty that the two were concerted. Only Somerset's men remained true to their colours, a striking example of what the personality of a single senior officer of the best quality can do with half-civilized soldiers.

Smith, in a fashion typical of him, decided that the only course open to him was to strike as hard as he could with what he had got. Word was coming in that the future of the Kat River prisoners was the moving force behind the mutinies and that a serious attempt was going to be made to release them. The deserters were all reported as having headed for the Amatolas and it was plain that the stroke would come from that direction towards Fort White where the prisoners were under guard. This was all Smith needed to know. With some 2,000 infantry, whose hard-core was the greater part of the 6th and 73rd, together with 3 guns and a small band of volunteer cavalry, his only mounted men, he moved on Fort White early on the 18th. At dawn next day he divided his little force into 4 columns with which he manœuvred the large body of Kaffirs opposed to him on to the slopes of an isolated hill named Pegu. As soon as they were all driven in, Smith stormed the hill with his regulars, driving the fleeing Kaffirs on to the spears of his Fingoes who were spread out to intercept their retreat. About 40 or 50 Kaffirs were killed; Smith's men had not a single casualty.

But he had by no means finished with them yet. After a day of rest at Fort Hare he set out again on the 23rd, westwards to the Keiskamma, where he collected 1,000 head of cattle and destroyed all the crops he could find. On a day of intense heat and with no water beyond what they carried in their canteens, his men covered 36 miles in 16 hours and fought many petty engagements in the course of which the Kaffirs were severely punished. His own casualties did not reach double figures and on 25 March he returned to King William's Town reasonably contented with what had been achieved. If it had not been exactly another Waterloo it had at least served to demonstrate to Hottentot and Kaffir alike that Harry Smith was still very much in the field and had no intention of walling himself up inside the forts.

All accounts tally, for once, in showing that these displays of energy and offensiveness put heart into his men from the toughest regular Highlander to the most peripheral Fingo camp-follower. Even so, the initiative was still with the insurgents and reports continued to flow in of plots and treachery, even in King William's Town itself. Nor was this all Smith had to contend with. Away to the north lay the kingdom of Moshesh, probably the most intelligent and statesmanlike leader black Africa had produced. From the debris of wrecked tribes left behind by the Zulu he had painstakingly built up a nation known as the Basuto with whom the colony enjoyed good relations and were conscious of no quarrel. Moshesh had been sedulously proselytized by some of the more thoroughly mission-trained Hottentots up to the point when he himself took the field. This was the catalyst that brought out the hangback Boers to ride knee to knee with the British; on 25 March they fell upon Moshesh and scattered his army, inflicting some 200 casualties in the process. It was a fortunate stroke for the Basuto were fighters to be reckoned with and were to be encountered again in greater strength. For the moment, however, a threat that might have developed into something extremely serious had been warded off. If the Boers of the old frontier districts had done their duty in the same way, the current war could have been greatly shortened. As it was, Smith could do no more than cling on to his line of outposts, hitting out whenever opportunity came his way, while the usual pillaging bands murdered and ravaged unchecked up and down the eastern marches of the colony.

The reinforcements he need so sorely were slow to come although the Duke, still Commander-in-Chief at 82, was throwing the weight of his great authority behind the Government in its efforts to conjure up numbers of trained fighting men from the army which it had so studiously neglected for so long. Only 300 details for regiments already in the colony came during April but on 12 May there arrived at Table Bay the ships bearing the 74th Highlanders (Highland Light Infantry), diverted from service in the Mediterranean. Steam had not yet worked any great wonders over shipping times, for the passage had taken 58 days. They were sent straight on to Algoa Bay having had time only to dump their heavy kit.

During the same month Smith, at his wits' end for mounted troops, elected to take the risk of re-enlisting some of the disbanded C.M.R. It seemed a reasonably safe bet, he argued to himself, for they had seen the speed and weight of his hand and were not blind to the fact that he, more than any other man but Somerset, had dominion over the debatable lands everywhere save in the Fish River bush and the Amatolas themselves. A hundred and twenty old soldiers came back and served for the rest of the war without giving further cause for anxiety; as time passed, more and more came in and the threat of organized mutiny seemed to have passed. Somerset and Mackinnon were regularly raiding the old grounds of the upper Buffalo and Keiskamma and were continuing to bring in cattle even though not in vast numbers. Now and then the pendulum swung back; as the 74th were marching from Port Elizabeth to Grahamstown the Hottentots of Theopolis, 25 miles south of that place, decided that the moment was opportune for them to revolt in their turn. What they expected to gain from an insurrection at this moment is not easy to understand but the conjoint preachings of certain missionaries and Umlanjeni seem to have achieved their natural consequence. However, far more important than the defection of one small mission was the fact that Pato continued not merely unnumbered amongst the enemy but a positive friend, as Smith readily acknowledged in his official reports. On 16 May, the 74th arrived within his dominions and were carried ashore by naked Fingoes, 'to the intense amusement of both parties' as Captain King of that Regiment tells us.

The 74th did not linger at Port Elizabeth, which King found to be 'rather a dull-looking place at first sight' but moved straight on towards Grahamstown. Again King tells us something of how the young Highlanders first came into contact with an older Africa than we know today. 'This dense and beautiful bush extends for miles on every side; its solitary depths, impassable except to Kaffirs and wild beasts hundreds of which latter roam through it undisturbed. Tigers, hyaenas, jackals and wild cats abound; and buffalos and elephants are still occasionally seen, of which we had convincing evidence in the fresh spoor of three of the latter, whose enormous footprints were distinctly visible and made one's heart beat with excitement at the idea of being in a country where such noble beasts roamed wild and unrestrained. The wagon track was in many parts very beautiful, sometimes so narrow that the overhanging trees, covered with festoons of grey pendant lichen, met above it; in others opening out into smooth green lawn-like patches surrounded by brilliantly flowered trees and shrubs as the crimson Boerboom and the yellow mimosa with its giant milk-white thorns, everywhere clusters of the beautiful pale blue plumbago with numberless aloes and occasional euphorbias rising to the height of 30 feet; the underwood filled with the "stapelia", "gasteria", and other

varieties of cactus. The heat of the sun was again most oppressive, shut in as we were between walls of bush so close that not
a breath of air found its way through. The oxen were so completely done up that they could scarcely draw the heavily laden
wagons through the deep sand and numbers fell to die by the
roadside or were abandoned a prey to the wild beasts and vultures. Halting for half an hour to rest the cattle at the top of a
heavy hill, a lovely view presented itself; in the foreground, the
road we had just passed, winding down into the bush below;
beyond that, a vast extent of flat, thickly wooded country; and,
far off, a fine chain of rugged mountains, mellowed by the purple
atmosphere of the distance into a mist-like softness'. There
sounds a touch of wistfulness in this for other purple mountains
but the buildings inhabited by man bore some striking differences
from Scotland. King tells of houses 'enclosed by stockades and
barricaded with boxes, chests and barrels filled with sand and
piled up against the doors and windows' and of churches turned
similarly into strong points.

The Highlanders in the course of their march heard many
stories illustrative of the horrors of a native rising and they
would not have been flattered had they known that certain newspapers at home were likening the perpetrators to the ancient
Scots fighting bravely for their hearths and homes. They were
not greatly taken by Grahamstown, 'a straggling place situated
in the midst of a bare piece of country surrounded by equally
bare hills' but they were not long detained there. The Hottentots
of the unfelicitously named Theopolis had gathered in a number
of deserters and, after murdering all who did not go along with
them, barricaded themselves in the mission buildings. From
Grahamstown to Theopolis is a matter of about 25 miles and
the 74th were marched out to deal with the rising, their pipers
at the head of the column. In the course of the day's march they
were joined by Henry Somerset, at last promoted Major-General
(as he had first seen battle at Vittoria as a Cornet of horse, his
advancement after nearly 40 years' unbroken service can hardly
be ascribed to unfair aristocratic influence). As the renegades
caught the sound of the skirling, mountain music they broke
without firing a shot and took refuge in the friendly bush where
they remained as a nuisance for a long time to come.

11. The Capture of Fort Armstrong, 22 February, 1851.

12. Kaffir women and children seek refuge from the war in a blacksmith's forge near Fort Beaumont.

13. The Attack on Colonel Fordyce's column by Macomo's men, 8 September, 1851.

14. Colonel Eyre of the 73rd Foot, who led one half of Mackinnon's patrol on the Fish River.

Having scattered the proselytes, the Highlanders continued their march to Fort Cox while Smith sent out Mackinnon to patrol the Keiskamma in case the dispersed Hottentots tried to link up with the tribes in that area. Nothing of substance happened and so Smith decided that, even though there was some threat to Grahamstown from the large vagabond bands, he could make another thrust into the Amatolas where the most and best of the Kaffir warriors were certain to be found. No less important than bringing them to battle was the fact that here also lay their main sources of supply of food and, little though he liked the idea, Smith was resolved on putting this out of his enemy's reach by one means or another. On 26 June, three convergent columns moved from their positions, Somerset heading northeastward from Fort Hare, Colonel Cooper marching due east from Fort Cox while Mackinnon worked north along the upper reaches of the Keiskamma and the Gwilli Gwilli. During the last 3 days of June they succeeded between them in carrying off 2,000 cattle and destroying large areas of growing crops in addition to inflicting some casualties in a score of tiny engagements. Destruction of foodstuffs on which a simple folk depend for their existence sounds a brutal means of waging war and Harry Smith, who was as convinced and instructed a Christian as any missionary, was revolted by it. Nevertheless, if the war was not to drag on for ever, the thing had to be done and all past experience had demonstrated that it was the most humane way to persuade the rebels to come in and surrender.

Successful though the enterprise had been, it was no more than one more laborious step towards a distant goal, for Smith still had nothing like enough men for a decisive stroke. If the Boers had been willing to turn out the war would already have been over, but they showed not a sign of willingness to do more than watch uninterestedly. Sandili and Macomo concentrated their fighting men more closely in the 20 square miles of high, broken and thickly wooded country to the western end of the Amatolas around Fuller's Hoek and the Blinkwater—names soon to become very familiar in England—while Kreili took care of the Fish River bush. Somerset made a foray into the Amatola fastness, compendiously known as the Waterkloof, early in July with the object of allowing the Kaffirs no respite. It was

241

excruciatingly hard work, for at that season of the year the ground is white with frost at 6 a.m. and such is the rate of change of temperature that within 3 hours the direct heat of the sun cannot be borne. Sandstorms are a commonplace. Somerset had no comfort not shared by the least of his men save for the small canvas dog-kennel called a patrol-tent which most officers used; at a time when the army officer at home was usually depicted as a witless, languid fop utterly ignorant of his business and incapable of constructing the simplest sentence without the helpful interjection of 'Haw haw' once or twice, it is refreshing to know that there was no shortage of gentlemen of another kind. Nearly all the officers of the South African Army, as it was called, studied their trade as meticulously as any other professionals.

The time coincided with great advances in the manufacture of fire-arms and the famous London makers were turning out beautifully finished weapons which were not only vastly more accurate and reliable than anything known before but which were also built with such skill and care as to be works of art in themselves. Every officer under orders for the Cape who could afford it provided himself with a rifle or pair of rifles whose case and mountings bore the name of Lancaster, Grant or some other famous maker. With these and with a muzzle-loading revolver of 5 chambers made by Colt or Adams, the officer's personal armoury was complete and his sword was relegated to the heavy baggage. Shooting became a fashionable sport with all ranks and the standard improved out of all knowledge. It was not only thanks to the private weapons, for every kind of experimental service arm was sent to Kaffirland for trial and report. The Minié was first fired there in battle; the Rifle Brigade arrived with the Brunswick rifle, issued eleven years earlier and possibly the worst arm ever given to British soldiers, and there was a large-bore rifle emanating from Edinburgh which projected a small conical shell. Men now began to consider the effective range of the infantry as something better than 800 yards and there were instances recorded of groups of Kaffirs being broken up at distances of nearly three-quarters of a mile. Musketry (the word is still correct, for 'rifle' is no more than a diminutive of 'rifled musket') was encouraged as never before, since there were now weapons available that would throw as straight as a man could hold them and prizes were freely given by units and individual officers. If the British public in the years immediately before the Crimean War had known more of the quality of the army officers not under its immediate eye, it might have realized that for every 7th Earl of Cardigan it could show several Fordyces and Mackinnons. Of the latter Bissett wrote that 'I have seen [him] advance on horse-back with an attacking party against an enemy posted in strong positions smoking his cigar in the coolest manner while bullets were falling about him like hail.'

Major-General Somerset remained in the Waterkloof beating about the bush to the full extent permitted by his meagre resources; in the end the Kaffirs managed to compel his withdrawal by the expedient of firing the grass and thus destroying all the forage for his horses. Harry Smith had been making life a misery for his former protégé, Kreili, in the Fish River bush; once more it was a series of paltry encounters by patrols but, inglorious though they were, they wore down the strength of the Kaffirs more than they did that of the colonists and in August there came feelers for peace put out through the agency of Pato. Smith was far from certain whether symptoms equally consistent with a change of heart or weariness of war meant the beginning of the end but before he was under the necessity of taking a decision it became plain that the explanation was only that Kreili was running short of ammunition. Commercial gentlemen with white faces soon put the matter to rights for him and the war went on.

Reinforcements, however, were now beginning to arrive in significant numbers. On 8 August the 2nd Queens touched at Cape Town after an 86 day passage and were sent straight on to East London. From there they went by march route to join the 73rd at Grahamstown, and before the end of the month the reserve battalion of the 12th (The Suffolk Regt) had come after an uncommonly long passage from Mauritius. September saw the further addition of the 60th Rifles and a couple of hundred drafts for regiments already in the colony and October at last brought a regiment of regular cavalry, the 12th Lancers.

Now Smith could begin to formulate plans for a serious offensive against the citadels of the enemy. Up to now he had reckoned himself fortunate that his combination of small forces and *ad hoc* levies had been able to prevent the colony from being submerged under a great Kaffir wave and the defenders of Whittlesea, Fort White and the other places alone had saved it from this fate. The two purposes now to be effected were to drive the Rarabe tribes across the Kei for good and to clean out the Amatolas in general and the Waterkloof in particular. The latter task was entrusted to Colonel Fordyce of the 74th, Captain King's C.O. and one of the very best officers ever to serve in South Africa.

King's description of the country over which he was to operate is well known but it can bear repetition. 'Nothing more difficult and trying can be imagined than our laborious progress through this all but impracticable forest, studded throughout with enormous masses of detached rock, overgrown with wild vines, twining asparagus trees, endless monkey ropes and other creepers, so strong and so thickly interlaced as almost to put a stop to our advance; concealed, moreover with dense thorny underwood, concealing dangerous clefts and crevices, and strewn with fallen trees in every stage of decay, while the hooked thorns of the "wait a bit" clinging to our arms and legs, snatching the caps off our heads and tearing clothes and flesh, impeded us at every step'.

To clear this out Fordyce was given 250 of his own Highlanders and 400 Fingoes. Ten times as many troops would not have been an excessive over-insurance but they were not there for Smith to give. Fordyce's immediate objective was the Kroome range with its offshoots, the Blinkwater and the Waterkloof, its forests and mountains being generally reckoned impenetrable. It was from these robbers' strongholds that the bands of marauders were ravaging the colony and Macomo was giving a convincing performance as the Old Man of the Mountains. Fordyce, like everybody else, had to learn by experience. He led his column to the top of the Kroome range from the south on 7 September and having made their way there by tremendous exertions, the men found an open space. Here Macomo attacked them, to be beaten off without great difficulty but with the expenditure of too much precious ammunition.

Fordyce, unable to remain, came back by the same route. As

soon as they were in the forest, Macomo's people hurled themselves at the column. The Highlanders stood their ground but
the Fingoes, or some of them, panicked; they rushed down-hill,
knocking over cursing Scotchmen in their flight, and there was
a moment of confusion when things looked very ugly. The Highlanders, however, remained masters of the situation and drew off
in decent order, though not unscathed. They were fortunate not
to lose more than 17 killed and wounded but the Bandmaster,
Mr Hartung (who probably had no business to be there) was
bowled over in the rush and fell into Macomo's hands unhurt.
Macomo personally helped in torturing him to death, an operation which took three full days and of which a detailed description survives; it was given by a Kaffir girl who was compelled to
watch it all and who fled later because she was starving. Her
deposition was later reduced into writing by a magistrate.

Mackinnon, in command of affairs in the south, was also
having his share of misfortune. He started to patrol the Fish
River at about the same time as Fordyce began in the Amatolas;
his force was a stronger one, two battalions (Queens and 6th)
each about 400 strong, 152 men of the 73rd and 50 Royal
Marines, with some 300 Fingo levies. The force was big enough
to warrant its division into two halves, under Colonel Michel of
the 6th and Colonel Eyre of the 73rd respectively. A company
of the Queen's, who had been only a very short time in Africa
and had almost no experience of bush-warfare, lost its way in
the pitiless jungle and was cut off. The all-seeing Kaffirs, hardly
able to credit their good fortune, attacked them and killed 32,
including an officer, wounding another 21. The casualties to the
remainder of Mackinnon's force did not exceed about a dozen.

To a generation brought up on losses of world war scales,
deaths and wounds numbering rather less than usually occur
during a slack week-end on the roads in summer hardly seem
matters over which too much excitement should be engendered.
It did not seem like that to the politicians of the year of the
Great Exhibition. The Cabinet had sent troops to South Africa
and had a right, according to their thinking, to expect a mighty
victory in return, but they had not got one. It must therefore
follow that the Commander-in-Chief was incompetent, a conclusion that Cabinets are seldom slow to draw. The fact that a

battalion, having arrived at the Cape, had a further sea voyage of 500 miles and a long march to endure before it had even reached the place from which it could begin operations was, to put it charitably, not comprehended by civilian intelligences. Even less would they understand that a regiment which had been engaged, perhaps, in keeping rioting weavers in order or maintaining some kind of peace in Connemara was not fully equipped to take on ten times its number of naked and ferocious savages in country the like of which the soldiers have never dreamt of.

British soldiers were well known to be able to overcome any adversary at any time and in any place against any odds and the failure to achieve a swift and decisive victory over some 15 to 20 thousand Kaffirs, well armed with sophisticated weapons, well supported by renegade Hottentots and well supplied by enterprising merchants, obviously must have been occasioned entirely by the personal shortcomings of Harry Smith, and the Cabinet began to wonder in its bewildered way whether he ought not to go. They did not consult the Commander-in-Chief of the Army, for the Duke had a habit of being short with the ignorant and presumptuous.

Smith, unconscious of the fact that he was now on probation, continued to unfold his plan. He had other things exercising his mind aside from the immediate operations; Moshesh and his Basutos were becoming restive and, if that were not enough, so was Panda, King of the Zulu. At the beginning of the war Panda had let Sir Harry know that his warriors were bored with doing nothing but listen to the veterans tell of their past glories and would not in the least mind washing their spears in the blood of the Xosa. Smith sent a polite message of thanks. Panda's impis would have minced Sandili and Macomo but would hardly have been agreeable neighbours in their stead. Now Panda's army seemed as if it might be getting out of hand in its desire to fight somebody. It was not really likely that they would take on Harry Smith but it would have been imprudent to withdraw the 600 regulars in the Sovereignty who would have been very useful to Mackinnon or Fordyce.

CHAPTER 16
The Strongholds Fall

CHIEF amongst the enemies behind his back with whom Harry Smith had to contend was the Member for East Cornwall, Sir William Molesworth. Sir William was a rancorous man in permanent opposition to almost everything; his reputation as a professional protester inevitably meant that any cause which he might be pleased to espouse became as a result suspect in the eyes of right-minded men. On 10 April, 1851, he made a savage and ignorant attack on Smith in the Commons, accusing him of burdening the Empire by the annexation of 105,000 square miles of new territory and provoking the troubles in the Cape by 'highhanded and despotic behaviour'. Smith's view of the matter comes out clearly in a letter to his sister:

'King William's Town, 18th June, 1851
Waterloo
'My dearest Alice,
 'I wish I was half the active fellow now I was then, for I have need of it, seeing I am Her Majesty's "Despotic Bashaw" from Cape Point to Delagoa Bay to the east, and to the great newly-discovered lake to the north-west—without a legislature, and in the midst of a war with cruel and treacherous and ungrateful savages and renegade and revolted Hottentots. These Hottentots have been treated as the most favoured people, enjoying all the rights, civil and religious, of the inhabitants at large of the

Colony—fed as a population when starving—yet have these ungrateful wretches in great numbers (not all) revolted and joined their hereditary and oppressive enemy the Kaffir, who drove them from the Kei over the Fish River, and who have destroyed them as a nation.

'I have had so much to do and some little anxiety of mind, although I sleep like a dormouse, that I have not written lately to one so dear to me, but Juana has. The war-making Kaffirs are cowed by the continued exertions among them of my numerous and vigorous patrols, but they are in that state of doggedness they will neither come in nor fight. By every communication I have open to me, I offer peace to the people, but the chiefs must await my decision, their conduct has been so treacherous, cunning, and deceitful. I have succeeded in maintaining in peace and tranquillity nearly one-half of the population of British Kaffiraria, those fortunately next to the sea, while the Gaika Kaffirs, natives of the mountains adjoining the Hottentot great location of the Kat Province, are all at war. This shows my system cannot be oppressive, or I should have no friendly Kaffirs, whereas the latter escort my wagons with supplies, slaughter cattle, carry my mails, assist me in every way in their power, which affords better argument in refutation of the Radical and garbled untruths, though founded on facts, of Sir W. Molesworth. I will give you an example of one among other accusations of my despotism. The Kaffir Hermanus, who by birth is a negro slave, was ever heretofore with his people an enemy to the Kaffir because it was his interest to be friendly to us. After the war of 1835–36, Sir B. D'Urban gave him a grant of a beautiful tract of country within the Colony upon the ever-supplying water, the Blinkwater stream. His title was disputed by some of the colonists, and it was complained that he paid no quit-rent as they all did. It was just, and only just, that if he was protected by the government, he should contribute, equally with others, his quota for its maintenance. I therefore, as part of a general system, exacted a quit-rent, a mere trifle, which was the best possible title and deed of occupation, yet does this throating Sir W.M. bring forward this as an act of despotism. It is really ludicrous.

'But for this inexplicable Hottentot revolution, I would have put down the Kaffirs in six weeks. These Hottentots are the most favoured race on earth, yet have a set of Radical London Society missionaries been preaching to them like evil spirits that they were an oppressed and ill-used race, until, encouraged by violent meetings all over the Colony upon the convict question, they have met with arms in their hands, arms given to them by us, for the purpose of joining the Kaffirs to drive the English over the Zwartkop River beyond Uitenhage. I have endeavoured to administer this government so as to allow the all-powerful sun to shine forth its glory upon all its inhabitants, whether black or white, equally, and I have no other object than the welfare of the people generally. I have said "Lay before me your wants; they shall be considered and your wishes met if practicable". This was appreciated until the d—— convict question arose. The emancipated blacks in Cape Town, the Hottentots in the Kat River, held anti-convict meetings got up by white Radicals, who have thus induced the coloured classes upon this frontier and in many other parts of the Colony to believe that separate interests exist for white and black. The Kaffir has been fostered by the most benevolent acts of kindness by me as a Governor. My study has been to ameliorate their condition from brutes to Christians, from savages to civilized men. They progressed in three years beyond all belief until some white-faced devils (the sable king often wears a white face) got in among them, persuaded the chiefs my object was their extermination, and while the people clung with avidity to my protection from the former tyranny they groaned under, the chiefs asserted their feudal authority, and such is man in a wild state of nature, he cleaves to the hereditary rule of oppressors of his forefathers—with tears in his eyes. I have seen many weep when they came to say to me Farewell; "Our country will be lost". Let Sir W.M. and his myrmidons deny this; he cannot, but, he can assert that just measures are foul, despotic and arbitrary acts.

'Juana is in better spirits now since the reinforcements have arrived, I hope. Since I have received the dear Duke's kind letter, Juana regards me as supported by old friends and present master [Lord Grey]. The latter gentleman and I understand each other. I will be censured by no man but I will endeavour to obey where I can. He affronted me by finding fault with "an abortive attempt to reform the Legislative Council", which made my blood boil, although my remonstrance was as mild as milk. I think the recent attempt he and his colleagues have made to form a government has been fully as abortive as mine, and they have discovered the impossibility of making legislators of men who will not undertake office. Since the outbreak all his communications have been most complimentary.

'Your brother,
'Harry.'

In believing that he and Lord Grey understood each other, Smith deluded himself. Having sent more troops to the Colony, Grey expected to see quick results. If these were not forthcoming, then it must be that Harry Smith was either ignorant of his profession or was not trying. 'Attrition' was not a word that featured in Lord Grey's vocabulary and his conception of time and space factors was limited. The fact that the 73rd had kept a careful record of their movements and had marched 2,838 miles between Christmas, 1850, and 8 August, 1851, would have impressed him not at all. By the time the Queen's and the 12th had arrived in August, the best intelligence reports showed that there were at least 6,000 Hottentots and Kaffirs armed and operational within the Colony, their forces being about equally divided between the Amatolas and the Fish River bush. Things were not looking too encouraging by the time the 12th Lancers and 60th arrived in October because Henry Somerset had not been able to drive Macomo from the Waterkloof and although Mackinnon had largely cleared the Fish River at the time of the misadventure to Captain Oldham's company of the Queen's in September, the enemy had returned to their fastnesses the moment he went away again. The levies raised by Mr Montagu had served the 6 months for which they had contracted and very few were willing to re-engage.

If that were insufficient to keep him occupied, Smith was now getting messages from Warden in the Orange River Sovereignty that the Boers there were unwilling to assist him against Moshesh and that their countrymen across the Vaal were at least as hostile to the British government. Warden was given the only orders possible in the circumstances, that he was to do no more than act on the defensive. He was not the most brilliant officer in South Africa and Smith, as he later wrote, would have liked to replace him; there was, however, no officer available who was likely to do better. Men wise in the ways of Africa were beginning to feel that Kreili was contemplating joining in the rebellion and even the new regiments which had arrived and were becoming accustomed to this singular mode of warfare would not suffice to carry out a victorious campaign in the mountains 30 miles to the north-west of Grahamstown and along the Fish River 30 miles to its north-east. On 15 October, Smith asked Grey to furnish him with two more regiments of infantry and another 400 British recruits for the depleted C.M.R.

Before his despatch reached Downing Street, however, he had some successes to put on record, for at the end of the month Somerset managed at last to eject Macomo from his stronghold. A column of 700 men drawn from the 12th and 74th with 350 Fingoes had been organized under Colonel Fordyce and another made up of the Queen's, 6th and 91st with the addition of 2 small field pieces was ordered to clear out the Kroome mountains. These are a rugged off-shoot thrown out to the south by a high table-land and connected with it by a narrow spur running between the heads of two deep, wooded valleys, each at right-angles to it. The valley on the west is the Waterkloof itself while that on the east is called Fuller's Hoek. Both were famous Kaffir fortresses, the Waterkloof in particular containing the *sanctum sanctorum* which no white man had seen called Macomo's Den. The plan was for Fordyce's column to ascend the Kroome range from the south as far as the spur just mentioned and which was known as the Horseshoe; Michel's task was to advance from the opposite direction, driving all the Kaffir he came across into the arms of Fordyce. Fordyce began his advance before dawn on 14 October and within three hours the two columns had joined up. Each had been involved in a little fighting but nothing more serious had happened than the driving off of bodies of Kaffirs which had attacked them. Somerset withdrew his force north-westwards over open country and made no effort to drive off those who felt brave enough to follow him. When he judged that they had come far enough from the shelter of the forest, he loosed his cavalry, all irregulars and not very many of them, which galloped through the Kaffirs, cutting down many, and then turned to repeat the process. He reached his bivouac site, a deserted farmhouse, at about 5 p.m. Fordyce's men, having been on the march for 18 hours under an African sun and without food, could hardly have continued further.

Somerset gave them a day of rest and then went back by a different way into the mountains; this time Fordyce drove up the valley of the Waterkloof while Michel came in at right angles to him from the north. The consequences were the usual ones, Kaffirs being driven out of their wilderness and casualties inflicted upon them; but then came the rain. All the troops had to be withdrawn to provide escorts for supply convoys as there were no others who could be employed on this essential but back-breaking work. During this time, however, the 60th arrived at Fort Beaufort and on 24 October they were put to work by Somerset, in common with the others, to carry out another drive. Michel, this time, was to comb Fuller's Hoek, Nesbitt (Colonel of the 60th) was to move through a ridge just to the north of it named Wolf's Back and Fordyce was to take on the northern ridge above the Waterkloof. The guns marked certain well-known spots into which it was the business of the infantry to drive the enemy; the rain continued to fall but during the next 3 days the whole area was crossed and re-crossed in several different directions by Somerset's men, the columns always converging on the Horse Shoe. The Kaffirs fought harder than anybody remembered, but the inefficacy of Umlanjeni's charms against musket balls was becoming daily more demonstrable.

After 3 days of deserved rest, operations started again on 6 November when the force suffered a sad loss. Colonel Fordyce stepped out into the open from behind a bush in order to focus his glass on something he had seen; before he could do so, he was shot dead by a 'huge Hottentot' who leapt out of the bush and ran away laughing. The death of so fine and popular an officer was felt throughout the army; Lord Grey, of course, wrote it down again to the personal shortcomings of Harry Smith. The work had not been done without scathe, for, in addition to Fordyce, the 74th lost on that day two junior officers and 6 Highlanders killed and another half-dozen badly wounded. The casualties inflicted on the Kaffirs were not heavy, being probably under 50 killed and wounded, but, far more important, their citadel was being wrested from them.

By 9 November Somerset was able to report that, although there were still small bands in the Kroome Range, most of the rebels had been cleared out of the Waterkloof. It was just as well, for operations could not have continued much longer. Michel's column, Smith reported, had been in the field since the end of September with no tents and only one blanket a man during unimaginable rains, sometimes turning to sleet, and chilling winds straight from the snow-capped mountains. Fordyce's men were in slightly better case, for late in October they had obtained an issue of small tents. During the day, invariably, the sun blazed down after the rain had stopped and the heat became intolerable. Fever, rheumatism and dysentery were beginning to waste the force away and there were none to replace them.

They had done their work, for the Gaikas, finding life in the mountains to be intolerable, were pulling out and moving eastwards. Seldom have British troops been called on to undergo hardship worse than this. 'No one without experience of virgin forest can have any conception of the physical labour of toiling through it, nor understand how, apart from creepers, and undergrowth, a huge fallen trunk, slippery as an eel, may bring a man abruptly to a stand. Yet the men had to circumvent or surmount such obstacles somehow; and their officers had somehow to keep them together and preserve the right direction, on pain, at best, of instant death, or if haply they were taken alive, of lingering dissolution by hideous torture. And nowhere could they feel assured that naked savages, unencumbered except by their arms, and at home in crag and thicket, were not lying in wait for them . . . However, the British soldier is a patient soul, and his dogged perseverance will, if time be granted to him, push any enemy out of any country.' This was Sir John Fortescue's view of the matter.

The Waterkloof being clear, it became necessary to consider where its former inhabitants would now take themselves. There was only one possible answer. Kreili had committed no overt act of hostility but everybody knew that his Galekas were obligingly taking care of any surplus cattle whose presence might be proving an embarrassment to their Gaika friends. Now it was clear that the Gaikas themselves were seeking sanctuary in the same direction. Smith, whose acquaintance with Kreili went back many years, decided that an expedition into the Upper Kei was called for. The 43rd had arrived at East London on 17 December, which would at least make up for the men lost by casualties and sickness during the drives and he was able to muster about 5,000 men for an expedition against Kreili. The 74th and 91st were left to watch the Waterkloof and Fuller's Hoek.

The column set out for Kreili's country on 17 November, in spite of heavy and continuous rain; it came back at the beginning of January, 1852, with 30,000 cattle and tales of many Kaffirs slain. On their heels came emissaries from all the Gaika chiefs asking for terms. Smith, knowing his men, demanded nothing short of instant surrender but this was beyond the powers of the delegates. Accordingly, Smith despatched seven columns into the Amatolas to destroy crops and devastate all they could find; they met with no resistance, for the heart had gone out of the rebellion.

The Gaikas were on the ropes but knowledge that they had friends in high places in London kept hope alive sufficient to warrant a refusal to throw in the towel. They were not without reason in their belief. Grey had been for some time past in the habit of sending carping and foolish despatches to Harry Smith complaining at the lack of decisive victory. On 14 January he posted the most fatuous of them all. Paragraph 2 reads '. . . . another month of this distressing warfare has passed away and though the force at your disposal has been increased to a very considerable amount no advantage of any real importance has been gained over the enemy, while the loss of Her Majesty's troops has been exceedingly heavy, that very distinguished officer, Lieutenant-Colonel Fordyce, being included among those who have fallen.'

The acuity of reasoning displayed in a dozen long paragraphs in no way falls short of this one. Somerset's efforts in the mountains are 'these successes (if they can be called so)'. The dismal farrago of nonsense ends with the recall of Smith and his replacement by General Cathcart.

Sir William Molesworth was, no doubt, highly gratified. The

war was, for all practical purposes, over and the rebellion had been put down, but it was too much to hope that those in Downing Street could understand it. The Duke was swift to make it plain that he had had no hand in Smith's undeserved dismissal and made a speech in the Lords giving him a fair meed of praise and spelling out a few of the facts about campaigning against a primitive enemy. Smith was, of course, bitterly chagrined; it was small comfort to know that his successor was a man in every way worthy of the post. Major-General George Cathcart came of a distinguished military family and was himself a thorough soldier; he did not arrive in the theatre of operations until 26 March and by that time much more had happened.

Sir Harry decided that he was not going to leave the Cape before he had seen the inside of the Waterkloof with his own eyes and he moved to Fort Beaufort on 5 March so that he might accompany Eyre when that highly skilled officer made his final push into the mountains. In a sweep lasting six days and which was, by common consent, the most arduous yet, Eyre penetrated to the last fastnesses and had the satisfaction of walking down the steps into Macomo's Den, the location of which had been betrayed by a woman. By 17 March all resistance seemed to be at an end; the Waterkloof, Fuller's Hoek and the Blinkwater were all empty and the columns of Eyre and Michel, rationed for 15 days, were directed at the heart of the main Amatola range to dislodge Tyalie while further mopping up operations were carried out by Somerset and the garrison of Whittlesea. As Smith wrote, in his last despatch to Grey and on the eve of the last drives, 'Every part of the rebel enemy's country will then be assailed'.

On 25 February there took place the tragic event by which the Kaffir Wars are most generally remembered. The steam-transport *Birkenhead*, bearing drafts for every regiment in the Colony, struck a rock off Danger Point whilst on passage from Cape Town to Port Elizabeth; it happened in a flat calm and at dead of night. The captain, very properly, had all boats hoisted out and then for some obscure reason gave the order 'Full Astern'. His ship being hard and fast, the natural result of this was that she was pulled in half; the forward part sank immediately with all hands, most men being drowned in their berths. The after part remained afloat and all the troops on board were paraded under Major Seaton of the 74th, O.C. Troops. The young soldiers fell in in disciplined silence; all the women and children aboard were loaded into the boats which lay off about half a cable's length from the ship. The troops, perfectly well aware that this was the end, remained in their ranks, obeying every order with complete calm. In a few minutes, the stern part of the *Birkenhead* tilted and plunged to the bottom. Five officers and 109 men swam ashore, though many did not survive the battering they received in the terrible surf; 14 officers and 349 other ranks went down with the ship.

The splendid behaviour, not of a regiment which had fought together as a body and had traditions of how to behave on such an occasion, but of young details, many not much more than recruits, caught the imagination of the world. The Duke made it the subject of one of his last speeches, dwelling not on courage but on discipline; the King of Prussia (who had been at Waterloo) ordered the account of it to be read out at a special parade of every regiment in his army.

The sinking of the *Birkenhead* established a standard of behaviour in shipwreck which the British, military and civil alike, have ever since aspired to match. It was not simply a pointless exercise in fortitude, like that of the Indian brave, for on at least two occasions since—when the troopers *Warren Hastings* and *Sarah Sands* were lost—discipline of the like kind saved entire battalions from death by drowning in confusion. Sir John Fortescue is not wrong when he says that freedom from panic, orderliness, patience and self-denial in ship-wreck have, since the *Birkenhead*, become a point of national honour. However, for Harry Smith and his men the work had to go on.

It was on 10 March that the last fighting in the Waterkloof region took place, Eyre going through Fuller's Hoek with eight small columns, including 2 companies of the 74th which had been added to him, his four guns being, by Herculean efforts, got up to a place from which they could command the north side of the valley. Napier had a hard fight preventing the Kaffirs from getting back into the Waterkloof, a business in which Michel came to his aid at a worrying moment, and the Lancers to the north cut off those minded to head back to the Kat River. On 15 March a party of 400 burghers, presumably having come to the conclusion that the war was all but over, joined in. Their arrival was welcome, for Michel on the same day had the hardest fight of the war at a place called the Iron Mountain. It was a strong position which nature did not allow to be turned and Michel, reluctantly, had to make a direct assault. He was driven back by the fire of well-concealed defenders and it was not until a second attack was mounted by the 60th with fixed swords that the place was stormed. The slaughter is described as great.

Harry Smith then left this theatre to Somerset and accompanied the columns of Eyre, Michel and Percival (who had been chasing Kaffirs out of the Fish River bush) to the Tyumie River; for 4 days they drove Kaffirs before them in the direction of the Kei and strong patrols were kept constantly moving from Fort Cox north-eastward to the Gwili-Gwili mountains, Keiskamma Hoek and Kabousie Nek, covering the Amatolas from the south while Somerset attended to them from the north. The Rifle Brigade arrived on the 24th and made camp in the Waterkloof to discourage any attempt to return there.

The Kaffirs acknowledged to have lost 6,000 warriors, including 80 chiefs to say nothing of more than 80,000 head of cattle and uncountable numbers of goats. With total victory in sight, Harry Smith had only one duty remaining, to hand over his command and return ignominiously home.

He met Cathcart at King William's Town at the beginning of April and gave him all the help and advice in his power. Cathcart readily appreciated how things stood and saw no reason to depart from Smith's strategy. The war petered out over a period of months; during July the Waterkloof was twice more purged of its returned inhabitants and in August 2 columns were sent to beat up Kreili. By November, Cathcart was able to report that, although Sandili and Macomo were still at large, the last gangs of Hottentots had been broken up and driven from the mountains. The Eighth Kaffir War was concluded.

This did not mean that no work remained for the army. With his feet cleared, Cathcart could now set out to punish Moshesh who had shown himself far from friendly.

Basutoland is a very different kind of country from Kaffraria, consisting of open mountains and its people were very different from the Kaffirs. The historian of the 12th Lancers says of them: 'Moshesh could put into the field 7,000 well-mounted men, riding a wonderful stamp of 14 hand pony, carrying good flint-lock muskets, and using saddles and wearing European clothing with cloaks of dressed skins. The Basuto horseman carried his musket slung over his shoulder, and a leather bucket carrying assegais, knobkerry and a special barbed spear for disembowelling his wounded enemy over his left shoulder. In his right hand he carried a light axe with half-moon blade mounted on a 2 foot handle, weighing up to 3 pounds and very sharp. It was used like a sword but could be thrown at close range with deadly effect.'

In mid-November, Cathcart assembled a force of about 2,300 all ranks at Burghersdorp, 150 miles north of Fort Beaufort. He had with him the 12th Lancers and about 220 C.M.R. for his mounted component, 250 Sappers with the rubber pontoon, 3 guns and a few rockets together with 5 regiments of infantry (Queen's, 43rd, 73rd, 74th and Rifle Brigade, none more than 400 strong. The Rifle Brigade could raise only 100 effectives).

The force, having endured a most gruelling march in the course of which both the Caledon and the Orange Rivers had been forded, arrived in presence of the Basuto and in sight of the tableland known as the Berea on 13 December. Colonel Eyre, who was in command of the field force, had no experience of the Basuto and wrongly equated them with the Kaffirs whom he knew so well. Moshesh visited the General on the following day but declined to pay the fine of cattle imposed upon him, asserting, not without reason, that he had grievances of his own that called for redress. His warriors had inflicted a palpable defeat upon a rather motley force commanded by Warden, whose only troops deserving the name had been 172 men of the 45th, at Viervoet six months before and authority in the country was shared between Moshesh, an independent body of Boer farmers led by Pretorius and the British Resident who counted for less than either of the others. Cathcart said firmly that if the cattle were not delivered he would come and get them and, to accomplish this, he moved a part of his infantry to the north of the

Berea, on which feature all Moshesh's cattle were known to be.

The Berea is about 12 miles east and west by 4 miles north and south, and the sides are precipitous in most places. Eyre with most of the infantry had an uneventful march to the top of the plateau while the cavalry under Napier made their way to the same place from the north slopes. Contrary to Cathcart's wishes, they decided on a glorious round-up of masses of cattle, leaving their commander isolated at the foot of the plateau with only 3 companies of the 43rd, some details of the 12th Lancers and C.M.R. and, by the greatest good fortune, 3 guns. With these, Cathcart maintained his position until Eyre returned an hour before dusk driving about 1,500 cattle. Napier, having got into a scrape on the way down, rejoined the main body and firing continued until 8 p.m. when Moshesh drew off. In truth, Cathcart was in a position of extreme danger, for his men were exhausted and greatly outnumbered. Moshesh, however, sent in a most diplomatic message to the effect that he had been suitably impressed by the sight of the forces of the Great Queen and would give no trouble for the future.

The bread cast on the waters returned to him after many days. In 1868 Moshesh's people became embroiled in a war with the Boers of the Orange Free State and would have been exterminated but for intervention on their behalf by the Governor of Cape Colony, Sir Philip Wodehouse. Three years later the country came formally under the Colony's protection.

Cathcart went thankfully back the way he had come. It was not a glorious return; many of the Basuto warriors were prancing about in the uniforms of dead Lancers, Captain Faunce of the 73rd had been captured and tortured to death unavenged and it had been very close to an earlier Isandhlwana. There were to be further wars with the Basuto until the 1880's but they fall outside the scope of this book. Suffice it to say that they were productive of more hard fighting and actual battle-casualties than those with the Kaffirs but never after Cathcart's expedition were they again under-rated.

In February, 1853, Sandili, from his hiding place on the Tsomo, sent in his plenipotentiaries to Colonel Maclean at Fort Murray and on 9 March there was a meeting at the Yellowwoods, six miles from King William's Town, attended by the Governor and the suppliants. Sandili, Macomo, Stokwe (son of the deceased Eno), and all the Gaika chiefs were there. Cathcart dictated his terms which they were in no shape to oppose. The whole Amatola Range was to be taken from the Gaika tribes for ever and any member found there would be dealt with under martial law. They might, however, occupy the great tract of open land from the Kei to the great northern road so long as they behaved themselves. On the part of General Cathcart there were sincere protestations of his sovereign's forgiveness to her erring children and on theirs a thoroughly insincere avowal of gratitude and loyalty. Umlanjeni, now an object of derision, died in the following August while Uithaalder, perhaps the most dangerous of the Hottentot rebels, blew out his brains. The chief Kama, who had remained loyal and had proved particularly valuable during the critical days of the attacks on Whittlesea, was rewarded with a handsome grant of land along the east bank of the Keiskamma and the Fingoes acquired some of the best locations in the Tyumie and upper Keiskamma valleys as well as a good deal of land further north. The Tembu, who had been the main assailants of Whittlesea, lost their land north of the Amatolas which was parcelled out amongst new European settlers, while the forfeited Gaika land remained a Government reserve. For reparation of the cost of more than 2 millions sterling, to say nothing of the lives of about 500 soldiers, the settlement can hardly be called excessive. Sandili, Macomo and Kreili still had many years left to them; General Cathcart, however, had only a little time to go, for he was killed in action, as he would have wished, fighting valiantly at Inkerman. Another familiar face left the frontier when the war ended; Henry Somerset after more than 30 years in the Cape moved on to India as Chief-of-Staff of the Bombay Army. He rose to be its Commander-in-Chief, a Lieutenant-General and K.C.B., dying at Gibraltar on his way to England in 1862. The map became enriched with more new names, Queenstown for the forfeited lands of the Tembu and the old hotbed of trouble at the Kat River providing the new village of Seymour, its donor being Cathcart's Military Secretary who was to fall by his side in the Crimea.

Cathcart's memorial (apart from the hill outside Sebastopol

which bears, or bore, his name) is a thriving township to the south of Queenstown; between the two lies a village named for Tylden, the defender of Whittlesea.

The chiefs and the missionaries returned to their respective charges and the farmers once more buckled down to restore and restock their farms. Most of the British troops sailed home to prepare for the war with Russia.

CHAPTER 17
Last Struggles

THE quarter of a century which followed upon the end of the Great Kaffir War can be treated only rather cursorily. The centre of gravity had already begun to move north and, before the war was over, there came the Sand River Convention of January, 1852, under which the British Government abandoned Harry Smith's Sovereignty and granted independence to the Boers beyond the Vaal River; two years later the Bloemfontein Convention performed the same office for those living between the Orange and the Vaal. Natal, of course, remained a British Colony and between it and the eastern boundary of the Cape Colony lay large areas of Kaffraria, notably Pondoland.

The old Colony had to decide on the military forces that it could sustain in the future, as the large-scale defection of the Hottentots of the C.M.R. hardly inspired much confidence in the value of that corps. It continued in existence until 1870 but was subjected to a gradual process of what would now be called Dehottentotization, the European component being proportionately increased. Even so, it was regarded as a broken reed and was only allowed to endure so that the loyal men should be given the opportunity of serving out their time. To supplement it, there came into existence a new and entirely British para-military force; it began in 1852 under the name of the Armed and Mounted Police and was raised in local detachments at Albany, Uitenhage, Somerset, Cradock, Albert, Victoria and Fort Beaufort some of which, under Captain Walter Currie, did extremely useful work against the bands of renegade Hottentots in the Fish River bush. At the close of the war only the detachments at Albany, Fort Beaufort and Victoria were retained and in 1855 they were constituted a permanent force with the title 'Frontier Armed and Mounted Police', or F.A.M.P. for short.

Currie, a veteran of the last two wars, was the first Commandant, of whom it was said that 'He was a born fighter . . . he could ride without boots but he couldn't move along without adjectives. Still, there was melody in his language, the same as in the case of Sir Harry Smith . . . he was much respected and loved by the corps and the whole frontier'. The F.A.M.P. originally comprised 4 Inspectors, 12 Sub-Inspectors and about 500 N.C.O.s and men. They were well armed with double-barrelled percussion guns (one barrel rifled and the other smooth), revolvers and bowie knives, all of which, together with their horses and saddlery, had to be provided by the men. The uniform was smart and serviceable, much the kind of thing that many officers had long been advocating for use in bush warfare. A loosely cut suit of brown bedford cord with large poacher pockets in place of pouches, overalls strapped under the boot and a slouch hat (a kind of *kepi* for officers) gave the air of gamekeepers rather than soldiers which was entirely sensible.

Their first duties outside routine came in 1857 during the national suicide of the Xosa mentioned at the beginning of this book. The girl Nonquanse, a Galeka of Kreili's tribe, under the influence of her uncle, Mdhlaka, a famous witch-doctor, announced her vision. All stocks of cattle must be destroyed and all crops with them. Then, precisely on 18 February, the old chiefs would come back bringing with them such cattle and crops as never men had seen before while a great storm would drive all the white men into the sea. The British agents were able to put a stop to it amongst the Gaikas before too much damage was done, but Galekaland was utterly ruined. It is said that 25,000 Kaffirs died of starvation and 100,000 wandered away from their homes in that part of Kaffraria which was outside colonial jurisdiction. The population of British Kaffraria fell within 7 months from 105,000 to 37,000 in spite of all the Government could do to relieve their distress. The F.A.M.P., rather in the style of the North West Mounted Police in Canada, were heavily engaged in coping with gangs of starving men bent on robbery and pillage. The Government found it expedient to move some of the remnant of the Galekas beyond the Bashee River and to replace them with friendly Fingoes and others.

In the same year came a considerable accretion to the strength of the Europeans in the Colony. During the Crimean War, there had been raised in England a body of German volunteers on the lines of the King's German Legion of Peninsular days. The force never left England and after the war the question of its future had to be settled. Common gratitude demanded that something more be done than merely discharge the men with the thanks of the Government, and, on the initiative of Lord Panmure, the Secretary for War, it was decided to give them the opportunity of emigrating to South Africa. The Germans jumped at the chance, for Germans have always made excellent colonists. The colony was a little apprehensive, for among about 2,300 men there were only just over 500 women and children and the influx of so many lusty bachelors was expected to pose a considerable problem. It seems to have solved itself somehow. Later in the year they arrived, in a formed military body known as the Settlers Regiment, fully armed and equipped. The arrangement was that, on arrival in the colony, the command of Graf von Stutterheim would come to an end (though he was granted the honorary rank of Major-General) and all should revert to civilian status, though forming a reserve for emergencies. Grants of land were freely given and the names of Stutterheim, Berlin, Hamburg, and others began to enrich the map in an arc facing eastwards on the Kaffrarian side of King William's Town. The Germans were admirable settlers, patient, frugal and uncomplaining. Many of them enlisted in the ranks of the C.M.R. and the F.A.M.P. where they were most welcome recruits. It is, perhaps, not too cynical to suppose that the removal of the Galekas further east was not entirely coincidental.

On an evil day for South Africa, diamonds were discovered near Kimberley in 1870, to be followed by strikes of gold elsewhere. From that time on the importance of the old Colony diminished, for it could not compete in riches with these newer places. It remained the agricultural country it had always been, but it was not free from troubles. In 1869 the Tembu had another bout of witch-doctor trouble which was put down almost bloodlessly by the F.A.M.P., armed with the first breech-loader, the Snider, for the occasion. In 1873 came the rebellion of Langalibalele, beginning in Natal but ending with a smart little action at Leribe in the Colony, where he was captured by a detachment of the F.A.M.P. under Inspector Surmon.

The year 1877, in the reign of Sir Bartle Frere, brought the beginning of the Ninth and last Kaffir War. It was not of the pattern of the others for it was caused by a purely Kaffir quarrel. The Fingoes had been rewarded for their steadfastness in war in a fashion which many other tribesmen felt to be excessive. They had, since their recovery of an identity, acquired the reputation which in other communities is held by the Jews, the Armenians, the Basques and the inhabitants of Paisley, for they never failed to get the better of a bargain with their simplerminded kinsmen. Resentment against their favoured treatment had long been smouldering and in September, 1877, it burst into flame at a beer-drinking near the old mission station of Butterworth. It happened that Frere was near at hand, for he had just been on a visit to Kreili and was passing through King William's Town when the news reached him that a bar-room brawl had spread into a regular tribal fight and that opportunists on both sides were helping themselves to each other's cattle. Later the same day, the Galekas attacked a police post in the Gwadana mountains where there was a troop of the F.A.M.P. under Sub-Inspector von Hohenau. A body of Fingoes came to the aid of the police but the gun with which they were reinforced (the F.A.M.P. had its own artillery troop now) broke down, von Hohenau and half a dozen troopers were killed and an ignominious retreat followed.*

Sir Bartle moved his quarters to the barracks of the 24th

* The quality of the equipment of the F.A.M.P. can be judged from this incident. There were 3 guns in the Artillery troop, a 9-pdr R.M.L. brought out in 1874 by Lieutenant J. C. Robinson, a Gunner officer lent to the Police, and two M.L. 7-pdr mountain guns. The latter arrived without any sort of carriages and a local carpenter was employed to make the best he could. They were so flimsy that the trail of the gun at Gwadana broke after a few rounds had been fired and the other did the same a few days later at Ibeka.

where he remained for seven months. To show the extent to which even a colonial administrator of Frere's quality was ignorant of the recent past of his own bailiwick, the following passage from one of his letters dated 17 October speaks: 'I was hurried up in consequence of the alarm of a Kaffir War, and found that hostilities had broken out between the Fingoes, who are British subjects and live in British territory, and the Galekas of Kreili—an old chief, son of Hintza, Sir Harry Smith's opponent, who was unfortunately killed when he had come in under a safe conduct'. Such ignorance cannot be readily excused.

The Fingoes were, as always, ready to come to the aid of any foe of Hintza's son. Frere saw this at first hand. 'Last night, just as it was getting dark, on my way back by the Queenstown Road from Peelton, Hodson and I came on some 35 native men, armed with Enfields and fully-equipped with ammunition-pouches, haversacks, water-bottles etc. for field service . . . George, the commandant of the party, assured us that it was "all right". He was a "good man" and all his people "good men"—"Ayliffe's Fingoes".' The silent reserves were reporting to the Colours. They would be needed, for the war was Kreili's last throw of the dice. The old man had watched impotently as his once proud tribe had sunk lower and lower, never having recovered from the self-inflicted wounds of 20 years ago, while their former 'dogs' had taken to sheep farming and the use of the light American plough with the result that they throve exceedingly. The old chief was seen by Colonel Eustace, the Resident, to have painted the 'war charm', a black spot, on his forehead as long ago as 26 August and the brawl may well have been engineered by his people.

The only regular troops on hand were the 1/24th (South Wales Borderers) with 6 companies of the 88th Connaught Rangers on the way from Cape Town. Commandant Griffith had only suc-ceeded to command of the F.A.M.P. a few days previously but Frere had sent for Sir Arthur Cunynghame from the diamond fields to assume overall command. He at once appointed Griffith to the head of all Police and native levies in the Transkei and left Colonel Glyn of the 24th to lead all troops in the Ciskei, to be deployed to prevent any new irruption into the Colony.

It looked for a time as if this was a real possibility, for on

29 September a body of about 8,000 Galekas attacked the police post at Ibeka. They had, it seems, been egged on by their women who taunted them that they were no longer warriors nor even men to allow the dogs such licence. As the Fleet Surgeon of H.M.S. *Active* sagely observed, 'There is no mischief in the world that has not a woman at the bottom of it.' The F.A.M.P. repulsed all attacks, the Snider for the first time providing a firearm that could be reloaded without its owner making himself a target while he went through the drill, and when Griffith arrived with more men they rode out and burnt Kreili's kraal.

On the same day, 9 October, another force under Major Elliot with a troop of F.A.M.P. defeated a minor chief, Sitcheka, on the eastern border of the Transkei but Inspector Hook's troop was hard put to it to repel an attack on the post at Lusizi. Griffith, promoted Colonel after the Ibeka affair, got all the levies together and drove the Galekas across the Bashee and the Umtata and took most of their cattle. It looked as if a revolt had been put down by policemen and special constables; George and his friends, together with the other levies, were sent home with thanks. But it was all rather premature, for Kreili's braves had fallen back upon friends and soon returned for a second round. They had lost 700 men killed and 13,000 cattle taken but Kreili (whose chief adviser was the notorious Mr Crouch) was determined on a battle of Armageddon. Some of his men slipped across an unguarded ford of the Bashee to go to Sandili, elderly but rancorous as ever, to persuade him that this was his last opportunity also.

Sandili joyfully agreed and his warriors made a start by burning and sacking the Draaibosch Hotel, 30 miles north of East London on Boxing Day, 1877. This presented a serious situation, for no volunteers remained in arms and the F.A.M.P. were near exhaustion. Frere, who had witnessed the Indian Mutiny, had no enthusiasm for volunteers for he regarded them as men who would, for no provocation at all, visit on their prisoners the condign punishment exacted by Neill's Blue Caps at Cawnpore. He had a good deal of sympathy with the rebels, and indeed there were some points in which they were more sinned against than sinning. His Attorney-General, the third generation of the Stockenstroom family, gave his opinion: 'Rebels in arms may be shot without mercy or trial. Investigation at drum head suggested by me merely to distinguish between rebels and other enemies, and allow instant execution of former in the field'. Frere refused to accept his advice.

A private war was raging between the Governor, Mr Merriman (Commissioner for Crown Lands) and Mr Molteno (Colonial Secretary) which bid fair to distract the attention of all of them from the uprising. Frere, who was soon to have a full-dress constitutional crisis on his hands, wrote of the former 'Merriman's insane attempts to ape Gambetta had caused a serious aggravation of war fever. Years of good management will not repair the evil this war has already done in the Gaika and Tambookie locations by his amateur campaign under civilian soldiers.' Controversy has raged around the name of Sir Bartle Frere for generations and it is not yet stilled. The only comment called for in this book is that it would have been far better for the colony and all its inhabitants if Sir Harry Smith or Sir George Cathcart had still been living and in office. When a civilian Governor upbraids a civilian Minister in the course of a war as an amateur strategist, then the outlook for the professional soldier is bleak indeed.

Both Molteno and Merriman were anxious that the rising should be put down by Colonial forces alone and they insisted on maintaining complete control over everything that affected them, even to the extent of making it impossible for the General officer commanding the Queen's troops to give orders to a Corporal of Police. This led to ill-feeling between regular and irregular, not diminished by the fact that the most useless volunteer drew 5/- a day in contrast to the soldier's traditional 1/-, and there were to be heard ugly accusations and counter-accusations of running away. Peace was only restored when Frere dismissed both men and appointed as Prime Minister Mr Gordon Sprigg, a farmer with no experience of public office. He made a surprisingly good one.

The Kaffirs, conscious perhaps that the traditional Africa of the chiefs was melting away before their eyes in a world of railways and electric telegraphs, were determined to see the business through. They had lost more than 700 men to the guns and rifles of the F.A.M.P. and their associates by the end of

October, largely as a result of the throwing to the winds of the old methods of warfare and by trusting to numbers to swamp the F.A.M.P. by mass attacks. Nevertheless, with their forces augmented by Sandili's people and with the battlefield now extended to Queenstown in the north and Fort Beaufort in the west, the cause did not seem lost for the troops in the Colony were few indeed by contrast with the numbers General Cathcart had disposed in the previous war. Their quality also was in question, for the F.A.M.P. had undoubtedly suffered defeats in the early stages. Frere had always held to the opinion that their discipline left a lot to be desired and that their equipment was not good for more than ordinary police work though their courage was never in issue.

The real miscalculation by Kreili and Sandili was about the attitude of the Fingoes whom they expected would desert in substantial numbers and come over to their kinsmen; the Fingoes, however, knew perfectly well on which side their bread was buttered and had no romantic dreams of a past and vanishing age. Many of them gave point to the aphorism that 'A Kaffir civilized is a Kaffir spoiled' for there were too many instances of cowardice on their part, of which their fathers would never have been guilty. Nonetheless, they stayed loyal and without their aid the war could not have been won except by demanding large reinforcements from England.

The Germans too were invaluable. Twenty years had not caused them to lose their old skill at arms but had merely ripened their experience of Africa and its ways; many of them had strong sons who could track and shoot as well as their fathers and their farms were at strategic places which inhibited any concentration of Kaffirs.

We get here a glimpse of George Theal in a capacity other than historian; he had for some time been running a school at Lovedale where he personally taught Kaffir boys useful trades from carpentry to cultivation. He makes an obscure but typically modest reference in one of his many books to his having been sent to one of the most troublesome tribes and that, as a result of his labours, they took no part in the war. It was probably amongst Macomo's branch of the Gaika family; the old chief had died in 1873 after a spell in prison on Robben Island for the murder of a petty captain. His son, Tini, was out in the Waterkloof again but that no operations occurred in that un-hallowed place may well have been due to the greatest historian South Africa has produced.

There were many small battles at the end of 1877 and the beginning of 1878 in the Transkei, during one of which Major Moore of the Connaught Rangers won the first Victoria Cross in South Africa when he fought a postal convoy through a Galeka ambush. On 12 January the Galekas suffered a severe defeat at N'Amaxa where a company apiece of the 24th and 88th plus 50 bluejackets and a couple of troops of F.A.M.P. killed about 150 of them without loss to themselves. The campaign in Galekaland really ended when, on 7 February, Kreili and Sandili were both present to see the last attack, on the police post at Kentani, mounted by about 5,000 of their men. Captain Upcher commanded the little forces, mainly the 1/24th and Fingoes but including for once a body of irregular cavalry named Carrington's Horse.

Frere wrote to Lord Carnarvon about it on 17 February: 'They seemed to have had great hopes of crushing Upcher by enveloping his position, and then of raising the Colony. They came on in 4 divisions very steadily and in the days of Brown Bess would certainly have closed, and being 8 or 10 to 1 would possibly have overwhelmed our people. They held on after several shells had burst among their advanced masses but they could not live under the fire of the Martini-Henry. The 24th are old, steady shots and every bullet told, and when they broke Carrington's Horse followed them up and made the success more decided than in any former action. It has been, in many respects, a very instructive action, not only as regards the vastly increased power in our weapons and organization, but as showing the Kaffir persistence in the new tactics of attacking us in the open in masses. At present this is their fatal error, but it might not be so if they had a few renegade foreigners as drill-masters; and we find many indications that they may, ere long, possess them-selves of such desiderata, cannon and artillerymen included.' He told the Duke of Cambridge that 'From the very first, the Royal troops, though consisting of but a single battalion, without cavalry or artillery, were the backbone of everything, the one force on which we could rely, and while H.M.'s 1/24th held the line of railway and towns, the volunteer forces were able to go forward.' This seems a little wanting in appreciation to the forces which went forward but Frere was not alone in his opinion. The future Major-General W. C. F. Molyneux said that 'Colonial troopers were mad after looting cattle for the sake of the prize-money' and related how they were constantly falling into traps baited with a few head of them.

After Kentani, the war in Galekaland tailed off and patrols were able to move fairly freely. The Naval Brigade furnished by H.M.S. *Active*, in their gaiters and sennit hats and armed with Sniders and cutlasses, marched far and wide without seeing much fighting.* Their ship fought the only naval action of the wars when she lobbed a few shells into a body of Kaffirs on the sea-shore. It seems to have been the ship's chaplain who left on record the classic observation that 'In the Cape every dog is called Footsack and runs away when you call him'.

In the country of the Gaikas, however, the war was by no means over. This was largely the business of the regular troops, mainly the 90th who relieved the 88th at Fort Beaufort in February. General Thesiger, soon to be Lord Chelmsford, arrived in March at King William's Town and found that his predecessor, Sir Arthur Cunynghame, had already established a line of posts between Cathcart and King William's Town and along the line of the railway which now connected that place to the port of East London. Modern names begin now to appear, for Thesiger's field commander was Colonel Evelyn Wood and one of the latter's best fighting officers was a Major of the 60th Rifles named Redvers Buller. The battle ground was a new one, no more than 20 miles from King's William's Town at its most distant point. Thesiger found the town crowded, as it had been when Frere first arrived, and that every farm within a radius of about 7 miles to the north and east had been burnt out. Wood, an officer of the greatest distinction whose career had begun as a midshipman in the Crimea and was to close as a Field Marshal with a Victoria Cross, went out to inspect things for himself. 'I was glad to see the Waterkloof, of which I had read a good

---

* The Naval Brigade also took with them a Gatling, the first machine-gun to be seen in South Africa but it does not seem to have been used.

deal. It appeared to our forefathers very difficult, but they never penetrated the Perie bush with which it cannot compare as a natural stronghold for the black man. The Waterkloof ravines are not nearly so deep and rugged as those in the Perie'. Here, to the south of the Amatola Range and around the slopes of the Gwilli-Gwilli mountains and those of Mount Kemp [it was originally Kempt, after Sir James Kempt the famous Peninsular General but the modern cartographers have dropped the final 't'] were concealed the Gaikas with elements of the Ndlambe clans, the Tambookies. They numbered about 2,000 in 3 groups one of which was led by Sandili's son. Edmund. In the ordinary way Edmund was an interpreter in the office of the magistrate at Middle Drift and went daily to work in frock-coat and stove-pipe hat. To his credit. he abandoned these at his father's summons and took to the bush with kaross and assegai as a chief's son should. Wood established his headquarters in the old mission station at Pirie and set to work to encircle his enemy. He never had anything like enough troops for the purpose and those he had were of unequal quality. Brabant's Colonial Horse went off on a cattle raid of their own, fell into a trap and were badly worsted; a body of Fingoes raised by Mr Haynes, the proprietor of the saw-mills, ran away at the first encounter. Molyneux, a light-hearted young man who would, one feels, have got on famously with Caesar Andrews (who was still alive and writing up his 1835 experiences) noted many anecdotes of what he saw and heard. One that deserves preservation was his description of what it felt like to be on the receiving end of Kaffir musketry. 'They fired iron pot legs, slugs, stones or any heavy thing that will go down. The musical notes of the various missiles in a Kaffir fight is a thing to hear'. Bissett had said much the same thing during the War of the Axe. Molyneux, too, tells how Captain Stuart Smith of the Royal Artillery managed to get one of his 7-pdr guns to the summit of the Rabula mountain. He was assured that the feat, though highly desirable, could not be accomplished but Smith was a thorough gunner. With 48 oxen yoked together and his two most powerful wheelers attached to the horns of the leaders the thing was somehow done and case-shot and shrapnel tore into the unreachable kloofs. By painful degrees, with his men working in groups of four, Wood shepherded the Kaffirs north over the Kabousie Nek which joins the Buffalo Mountain to the Amatolas and into the bush around the Thomas River. On 8 March, Commandant Griffith with the F.A.M.P., the Volunteers and the Fingoes went in after them. By a piece of carelessness, a gap was left in the cordon through which Sandili slipped for the last time. A month later he was killed at Isidenge by a stray bullet and soon afterwards his son Siyolo was brought down in the Fish River bush by a patrol of German volunteers commanded by the veteran Von Linsingen who had been Brigade Major of the German Legion at Chobham. It was ironic that of all the refractory chiefs only Sandili, whose lameness kept him out of battle, did not die on his mat. Although he had been a consistent enemy of the settlers, in spite of all protestations made to the contrary, he was a man from whom one should not withhold all sympathy. In 1860 he had been taken on board H.M.S. *Euryalus* to meet Midshipman H.R.H. Prince Alfred; the ship, its guns and its engines impressed him not at all, but he was pleased to meet the son of the Great Queen. His philosophy was not ours but, according to his own lights, he had behaved as a chief should. *Molliter ossa cubent.*

The rest is shortly told. The Transkei was taken over in September, 1878, though not formally annexed to the Colony until 1885. There was an uprising in 1880 when the clans beyond the Bashee rose up and murdered half a dozen Europeans (including Von Linsingen and his son) together with 30 Fingoes but it was soon put down by the Cape Mounted Riflemen, the new title of the F.A.M.P. The Pondoland Protectorate was proclaimed in 1885, followed by annexation in 1894, and the gap between the Colony and Natal was finally closed.

Thesiger, Wood and Buller moved on to Zululand, where the splendid 1/24th was all but wiped out at Isandhlwana. On the face of things, the tribes of Holland, Huguenot France, Britain and Germany were the victors in the long contest. The vanquished, however, began from that day to thrive and multiply. In material terms, they were better off than they had ever been. An event in 1878 was of mildly topical interest for the great Russian scare was again uppermost in men's minds; a very short inspection showed that a solitary Russian warship with a good rifled gun could knock Cape Town to pieces without the slightest

273

risk to itself and could then move on to attend to all the other sea coast towns in like fashion. This was put to rights with all possible speed.

One sees the inevitability of it all from the moment Van Riebeeck first set foot on shore and the first Kaffirs drank from the Fish River. One can see also how easily the tragic Balkanization of South Africa could have been avoided had it not been for relays of meddlesome and ignorant politicians in London. Briton and Boer got on well enough from the beginning; they farmed together, hunted together and rode to war together, as they have done since, and left to themselves, they could have hammered out a *modus vivendi* acceptable to both and inoffensive to the consciences of all save the zealots of Exeter Hall. That they failed to do so is a standing reproach and the lesson to be learned from it comes too late.*

For generations of soldiers it was an experience without parallel anywhere else in the world. The men who had fought in the squares of Waterloo had to learn as they went along how to cope with an enemy who could conceal himself totally in a bush 18 inches tall or hide at the bottom of a pond breathing through a reed, a trick as old as Gaius Marius and as new as the Viet Cong. Heat and cold, sun and snow, rain and sand-storm, jungle, ravine and mountain, they endured them all without flinching. Few, if any, other armies could have found officers of the quality of 'Tiger Tom' Willshere, Harry Smith, Henry

---

* As was said at the beginning of this book, it is fashionable today to assert boldly that the Colonists stole the land from the black man in South Africa; by inference, nothing of the same kind happened elsewhere. There can be no harm in the reminder that, during about the same period as that covered by the Kaffir Wars, the young United States was thrusting westwards and driving the long-settled red men from their hunting-grounds by force, fraud and the deliberate breaking of treaties. Holy Russia was absorbing the Central Asian Khanates of Khiva, Samarkhand, Bokhara and Tashkent, of which little enough trace remains. Neither the French in Algeria nor the Spaniards in Cuba and the Philippines have escaped reproach for acts of cruelty which stain their reputations. At the end of the story in most cases, the original owners were dispossessed and left to fend for themselves, a process which resulted in the practical extinction of many tribes in many lands. No treaty ever was broken by the Cape settlers, no land granted to them by fraudulent means, nor did any massacre of those incapable of defending themselves ever take place. By contrast with the settlers in most other places, the hands of the Cape Colonists are clean.

Somerset, Peregrine Maitland, Eyre, Michel, Fordyce, Evelyn Wood and many others, generation after generation. With no doctrine drawn from past experiences to help them and having to plan and execute every move by the light of nature, they hardly ever failed. The former, long-service, British soldier was a man indeed. If their names are spread thickly over the map of the old colony, even though most people now have no idea who Alice or Cox or Cathcart might have been, and the Queen's writ runs no more in the land where their bones lie, it is no more than they deserve. May these names remain there for ever, and may those who farm above their heads learn and remember to whom they owe what they have.

BIBLIOGRAPHY AND A NOTE ON SOURCES

CHAPTER ONE

Theal's *History of South Africa*, Swan Sonnenschein, 1880, vol. I, is the most informative work on the subject. The Report of the Chief Magistrate, Umtata, dated 9 February, 1888, explains the results of an enquiry into the migrations of Bantu from the north and the dates of arrival of the tribes in various places.

The Early Cape Hottentots, Publication No. 14 of the van Riebeeck Society, is important and the Resolutions of the Council are extracted from the official English translation of the Cape Archives.

The AmaXosa Life and Customs, J. H. Soga, Lovedale Press, Cape Province, 1931.

Tobacco in South Africa, H. W. Taylor, Cape Town, 1927.

CHAPTER TWO

On the Second Kaffir War there are no English documents, for obvious reasons. The authoritative work is P. W. Marritz' *Verhaal van de Overgaave van de Kaap de Goed Hoop etc*. The original is at The Hague and a copy exists in the Cape Archives.

The British occupation of the Cape is dealt with by A. J. Sluysken in *Verhaal gehouden by den Commisaris van de Kaap de Goed Hoop* (The Hague, 1797) and H. D. Campagne in *Memorie en Byzonderheden wegens Overgaave der Kaap de Goed Hoop* (The Hague, 1795). See also S. C. Nederburgh, *Echte stukken etc*., 1803 (Original at The Hague, copy in Cape Archives).

The Annual Register, 1795.

The Influence of Sea Power over History, A. T. Mahan, Little, Brown & Co., Boston, Mass., 1890) pp. 422 et seq.

CHAPTER THREE

Theal, vol. I.

History of the Cape Mounted Rifles (Cannon Series) War Office 1837.

An Account of Travels into the Interior of South Africa, J. Barrow, vol. II, p. 130.

The Loyal North Lancashire Regiment, *R.U.S.I.*, 1932.

History of the 8th Light Dragoons, pp. 81–2, Smet. Quoted in *The VIIIth Royal Irish Hussars*, R. H. Murray, Heffer & Son, Cambridge, 1928. All letters quoted are in the Public Record Office under W.O. 332.

CHAPTER FOUR

A full description of the activities of De Mist and Janssens appears in Theal, vol. I, chapters 4 and 5.

For the taking of Cape Town see Sir John Fortescue's *History of the British Army*, vol. VII.

CHAPTERS FIVE AND SIX

The best and most detailed account of the events described in these two chapters appears in Theal, vol. I.

CHAPTER SEVEN

Bryant's *Olden Times in Zululand* is the *locus classicus* on the subject.

Shaka Zulu, E. A. Ritter, Longmans Green, 1955.

CHAPTER EIGHT

The Slachter's Nek Rebellion of 1815, H. C. V. Liebrandt, Cape Archives.

Plantagenet in South Africa, A. Millar, O.U.P., Cape Town, 1963.

Theal, vol. I.

BIBLIOGRAPHY

CHAPTER NINE

The best account of the Fifth War (an episode distinguished by a paucity of documents) appears in *Battles in Southern Africa*, vol. I, by Duncan Moodie (Murray & St Leger, Cape Town, 1888). This sets out *in extenso*, beginning at p. 197, the only eye-witness account, that of Captain Stretch. He was a Volunteer officer, apparently attached to the 38th for he deals only with that Regiment and the part played by Boesak and his men.

Stretch reckons the Kaffir army as numbering about 9,000 but too much reliance should not be placed on his figures which cannot have been more than an intelligent guess and were committed to paper more than 50 years after the event.

Theal deals well with the period and is usually reliable.

CHAPTER TEN

Settlers' Heritage, F. C. Slater, Lovedale Press, Alice, C.P., 1954. (An excellent account but, in my view, less than just to Lord Charles Somerset).

Theal, vol. I, pp. 286–363.

Philipps, 1820 Settler, A. Keppel-Jones, Shuter & Shooter, Pietermaritzburg, 1960. A well-edited selection of letters from an observant and educated man. Readable and essential.

The 1820 Settlers in South Africa, H. E. Hockly, Juta & Co., Cape Town, 1949.

Masken's *Miller's Africana Gallery*, Cape Town, contains memorable pictures.

Grahamstown Journal, 1831 onwards. Edited by K. J. Meurant.

Plantagenet in South Africa, A. Millar. Quoted above.

The Somerset Sequence, Honoria Durant, London, 1951.

Annual Register 1820.

P.R.O. File CO/48/33.

CHAPTER ELEVEN

A History of the Zulu and Neighbouring Tribes, A. T. Bryant, Cape Town, 1964.

The Washing of the Spears, D. R. Morris, Simon & Schuster, New York, 1965.

On the destruction and re-formation of the Bantu tribes, see Theal, *History of South Africa since 1795*, vol. I, pp. 368–428.

CHAPTER TWELVE

The Autobiography of Lieut-General Sir Harry Smith, John Murray, 1903.

Historical Records of the 72nd Highlanders 1777–1856, Blackwoods, 1856.

Theal, *Documents relating to the Kaffir War of 1835*, Government of South Africa, 1912.

A Narrative of the Irruption of the Kaffir Hordes into the Eastern Province of the Cape of Good Hope in the year 1835, Godlonton, Grahamstown, 1836.

The Unpublished Papers of Caesar Andrews. Copy in the R.U.S.I., London.

Notes on South African Affairs from 1834–1838, Boyce, Grahamstown, 1838.

British Military Firearms, Blackmore, Herbert Jenkins, 1961.

CHAPTERS THIRTEEN TO FIFTEEN

Fortescue, *History of the British Army*, vol. XIII, pp. 500–61.

Moodie, *Battles in Southern Africa*, previously cited.

History of the Sherwood Foresters, Colonel C. H. Wylly, privately printed, 1929.

History of the XIIth Royal Lancers, P. F. Stewart, O.U.P., 1950.

History of the Rifle Brigade, Sir W. Cope, Chatto & Windus, 1877.

Scenes in Kaffirland, Graham and Robinson, Cape Town, 1854.

Campaigning in Kaffirland, Captain W. R. King, Saunders and Ottley, 1853.

Five Years in Kaffirland, with sketches of the late war in that country, Harriet Ward, London, 1848.

The Present Kaffir War, Colonel Napier, *United Service Magazine*, July, 1851.

Operations in the Waterkloof, Anon, *United Service Magazine*, April, 1852.

The Diaries of Captain William King-Hall, R.N., are contained in *Sea Saga*, Gollancz, 1935.

Correspondence of Sir Harry Smith and Major-General Somerset, P.R.O., WO/1/446.

BIBLIOGRAPHY

CHAPTER SIXTEEN

Life and Correspondence of Sir Bartle Frere, vol. II, J. Martineau, John Murray, 1895.

Records of the Cape Mounted Riflemen, Basil Williams, Cawston & Son, 1909.

Campaigning in South Africa and Egypt, Major-General W. C. F. Molyneux, Macmillan, 1896.

Battle in Southern Africa, Moodie (previously cited), vol. II.

From Midshipman to Field Marshal, F.M. Sir Evelyn Wood, V.C., Methuen, 1906.

The Naval Brigade in South Africa, Fleet-Surgeon H. F. Norbury, Sampson Low, 1880.

Theal, vol. V.

Theal's *Compendium of the History and Geography of South Africa*, Edward Stanford, 1878.

INDEX

INDEX

INDEX

Moshesh, Basuto chief, 236, 257–60

Motte, M. de la, 40

Murray, Captain, 165, 189

Nambili, 131

Natal, 34

N'Amaxa, 270

Naudes Hoek, 38

Napier, Lieut-General Sir George, 188, 215

Ndlambe, Xosa chief, 41, 44–5, 56, 60, 70, 77, 83 et seq, 110, 113, 131

Nel, Commandant, 167

Nomsa, 167

NSutu, 175, 223, 225

Nutka, Hendrik, 117

Oertel, Secretary, 52

Olivier, Field Cornet, 100

Orange River, 76

Orange River Sovereignty, 218

Paarl, 33

Palo, chief, 34

Panda, Zulu King, 246

Panmure, Lord, 264

Parker, Mr, 129

Pato, chief, 122, 177, 226

Peddie, Colonel John, 161–4

Perie Bush, 272

Philipps, John, 130–3

Philip, Rev John, 161, 175, 180 et seq, 201

Pondo, tribe, 26, 216

Pondoland, 34

Popham, Cmdre Home, R.N., 72

Port Elizabeth, 62, 128, 131

Post Victoria, 193, 197

Pottinger, Sir Henry, 207–10

Pretorius, Andries, 187, 216–7

Prinsloo, Hendrik, 102

Prinsloo, Marthinus, 36, 50, 58, 66

Prinsloo, Willem, 36

Qokli Hill, Zululand, 136

Rarabe, Xosa chief, 38, 41, 111

Rademeyer, Cmdt, 163

Read, Rev Mr, 96, 161, 162

Regiments & Corps—see separate Index

Rensburg, Cmdt van, 64, 70

Retief, Piet, 185

Riebeeck, Jan van, 29

Rivers, Landdrost, 131

Ross, Hercules, 46, 49

Ross, Captain W., C.M.R., 173

Rousseau, Sjt, C.M.R., 100 et seq

Ruiter, Hottentot, 43

Saldanha Bay, 27, 52

Sandili, Xosa chief, 145, 193–4, 208–9, 224–6, 259–60, 267, 273

Settlers Regiment, 264

Shepstone, Sir Theophilus, 168 et seq

Sherlock, Major, 67

Shilling, Captain, 27

Shiloh, 209

Simonstown, 47

Siyolo, Xosa chief, 199

Sluysken, Governor, 46

Smith, Lieut-General Sir Harry, 144, 150, 179, 183, 210, 217–20, 222 et seq, 234 et seq, 237, 247–50, 252–4

Smith, Juana (Lady Smith), 144–5

Smith, Captain Stuart, 272

Smith, Major T., 216 et seq

Somerset, Lord Charles, 98, 103–5, 108, 120–2, 126, 132, 141, 146

Somerset, Major-General Henry, 129, 132, 139, 142, 161, 164, 194–5, 206, 227–9, 232, 240, 243, 255, 260

Somerset West, 36

Southey, George, 170–2

Southey, Richard, 166

Sprigg, Gordon, 268

Stel, Simon van der, 33–4

Stellenbosch, 33, 50

Stockenstroom, Andries, the elder, 71, 83 et seq

Stockenstroom, Sir Andries, 85, 94, 100, 119, 133, 181, 190, 197, 203, 222

INDEX

INDEX OF REGIMENTS AND CORPS
engaged in the Kaffir Wars